A Biblical Theology of Water

A Biblical Theology of Water

Initiating, Cleansing, and Sustaining Life

Eric R. Waller

☙PICKWICK *Publications* • Eugene, Oregon

A BIBLICAL THEOLOGY OF WATER
Initiating, Cleansing, and Sustaining Life

Copyright © 2024 Eric R. Waller. All rights reserved. Except for brief quotations in critical publications or reviews, no part of this book may be reproduced in any manner without prior written permission from the publisher. Write: Permissions, Wipf and Stock Publishers, 199 W. 8th Ave., Suite 3, Eugene, OR 97401.

Pickwick Publications
An Imprint of Wipf and Stock Publishers
199 W. 8th Ave., Suite 3
Eugene, OR 97401

www.wipfandstock.com

PAPERBACK ISBN: 978-1-6667-8502-9
HARDCOVER ISBN: 978-1-6667-8503-6
EBOOK ISBN: 978-1-6667-8504-3

Cataloguing-in-Publication data:

Names: Waller, Eric R., author.

Title: A biblical theology of water : initiating, cleansing, and sustaining life / Eric R. Waller.

Description: Eugene, OR: Pickwick Publications, 2024. | Includes bibliographical references.

Identifiers: ISBN 978-1-6667-8502-9 (paperback). | ISBN 978-1-6667-8503-6 (hardcover). | ISBN 978-1-6667-8504-3 (ebook).

Subjects: LSCH: Water in the Bible. | Water—Religious aspects—Christianity. | Biblical theology.

Classification: BS1199.W22 W35 2024 (print). | BS1199 (epub)

VERSION NUMBER 05/14/24

Unless otherwise stated, Scripture quotations are taken from the (NASB®) New American Standard Bible®, copyright © 1995 by The Lockman Foundation. Used by permission All rights reserved. lockman.org.

Scripture quotations marked ASV are taken from the American Standard Version, in the public domain.

Scripture quotations marked CEB are from the COMMON ENGLISH BIBLE. © Copyright 2011 COMMON ENGLISH BIBLE. All rights reserved. Used by permission.

Scripture quotations marked NIV are from the New International Version, copyright @ 1973, 1978, 1984 by International Bible Society. Used by permission of Zondervan Publishing House. All rights reserved.

Scripture quotations marked NRSV are from the New Revised Standard Version, copyright @ 1989, Division of Christian Education of the National Council of the Churches of Christ in the United States in the United States of America. Used by permission. All rights reserved.

Contents

List of Figures and Tables | ix
Acknowledgments | xii
How to Use This Book | xiii
List of Abbreviations | xv

1 Introduction | 1
2 Water and the Initiation of Life | 11
3 Water and Cleansing | 67
4 Water and Sustaining Life | 93
5 Synthesis of Evidence | 124
6 Theological Ramifications | 144
7 Summary | 183

Bibliography | 187

List of Figures and Tables

FIGURES

Figure 1.1 Representation of author's visual image of Gen 1:2 | 132

Figure 1.2 Representation of author's visual image of Gen 1:6–7 | 133

Figure 1.3 Representation of author's visual image of Gen 1:9–10 | 134

TABLES

Table 1.1 OT uses of water (reviewed) | 128

Table 1.2 NT uses of water (reviewed) | 129

Table 1.3 Water and water-related terms used in Gen 1–2 | 131

Table 1.4 Water and water-related terms used in Rev 21–22 | 137

Acknowledgments

Failing to praise God for his provision of time, health, stamina, and guidance would dishonor him. Without his blessings this book would not have occurred. One of God's blessings has been the understanding and patience of my wife, Angela. Her encouragement and suggestions have made this effort much easier than it might otherwise have been.

Gratitude is extended to the faculty and library staff at Liberty University who were instrumental in various phases of this work when it began as a doctoral dissertation. Special thanks is due to Richard Alan Fuhr Jr. for his oversight and input in the initial stages of this effort. He helped assess the narrow focus required to complete this work. I am also thankful to Andreas J. Köstenberger, who has offered encouragement and suggestions that kept me within boundaries during the course of this writing. These men are greatly appreciated not just for their assistance, but also for the Spirit of Christ that is evident in each of them. The staff at Pickwick Publications has also been enormously patient, extremely knowledgeable, and helpful through every step of the process.

How to Use This Book

The reader of this book likely has an academic focus and a wait-list of other books to be read. Time is precious. Quickly tasting the sausage may be more important than knowing the laborious and painful process of how it is made. If such is the case, it is suggested that one first read the introduction, and then skip to chapter 5, where the intervening chapters are synthesized into presumably clear and warranted conclusions that verify the thesis. If more evidence is demanded, then one may back up and read the compelling underlying evidence for further corroboration.

This book is intended to provide proof of its thesis, period. It is anticipated that others will affirm this thesis and build upon it. This is particularly true of the theological ramifications which encapsulate several concepts and applications worthy of additional exposition. This book is intentionally written within a very narrow scope due to the nature of the subject and the demands of its origin as a doctoral dissertation. Repetition is intentional and believed necessary to ensure focus on the topic at hand. Hopefully, such duplication is not wearisome. This book is a republication of my dissertation, amended only by correcting typos and rewording a few phrases for clarity.

God's blessings are wished upon each reader!

—Eric Waller

Abbreviations

ABRL	Anchor Bible Reference Library
ACCS	Ancient Christian Commentary on Scripture
AMP	Amplified Bible
AMPC	Amplified Bible, Classic Edition
ASV	American Standard Version
AYBRL	Anchor Yale Bible Reference Library
BCOTWP	Baker Commentary on the Old Testament Wisdom and Psalms
BDAG	Danker, Frederick W., et al. *Greek-English Lexicon of the New Testament and Other Early Christian Literature.* 3rd ed. Chicago: University of Chicago Press, 2000
BDB	Brown, Francis, et al. *A Hebrew and English Lexicon of the Old Testament*
BECNT	Baker Exegetical Commentary on the New Testament
BTB	*Biblical Theology Bulletin*
BZ	*Biblische Zeitschrift*
CC	Continental Commentaries
CEB	Common English Bible
CEV	Contemporary English Version
CJB	Complete Jewish Bible
CSB	Christian Standard Bible
CTJ	*Calvin Theological Journal*
ECC	Eerdmans Critical Commentary

ECNT	Exegetical Commentary on the New Testament	
EGGNT	Exegetical Guide to the Greek New Testament	
ESV	English Standard Version	
EvQ	*Evangelical Quarterly*	
HALOT	The Hebrew and Aramaic Lexicon of the Old Testament. Edited by Ludwig Koehler and Walter Baumgartner. 2 vols. Study ed. Leiden: Brill, 2001	
HB	Hebrew Bible	
HCSB	Holman Christian Standard	
HvTSt	*Hervormde teologiese studies*	
ICC	International Critical Commentary	
JANESCU	Journal of the Ancient Near Eastern Society of Columbia University	
JBL	*Journal of Biblical Literature*	
JBQ	*Jewish Bible Quarterly*	
JETS	*Journal of the Evangelical Theological Society*	
JSOT	*Journal for the Study of the Old Testament*	
JSOTSup	Journal for the Study of the Old Testament Supplement Series	
JTS	*Journal of Theological Studies*	
JUB	Jubilee Bible	
KJV	King James Version	
LHBOTS	The Library of Hebrew Bible/Old Testament Studies	
MSG	The Message	
NAC	New American Commentary	
NASB	New American Standard Bible	
NBCB	New Beacon Bible Commentary	
NCCS	New Covenant Commentary Series	
Neot	*Neotestimentica*	
NET	New English Translation	
NICNT	New International Commentary on the New Testament	
NICOT	New International Commentary on the Old Testament	

NIDOTTE	*New International Dictionary of Old Testament Theology and Exegesis.* Edited by Willem A. VanGemeren. 5 vols. Grand Rapids: Zondervan, 1997
NIGTC	New International Greek Testament Commentary
NIV	New International Version
NovTSup	Supplements to Novum Testamentum
NRSVUE	New Revised Standard Version Updated Edition
NSBT	New Studies in Biblical Theology
NT	New Testament
NTL	New Testament Library
OT	Old Testament
OTE	*Old Testament Essays*
OTL	Old Testament Library
OtSt	*Oudtestamentische Studiën*
RB	*Revue biblique*
RSV	Revised Standard Version
SJT	*Scottish Journal of Theology*
SP	Sacra Pagina
SSN	Studia Semitica Neerlandica
THNTC	Two Horizons New Testament Commentary
THOTC	Two Horizons Old Testament Commentary
TNTC	Tyndale New Testament Commentaries
TOTC	Tyndale Old Testament Commentaries
VT	*Vetus Testamentum*
VTSup	Vetus Testamentum Supplements
WBC	Word Bible Commentary
WEB	World English Bible
WTJ	*Westminster Theological Journal*
ZAW	*Zeitschrift für die alttestamentliche Wissenschaft*

1

Introduction

SIMILARITIES AMONG VARIOUS PORTIONS of Scripture abound fostering speculation and debate over such issues as authorship, provenance, redaction, and theological significance. For example, the books of Kings and Chronicles share significant common ground in terms of characters, topics, and time frames, although each is distinctive from the other. Prophetic figures are more central to Kings, while Chronicles seems more interested in the temple and priestly matters.[1] Ezekiel and John both share interest in the "son of man," but even casual observation detects differences in authorship, audience, message, purpose, and setting.[2] The first two chapters of Genesis detail the beginning of the created world, while the last two chapters of Revelation describe the future new creation. Both depictions use remarkably similar concepts and terms supplying a series of intriguing parallels. The freshly created heavens and earth in Gen 1–2 corresponds to a new heaven and earth forecast in Rev 21–22. In Genesis God interacts with, and speaks to, the first humans (Gen 1:29–30; 2:16–17).[3] Revelation similarly depicts God cohabitating with his people, even inviting entrance into the new heaven and earth where he and the Lamb dwell as its temple (Rev 21:3–7, 22–23; 22:3–4).

---

1. Grabbe, *1 & 2 King*, 6; Mabie, *1 and 2 Chronicles*, 40.
2. Fowler and Strickland, *Influence of Ezekiel*, 109–12; Udoibok, "Significance"; Vawter, "Ezekiel and John."
3. God's interaction with the first humans is also vividly portrayed in Gen 3:8–24.

God purposed the first humans to co-reign with him and the renewal of that regal relationship is forecast in the new heaven and earth (Gen 1:26–29; 2:15–16, 19–20, 22–23; Rev 22:5). Each text references the "tree of life" (Gen 2:9; Rev 22:2). Both texts describe a sinless habitat (Gen 1:4, 10, 12, 18, 21, 25–27, 31: Rev 21:7–8, 24–27; 22:14–15).[4] Genesis 1–2 is set in a pre-sin state, while its counterpart in Revelation is described as a post-sin state (Gen 1:31; 2:25; Rev 21:4–7, 27; 22:3–5, 14–15).[5] Genesis details God "birthing" the first humans in his likeness and image, as Revelation proclaims a new parent/child relationship where the children continue to bear evidence of God's imprint (Gen 1:26–28; 2:18–23; Rev 21:7; 22:4). The correlation between these two Bible bookends, Gen 1–2 and Rev 21–22, is undeniable and striking.

WATER-RELATED TERMS

Numerous water-related terms found in these two canonical end points are of particular interest, and are the launchpad for this research. An especially strong affinity exists with terms such as "the deep," "the waters," "water," "the sea," "seas," "stream," "river," "flow," "flows," and "rain" from Gen 1–2, which correspond, to varying extents, to the Rev 21–22 terms "water of life," "river of the water of life," "thirsty," "spring," and "lake." While there is similarity in the individual words themselves, the similarity also extends to the concepts, theological and otherwise, these words convey. For example, Gen 2:10 describes a river that was to "water the garden," which implies the broader concept of its life-giving and life-sustaining purpose. Revelation 22:1–2 speaks of the "river of the water of life" which likewise implies within its title a life-giving and life-sustaining purpose.[6] It also appears to support, or work in consort with, the "tree of life" to provide nourishment and healing.[7] These terms are similar, and the notion each communicates is also similar. That the traditional Protestant canon begins and ends with such analogous concepts and terminology is conspicuous. It appears to create an inclusio that demands further inquiry. An inclusio is "sometimes called a *sandwich structure*" in which

---

4. Smalley, *Revelation of John*, 562–63.

5. The pre-sin state is implied by Gen 1:31; 2:25, but is more clearly attested in Gen 3 when sin first appears to alter the previously sinless habitat.

6. Smalley, *Revelation of John*, 562–63; Koester, *Revelation*, 834–35.

7. Koester, *Revelation*, 834–35.

"a word, image, or idea from the beginning of the passage is echoed at the end."[8] Granted, this would be among the broadest literary brackets in the canon, but it is believed supplemental and complementary evidence within the canon (between these end points) uphold the presence of this inclusio, and support a biblical theology of water that extends from the beginning of the Bible to its end. This interpretive perspective is explained by Graham Cole:

> Biblical theology as a discipline traces the great themes of Scripture from their first appearance in the canon to the last, whether the key term (or terms) appears or the idea does. Key ideas such as covenant, election, sacrifice, kingdom, the land, inheritance, and presence, among many others, become the lens through which the unfolding biblical story is viewed.[9]

Sometimes the Bible uses a term or concept so frequently, or a term or concept becomes so commonplace in human vernacular, that its broader scope, or alternative potential meanings, remain veiled. For the Jews, this was true with the OT concepts of the temple, murder, adultery, circumcision, faithfulness, divorce, sacrifice, vows, love, worship, and more. Their failure to visualize anything beyond the raw elementary external of these concepts prevented many Jews from accepting Jesus and his message (Matt 15:9; John 4:23; 14:17; Rom 2:17–24). Jesus confronted this mental and spiritual blockage when he says six times, "You have heard it said . . . But I say to you" (my paraphrase of Matt 5:21, 27, 31, 33, 38, 43). Regarding eschatology, Eckhard Schnabel says, "It seems provocative that . . . among evangelicals, systems of theological thought have been more important than the biblical text."[10] This same flaw may be applicable to the subject of water, and it may be that certain theologies have taken precedence over and obscured a biblical theology of water. Common usage, familiarity with the term, and its pervasiveness in Scripture may inhibit a broader, deeper, or alternative perspective. Taking a precautionary lead from Schnabel, this presentation will look at the biblical text first, and from it unwrap a biblical theology of water, rather than allowing a predetermined theological stance to influence or overlook the biblical text. While commentary on every canonical water-related text or term would be a daunting task beyond the scope of this presentation,

---

8. Michael Gorman, *Elements of Biblical Exegesis*, 40.
9. G. Cole, *God Who Became Human*, 115.
10. Schnabel, "Viability of Premillennialism," 785.

this research centers around three major theological constructs of water, which necessitates discussing significant portions of the canonical texts that reference water and its related terms.

THREE ASPECTS OF WATER

This study will unveil the use of water as an element initiating physical and spiritual life, providing physical and spiritual cleansing, and sustaining physical and spiritual life. Each of these three aspects of water interrelate. When properly understood, they offer implications for God's usage of water as an instrumentality by which at least some of his purposes are accomplished. They also oblige reconsideration of certain church dogma, particularly doctrinal positions on the gift and work of the Holy Spirit, salvation, and baptism. While not the primary focus of this work, it is believed that an argument can be made from this investigation for the coherence and uniformity of the existing sixty-six-book canon of Protestant Scripture. Deeper exploration of this belief, however, may be better served by separate research. The longer thesis of this dissertation is that there exists a biblical theology of water within the traditional canon of Protestant Scripture whereby water is an instrument that initiates physical and spiritual life, provides physical and spiritual cleansing, and sustains physical and spiritual life, and that these three aspects are interrelated, forming a biblical theology of water. The shorter thesis is that God uses water to initiate, cleanse, and sustain life, and these three constructs interrelate forming a biblical theology of water. There currently exists numerous books and monographs touching on specific portions of this thesis, but none known that consider them all, and combine them into a proper theology. For example, the cleansing aspect of water has regularly been associated with baptism at least since Acts 22:16 was penned. It says, "Get up and be baptized, and wash away your sins." Discussion of this text, and debate over whether it refers to a cleansing aspect of water, has continued from the time of Hippolytus (170–235 CE) into recent times.[11] The intensity and variation of discussions of such single focal points, and splinter debates arising from them, may have obscured the existence of a comprehensive theology found in Scripture which this presentation expects to disclose.

---

11. Beasley-Murray, *Baptism in New Testament*, 37–44, 127, 163–67; Nettles, "Baptism as a Symbol," 31; Pratt, "Reformed Response," 45–46; D. Wright, "Origins of Infant Baptism," 4.

Introduction

ANCIENT NEAR EASTERN CULTURE

This research will examine these three aspects of water by citing significant biblical texts that substantiate each aspect. There will be a degree of overlap as a given biblical text may advocate more than one of the three aspects, or even all three. In some cases, extra-biblical texts will be cited to enhance and contrast the significance of water as an instrument of God. This will also capture the frame of reference of the first recipients which helps juxtapose and clarify the biblical view. For example, the worldview of the sea as being a dark or demonic-type existence is well founded in ancient Near Eastern literature and its influence may be evident, even if somewhat cryptic, in various biblical texts, both in the OT and in the NT.[12] Considerable discussion has occurred regarding the impact of ancient Near Eastern mythology and culture on present understandings of the OT.[13] John Walton has been outspoken in advocating "cognitive environmental criticism" which intends "to recover the cultural layers from the world behind the text that were inherently understood by the ancient audience but have been long lost to our modern world."[14] While no one denies a broader environment encircling Israel's culture, the degree to which that influence impacted the writing of Scripture, or the extent to which Scripture was used polemically against such influence, is not yet conclusive. The attempt to recover the ancient cultural environment surrounding the Genesis account of the presence of water in creation has given rise to a theory known as *Chaoskampf*, popularized by Hermann Gunkel. It has been accepted, to varying degrees, and discussed in depth by such scholars as John Walton, Debra Scoggins Ballentine, David Tsumura, and others, with Tsumura largely rejecting it.[15]

CHAPTER OVERVIEW

Chapter 2 will discuss water as the initiator of life. It will delve more in depth into the ancient worldview and its impact on understanding

---

12. V. Matthews and Benjamin, *Old Testament Parallels*; Currid, *Against the Gods*; Albrektson, *History and the Gods;* Batto, *In the Beginning*; Niehaus, *Ancient Near Eastern Themes*.

13. Currid, *Against the Gods*, 11–23; Childs, *Introduction to Old Testament*, 109–35.

14. Walton, "Interactions," 333; see also Walton, "Creation in Genesis 1:1—2:3."

15. Ballentine, *Conflict Myth*; Tsumura, *Creation and Destruction*; Scurlock and Beal, *Creation and Chaos*; Walton and Sandy, *Lost World of Scripture*.

Scripture, particularly the Genesis creation account and the use of water in the flood or re-creation (Gen 1–2; 6–9). Discussion of water initiating life will track various other OT texts such as water providing life to Moses (Exod 2), Moses turning water to blood (Exod 7), water initiating new life to Israel by crossing the Red Sea (Exod 14–15), and by crossing the Jordan River (Josh 3–6). Significant attention will be devoted to the Gospel of John where water is a significant symbol throughout the book, particularly in the early chapters.[16] The water to wine episode is instructional in announcing the new ministry that brings life (John 2). It is in John 3:3–5 where water reflects or reaffirms the Genesis creation motif and directs the individual seeking life in the kingdom of God. Living water is offered in John 4 and John 7 which by its very name heralds its life-giving purpose. Jesus uses water to heal providing what amounted to new life to a blind man (John 9). Water flows from the side of Christ in his final life-giving redemptive act (John 19). John obviously mentions water numerous times in a wide variety of circumstances, most of which bear upon the thesis.[17] Other NT texts, such as 1 John 5 and Rev 21–22, will also be explored as they describe water as initiating life.

Chapter 3 will follow a similar thorough examination of the biblical texts to establish the second aspect of the thesis, that God uses water to cleanse or purify. This chapter will follow a similar chronological path through the OT canon as in chapter 2, and will start by examining the creation story (Gen 1), then the flood (Gen 6–9). This chapter will find in Israel's purification rites an additional basis for the concept of purification by water which is echoed by Ezekiel, and carries over into the NT with the baptism of John, the baptism of Jesus, and numerous texts on believer's baptism (Ex 19, 29; Lev 1, 8; Ezek 36:25; John 1:26; 3:22–23; Acts 22:16; Heb 6:2; 10:22; 1 Pet 3:18–22). The cleansing of Naaman by water is related and paradigmatic (2 Kgs 5). It will be reviewed as well.

A similar path in chapter 4 will demonstrate the third portion of the thesis, that God uses water to sustain life. Continuing to follow a chronological path through the OT, several texts will be considered again, but this different aspect of the thesis will be explored. These texts include Gen 1–2, Gen 6–9, and Exod 2. New texts to be investigated that discuss water sustaining life include Hagar's departure from Sarah (Gen 16), the expulsion of Hagar and Ishmael (Gen 21), finding Rebekah for Isaac (Gen

---

16. Köstenberger, *Theology of John's Gospel*, 162.
17. Köstenberger, *Theology of John's Gospel*, 350, 471–76.

24), Isaac's covenant with Abimelech (Gen 26), the Israelite wandering and water from rocks (Exod 15, 17), another look at Israel's purification rites (Exod 29–40), Israel's crossing the Jordan (Josh 3), Elijah sustaining Elisha (2 Kgs 2); and numerous texts that refer to water sustaining life in Psalms, Isaiah, Jeremiah, Ezekiel, and Zechariah. NT texts in Matthew, Luke, Acts, Romans, 1 Corinthians, Ephesians, Titus, and Hebrews will demonstrate the broad usage of water and its cognate terms for sustaining life. These will be joined by John 4, 7, and Rev 21–22, which reference living water, to help cement this third aspect of the thesis. Reference back to such OT writers as Jeremiah, Ezekiel, and Zechariah will be necessary as they also mention life-sustaining water.

Chapter 5 will synthesize the findings of the prior chapters to ensure cohesiveness of the thesis and its supporting biblical texts. This will include a recap of the discussions of *Chaoskampf* and polemic theology. In each of the prior three chapters, numerous biblical texts will have been drawn upon to establish each of the aspects of the thesis, and these will be combined in this chapter to collectively demonstrate the existence of a theology of water that spans the entire canon. Because these three components interrelate, there is necessarily overlap, and that enhances the credibility and coherence of the thesis. This synthesis will demonstrate how that the one substance, water, has been used by God to accomplish at least three of his purposes, and these three are interconnected. The interconnection of these three deployments of water are visible throughout the Bible from Genesis to Revelation making the case for an inclusio with Gen 1–2 and Rev 21–22 as end points. Such summarization is essential prior to considering the ramifications of this thesis. Chapter 6 will explore the ramification of the thesis as it is applied to the doctrines of the gift and work of the Holy Spirit, salvation, both presently and eschatologically, and baptism.

The Holy Spirit is connected to water in creation (Gen 1:2). Texts such as Matt 28:19; John 3:3–5; Acts 2:38, 8:14–18; 10:45–48; 19:1–7 connect the Holy Spirit to water baptism. The Holy Spirit is linked to water, along with blood, truth, and the coming of Jesus in 1 John 5:6–8. These and other texts will be examined to demonstrate the correlation of the Holy Spirit to water, but also the continuation of the Holy Spirit's work in and for believers to cleanse and sustain, the second and third legs of the thesis. For example, in creation, the Holy Spirit's presence was critical to the heavens and earth producing the "good" and "very good" outcomes

God intended (Gen 1).[18] Additionally, John 3:3–5 speaks of being born again of water and Spirit with further discussion of the mysterious work of the Spirit. The purpose of this rebirth by the Spirit is to qualify (cleanse) and equip (sustain) people for the kingdom of God (John 3:3, 5, 15–17). Such is not a one-and-done event, but a continuous endeavor that carries into the end-time.[19]

The biblical text will show that water plays a part in salvation, both now, and into the eschaton.[20] Jesus dispenses living water now that immediately eliminates thirst, and this water continues its efficacy for eternity, being present in the new creation (John 4:9–14; Rev 7:17; 21:6; 22:1, 17).[21] Considerable debate regarding baptism has existed for nineteen centuries.[22] While baptism is not the primary focus of this research, due to the historical controversy surrounding it, and its present day practice which continues to raise many of the same issues from centuries prior, it becomes necessary to examine baptism as part of the overall biblical theology of water to locate applicable theological principles related to it and this research. Having first an awareness of how God has used water, and continues to use water, and then establishing baptism as part of that broader scope, baptism will be shown to be far more meaningful than some suggest.[23]

Numerous texts link these elements, and these elements coalesce, whether symbolically or literally, in the eternal kingdom where the water of life, the Holy Spirit of God, and the saved whose names are in the book of life will reside (Rev 21:27; 22:19). Discussing the gift and work of the Holy Spirit, salvation, and the application of baptism as isolated topics fails to appreciate their interrelatedness. The Holy Spirit is connected to water and water baptism. Salvation is connected to the Holy Spirit, water, and water baptism. Baptism is obviously connected to water. These bonds are extremely strong and crisscross throughout Scripture. A clear and systematic regimen will carefully apply the three aspects of water to these applications. Such will help establish connection points on several

---

18. Allison and Köstenberger, *Holy Spirit*, 297–301.
19. Köstenberger, *Theology of John's Gospel*, 162–63.
20. Mark Gorman, "Reading with the Spirit."
21. Köstenberger, *Theology of John's Gospel*, 162–63.
22. Beasley-Murray, *Baptism in New Testament*, 37–44, 127, 163–67; Armstrong, "Introduction."
23. Witherington, *Troubled Waters*.

fronts resulting in a biblical theology of water that is coherent and well supported throughout Scripture.

A summary and conclusion will form chapter 7, which will summarize the primary points making up the thesis, briefly reasserting the underlying supporting biblical texts. This foundation will be shown to uphold its application and integration into the doctrines of the Holy Spirit, salvation, and baptism. This is expected to solidify the thesis as not merely a vague theoretical construct, but as a powerful theology woven throughout the biblical text from beginning to end, making repeated appearances that have been largely unnoticed and without adequate linkage from one to the other. It is this extensive presence from Genesis to Revelation that helps ratify the validity of the present Protestant canon. Succinctly, this summary expects to conclude that an inclusio exists between Gen 1–2 and Rev 21–22 in which a biblical theology of water expresses God's use of water to initiate life, to cleanse life, and to sustain life. The relationship of these numerous texts to each other, and their abundance throughout Scripture, support the current Protestant canon as a unified and completed whole. A bibliography will follow.

COMMENTS ON METHODOLOGY

While many biblical texts will be used more than once, and for different purposes, the intent is to follow the chronological sequence within the biblical canon as closely as possible. This will facilitate easier reading, and also provide the same familiar sequencing found in Scripture. One of the frustrations of this approach is that the underlying texts are so broad and numerous only a surface inquiry will generally be employed, rather than dissecting each word of a text in its original language, supplemented by linguistic, historical, and cultural data. While this generalized approach may appear academically light, or be viewed as cursory, it does demonstrate the breadth of the topic without the expansiveness and distraction of more detailed exegesis that might bog down the presentation. In this case, it is believed that less is more. It is hoped that as this presentation unveils the biblical theology of water, others will take it upon themselves to dig deeper into each of the many texts to further substantiate the merits of what is argued.

The reader may be annoyed by what seems to be a failure to include a specific point about a text, only to find that point is made in a later chapter for a different reason. For example, the water of creation both initiated life and cleansed the earth. But in chapter 2, only the initiation of life aspect is discussed, with the cleansing aspect being found in chapter 3. In the synthesis of chapter 5, the text will be consolidated to include both aspects. It is intended that the reader merge each component of a text with the aid of the charts and diagrams provided in chapter 5.

As in any investigation, springing novelties tempt side-bar discussions that veer from the core focus. That is especially the case with this topic due to the mere frequency of water-related terms in Scripture. My intent, however, is to concentrate on the central thesis, while judiciously refraining from extraneous, albeit interesting, tangential matters that contribute little or nothing to the primary thesis. In the end, a clear and coherent biblical theology of water will emerge.

2

Water and the Initiation of Life

CULTURAL INFLUENCES

THE BIBLE WAS NOT written in a vacuum. The Bible, and the interpretation of it, emerges out of a context and is also received within a context.[1] The OT arose from within Israel, a small nation surrounded by many other influential cultures. To interpret the Bible without considering the orbit within which it was synchronically positioned socially, politically, and culturally, as well as its diachronic positioning in time, history, and experience, is to miss some of its purpose and meaning.[2]

It has been advocated that the meaning of the original biblical text is achieved by using "cultural environmental criticism," which is the discipline of recovering "the cultural layers from the world behind the text that were inherently understood by the ancient audiences but have been long lost to our modern world."[3] Some consider this line of inquiry a "macro-sociological perspective" because it concerns itself with a comparative study of cultures.[4] These societies and traditions are viewed as being in a "state of flux" over time, but with certain features identifiable as cultural

---

1. Campbell, "Preparatory Issues," 3.
2. Longman, "What Genesis 1–2 Teaches," 107; Niehaus, *Ancient Near Eastern Themes*, 28–30.
3. Walton, "Interactions," 333.
4. Carter, "Social Scientific Approaches," 39.

patterns and environmental settings that may provide a backdrop for a biblical context.⁵ It is claimed that these features do not need translating, but rather readers need to "enter the culture," understanding it from intimacy with it.⁶ Not all agree, and counter that what God meant, not what ancient Near Easterners thought, should dictate purpose and meaning.⁷ Historical facts and contexts related to the earliest times of Genesis, such as the creation or the flood, are difficult to substantiate historically due the dearth of evidence.⁸ Because the Bible is literature, this inquiry into the ancient environment tends to focus more on the literary culture, rather than on other aspects of civilization, such as being affluent, being in exile, or living a subsistence lifestyle, even though these criteria may be influential in both authorial intent and reader interpretation.⁹

Many attempts have been made to identify and categorize the type of literature found in Genesis, and in the OT in general, with one calling it "narrative chronology" that gives way to a "thematic" style,¹⁰ even though also calling it "explicitly historiographic."¹¹ Another differentiates the attempts of many to define the OT in terms of various literary-critical styles, inquiries, and categories, noting considerable conflict among these efforts, but concluding that there exists an intentional structuring of the biblical text.¹² Still another also notes the conflicting efforts to categorize the Pentateuch, but envisions this portion of the Bible as part of a compositional strategy that is unveiled in a series of poems that comprise the text.¹³ Consensus obviously seems lacking in spite of effort to define and categorize in human terms.

It is out of this widespread endeavor to define and categorize the OT, and to explore the ancient cultural influences on the OT, that the concept of the OT as a polemic has recently become popular.¹⁴ The essence of this

---

5. Carter, "Social Scientific Approaches," 39.

6. Walton, *Lost World*, 9–10.

7. A. Morris, "Lost Truth of Genesis," 61–62, 65–67.

8. Coogan, *Brief Introduction*, 21–22; Lemaire, "Schools and Literacy," 207–9.

9. Waltke with Fredricks, *Genesis*, 17–43; Sailhamer, *Meaning of the Pentateuch*, 11–56.

10. Coogan, *Brief Introduction*, 3.

11. Coogan, *Brief Introduction*, 21.

12. Childs, *Introduction to Old Testament*, 30–45, 112–35.

13. Sailhamer, *Meaning of the Pentateuch*, 283–354; Sailhamer, *Genesis Unbound*, 237–56.

14. Currid, *Against the Gods*, 25; Walton, "Interactions," 334; Wenham, *Genesis*, 1:xlvii.

"polemic theology" is for biblical writers to express truths from Yahweh, and characteristics about Yahweh and his workings, in "thought forms and stories" that were common in ancient Near Eastern environments to both discredit the cultural norm and to promote the truth of Yahweh.[15] The promotion of the Israelite view of strict monotheism as contrasted with the prevailing worldview of polytheism, along with the implications of each, is the intent of polemic theology. These scripts come in the form of "expressions" and "motifs," and are presumably used to taunt those outside Israel.[16] It appears that the polytheistic gods and myths are not directly undermined, but lampooned or denied their claimed power.[17] It should be noted that viewing the biblical text as a polemic is not limited to Genesis or the Pentateuch, but applies generally to the entire OT and to the NT.[18] Some readily accept the polemical perspective.[19] It is important, however, to see this perspective as one of many lenses through which Scripture and ancient Near Eastern literature is potentially viewed, and not as the only lens.[20] This brief background is foundational to discussion of the ancient Near Eastern influence on the writing of the Bible, primarily Genesis, and to the discussion of the biblical theology of water.

WATER AND CULTURAL INFLUENCES

Before evaluating the merits of viewing the OT through the polemic lens, it is important to establish, at least to some degree, the literary landscape and theological environment of the cultures that surrounded Israel, particularly during the earliest times recorded in the OT.[21] To that end, the following represents a tiny portion of the ancient writings that reference water in Mesopotamian and Egyptian cultures, with attention given to water and its initiation of life. Additional texts will be proffered during the examination of biblical texts.

---

15. Currid, *Against the Gods*, 25.
16. Currid, *Against the Gods*, 26–27.
17. Walton, "Interactions," 334.
18. Quine, "Ritual and Polemic"; Hasel, "Polemical Nature"; Pregill, *Golden Calf*; Amit, "Hidden Polemic"; Richard, "Polemics, Old Testament"; Albrektson, *History and the Gods*, 112.
19. Vanderhooft, "Babylonia and the Babylonians," 135–36.
20. Currid, *Against the Gods*, 31–32.
21. Longman, "What Genesis 1–2 Teaches," 107.

Mesopotamian Myths

The Babylonian stories of Enuma Elish arise from fragments dated to 900–850 BCE.[22] While Enuma Elish was compiled around 1100 BCE from Sumerian and Amorite stories, the primary character, Marduk, was considered the patron of the divine assembly since Hammurabi (1972–1750 BCE).[23] The stories were popular during the reign of Nebuchadnezzar I (1125–1104 BCE) and remained so for the next five hundred years.[24] Some of the texts from Enuma Elish that reference water include the following.

> When on high, when no heavens existed
> When no earth had been called into existence,
> Godfather Apsu and Mumme-Tiamat, Godmother of
> All living,
> Their two bodies became one;
> Before a reed hut was erected,
> Before the marsh land was drained . . .
> Then, from the marriage of two divine waters,
> Lahmu and Lahamu were created,
> Their names were called. (Enuma Elish 1:1–22)[25]

The Enuma Elish text goes on to describe a chaotic situation dwelling amidst the waters, from which the deities, Apsu and Tiamat, create other gods, each representing an element of nature such as the earth, or the sky, which brought order, while the two primary gods, Apsu and Tiamat, preferred their passive existence amidst the chaotic waters.[26] This story lies at the heart of a theory called *Chaoskampf*, an idea popularized by Hermann Gunkel.[27] The theory envisions a disorganized and chaotic existence, *Chaoskampf*, out of which creation and order arose.[28] Gunkel found what he believed were parallels in the HB with a primeval sea, and chaos battling divine order, described under various motifs such as the

---

22. V. Matthews and Benjamin, *Old Testament Parallels*, 21.
23. V. Matthews and Benjamin, *Old Testament Parallels*, 21.
24. Vanderhooft, "Babylonia and the Babylonians," 119–20.
25. As cited in V. Matthews and Benjamin, *Old Testament Parallels*, 22–23.
26. Currid, *Against the Gods*, 36–37.
27. Scurlock, "Introduction," ix; Gunkel, "Influence of Babylonian Mythology"; Frymer-Kensky, "Creation Myths Breed Violence."
28. Sonik, "From Hesiod's Abyss," 1–2.

divine warrior, and the sea serpent.²⁹ More reference will be made to this as the various "water texts" of Scripture are explored.

Another Mesopotamian myth, the Epic of Gilgamesh, dates back to 3300 BCE. Because writing occurred only as recently as 2600 BCE in Mesopotamia, and the oldest copies of the epic available date from 2000–1550 BCE, the utilization and impact of the epic prior to its written form is somewhat uncertain.³⁰ This epic is diverse with its significance to this study found in its references to the "deep" which may be comparable to Gen 1:2, and its mention of a deluge and boat building that may compare to the flood story (Gen 6–9). Whether these actually do find parallels within Scripture will be discussed as the various water texts are investigated. Portions of the Epic of Gilgamesh include the following.

> He who saw the Deep, the country's foundation . . .
> [Gilgamesh, who] saw the Deep, the country's foundation . . .
> He brought back a tale of before the Deluge . . .
> Gilgamesh . . . who restored the cult-centers destroyed by the Deluge.
> (Epic of Gilgamesh 1:1–10, 35–50)³¹

> O man . . . build a boat . . . put on board all living things' seed!
> The boat you will build, her dimensions all shall be equal;
> Her length and breadth the same, cover her with a roof, like the Ocean below.
> The rich man was carrying the pitch, the poor man brought the tackle.
> By the fifth day I had set her hull in position,
> One acre was her area, ten rods the height of her sides . . .
> Six decks I gave her . . .
> Into nine compartments I divided her interior.
> I struck the bilge plugs into her belly.
> I saw to the punting-pole and put in the tackle.
> Three myriad measures of pitch I poured in a furnace,
> Three myriad of tar [I tipped] inside,
> Three myriad of oil fetched the workforce of porters.
> Everything I owned I loaded aboard . . .
> All the living creatures I had loaded aboard.
> I sent my kith and my kin, the beasts of the field, the creatures of the wild.
> (Epic of Gilgamesh 11:10–85)³²

---

29. Sonik, "From Hesiod's Abyss," 1–2.

30. George, *Epic of Gilgamesh*, xviii; V. Matthews and Benjamin, *Old Testament Parallels*, 38; Lemaire, "Schools and Literacy," 207–9.

31. As cited in George, *Epic of Gilgamesh*, 1–2.

32. As cited in George, *Epic of Gilgamesh*, 86–88.

Egyptian Hymns

The Egyptian Hymn to Atum was composed in 1307–1070 BCE. Atum was the chief god who created and protected. Atum lived on a boat traversing the sea, constantly being threatened by the serpent, Apophis, which makes this portion of the story potentially identifiable with *Chaoskampf*.[33] Aside from the similarity to the Gen 3 story of the serpent in Eden, the hymn points to a single creator, the creation of dry land, creation by aforethought and design, and the existence of water and the sea prior to other life forms. Some of it reads as follows.

> I alone am the creator . . .
> When the almighty speaks, all else comes to life.
> There were no heavens and earth,
> There was no dry land . . .
> When I first began to plan their creation . . .
> I alone began to plan and design . . .
> Before I spat Tefnut the rain,
> There was not a living creature . . .
> Shu the wind and Tefnut the rain played on Nun the sea.
> (Hymn to Atum, Cols 26:21—27:15)[34]

When viewed geographically, Israel was somewhat surrounded with alternative accounts of creation. From the East, the Mesopotamians offered Enuma Elish and the Epic of Gilgamesh, while Egypt's Hymn to Atum spoke from the South. Each of these specifically reference water as instrumental to the creation of the world and life. While not the subject of this presentation, numerous additional ancient sources reference creation or water, which may, to some extent, parallel the Genesis creation account. Some of these sources include the Hymn to Ptah, Stories of Atrahasis, Stories of Aqhat, and the Hymn to the Aten.

The geographic proximity of Mesopotamia and Egypt to Israel is not the only nexus. The Levant was dominated at various times by Egypt, and by Mesopotamian cultures, such as Assyria and Babylonia.[35] At other times these political powers were threatening Israel or each other,

---

33. V. Matthews and Benjamin, *Old Testament Parallels*, 3.

34. As cited in V. Matthews and Benjamin, *Old Testament Parallels*, 3–4.

35. The presence and influence of various nations and cultures in the Levant, and upon Israel in particular, is a separate and broad study. General information may be obtained from the following resources: Van de Mieroop, *History*; Nissen et al., *Early History*; Arnold and Strawn, *World around Old Testament*; Greer et al., *Behind the Scenes*; Liverani, *Israel's History*.

making their presences known politically and otherwise throughout the Levant. It is not just that a nation neighboring Israel possessed some mythological writings about creation or water. Whatever religious, social, political, and cultural viewpoints these geographic neighbors held were persistently introduced into the regions of Israel by military force, or voluntarily by international travel, trade, intermarriage, and general socialization.[36] Abraham, the founding father of Israel, had origins in Mesopotamia (Gen 11:31). It is unlikely that his call from God instantly removed from him his decades of intimacy with polytheistic beliefs and mythology. His move from Ur to Canaan, and then to Egypt and back to Canaan, is a good example of cultural transference that surely occurred with more than just Abraham (Gen 11:31; 12:5—13:1).

Israel was monotheistic, but the surrounding worldview was polytheistic.[37] This was a primary distinction between not only the nation of Israel and other nations, but within the creation stories and their use of water as part of the creation process. Israel's God was self-existent, holy, and omnipotent, while the polytheists' gods were often created, depraved, and weak, even succumbing to death.[38] To the polytheists, water was pre-existent, or eternal matter, while Gen 1 presents the eternal God creating the world, including its water, ex nihilo.[39] Both Israel and surrounding cultures believed God, or the gods, had power and prowess. Because the creation itself reveals something about the nature of the Creator, Israel stands alone in presenting its God as self-existent, love, disciplined, orderly, benevolent, and concerned with the welfare of his creation. This is contrasted with polytheistic gods who often were arbitrary, capricious, self-indulgent, lazy, and vindictive.[40] Some of these differences may be merely of degree, but they are still differences.[41] One difference is that the surrounding nations saw in water chaos, conflict, death, and the

---

36. Garcia, *Dynamics of Production*. The intermarriage of Israelites with foreigners is frequently noted in Scripture (Gen 41:45; Ruth 1:4; 1 Kgs 3:1; 11:1; Ezra 10:10). Trade, socialization, and military alliances are frequent topics of the OT (Gen 12:10; 16:1; 25:18; 37:25–36; 41:57; 42:2–3; 2 Sam 5:1; 1 Kgs 5:1; 9:26; 10:22; 2 Kgs 15:19).

37. Currid, *Against the Gods*, 25.

38. Currid, *Against the Gods*, 40–43; Lynch, "Monotheism in Ancient Israel."

39. Currid, *Against the Gods*, 41–43. Sailhamer, *Genesis Unbound*, 113–14.

40. Albrektson, *History and the Gods*, 68–99.

41. Albrektson, *History and the Gods*, 89, 96–97.

emergence of new gods to fill their pantheon, while Israel saw in water "putty in the hands of the Creator."[42]

While *Chaoskampf* has a rich history and many well-known adherents, it also has its opponents. One of the most outspoken, David Toshio Tsumura, believes understanding the imagery of water in Enuma Elish as a creation motif is incorrect, and that this misperception has erroneously been applied to Gen 1. He denies that the Genesis creation story portrays an "order from chaos" motif, and denies that water represents chaos, which is an enemy of God.[43] Tsumura finds varying degrees of support for his viewpoint from Terence Fretheim and others.[44] Some of his argument against *Chaoskampf* is based on specific Hebrew word meanings and usages, and here again, complete agreement cannot be found.[45]

While not diminishing the importance of this line of investigation, it seems important to exercise caution as to the danger of investigating one aspect of the Bible so narrowly, or to be so concerned with proving a particular point, "that the question of *what* is revealed . . . [is] neglected."[46] Reading Genesis, or other biblical texts, exclusively through the lens of ancient Near Eastern literature, *Chaoskampf*, or polemic theology, carries with it the danger of failing to recognize what the text positively affirms. It is important to recognize that water is used in different ways in Scripture. For example, it is used for initiating life and for terminating it, even within the same context, which cautions against premature conclusions (Gen 6–9; Exod 14:21–31). To what extent the biblical use of water reflects *Chaoskampf* or polemic theology will likely fall to the evaluation of each individual water text as evaluated by each reader. A certain tension may exist until a proper interpretive balance can be attained. Accepting or rejecting *Chaoskampf* or polemic theology, partially or completely, is not required to accept the fact of God's use of water to initiate life and accomplish some of his objectives.

---

42. Currid, *Against the Gods*, 46.
43. Tsumura, *Creation and Destruction*, 1.
44. Tsumura, *Creation and Destruction*, 2–5.
45. Tsumura, *Creation and Destruction*, 7–140.
46. Albrektson, *History and the Gods*, 113.

WATER AND THE INITIATION OF PHYSICAL LIFE

The presence of water at the creation of the earth is well attested in Gen 1. The presence of water at the creation of human life is also well known, even if water is not the first thing that comes to mind with human birth. The presence of water in the earth's creation and in human creation share several parallels that are pertinent to this presentation.

Creating Human Life

"And then my water broke" is a typical part of the child-birthing description. What is commonly called water in this context is actually amniotic fluid that is housed inside the amniotic sac. The fluid is 99 percent water, making the water label appropriate.[47] The placenta and the membranes of the amniotic sac filter contaminants such as mercury, lead, cadmium, and other inorganic substances to provide the unborn child biological protection as the amniotic fluid supplies it nutrients.[48] The sac and fluid also provide a protective cushion for the unborn child to prevent its injury from external forces or from the pressure of the mother's organs against it.[49] It is common knowledge that this water plays an integral part of the human birth process.

This utilization of water parallels the utilization of water in the creation of the earth recorded in Gen 1. The amniotic sac, filled with its complex fluid (water), houses and protects the unborn child, just as water enveloped the earth before the expanse separated the waters "which were below the expanse" and the waters "which were above the expanse," and this encasing water kept the earth hidden until dry land appeared (Gen 1:7–9). Prior to this time, like the preborn child, the land was surrounded by darkness, being submerged in water (Gen 1:1–9). Just as the preborn child is birthed into dry land from water, and into light from darkness, the earth was comparably birthed into dry land and light from water and darkness (Gen 1:1–9). Peter says, "The earth was formed out of water and by water" (2 Pet 3:5). The formation of a child in water, and its birth by breaking water, bears strong resemblance to the earth's creation out of water and by water. As it relates to *Chaoskampf*, the preborn child does

---

47. Oughton and Peters, *British Medical Association*, 37.
48. Henriquez-Hernandez et al., "Assessment."
49. Oughton and Peters, *British Medical Association*, 37.

not appear to be in a battle amidst or against evil, nor does it appear to be overwhelmed with chaos. Quite the contrary, its locus is within a highly protective, organized, and efficient atmosphere that provides all that is needed to bring a baby from conception to birth.

The filtration of the amniotic membranes and production of amniotic fluid has its own schedule by which more effort is expended in early pregnancy, and less near the end of the pregnancy as the birth date approaches. Physicians advise against forcing delivery by breaking the amniotic sac and releasing the fluid (water), barring medical necessity.[50] In other words, the human birth process has its own timetable. So did the creation of the earth. First, the earth was "formless and void, and darkness was over the surface of the deep" (Gen 1:2). At some point, presumably at "the beginning" (Gen 1:1), "the Spirit of God was moving over the surface of the waters" (Gen 1:2). God created light, and separated light and darkness, making night and day, establishing the first day (Gen 1:3–5). Waters above and waters below were separated by an expanse called "heaven" which marked the second day (Gen 1:6–8). The waters below the heavens were gathered together and were called "seas," and dry land called "earth" appeared, from which vegetation was willed into existence and grew, marking the third day (Gen 1:9–13). The similarities between the birth of the earth and the birth of a human seem stark! Each is found in a pre-birth holding place surrounded by darkness and water. Each becomes visible and possesses form detectable by the naked eye only when water is separated or broken. Each has its own birthing time schedule.[51]

Psalm 127:3 says, "Behold, children are a gift of the Lord, the fruit of the womb is a reward." In this text, the Hebrew term נַחֲלַת is translated "gift," meaning "inalienable, hereditary property," an inheritance, a possession, often what God gives as one's personal share.[52] A child is a gift bestowed by God to continue the family lineage. It is one's share in the future, or one's legacy. Jacob expressed this concept to Esau by characterizing his children as "the children God has graciously given your servant" (Gen 33:5). It is said of God, "You formed my inward parts; you wove me in my mother's womb" (Ps 139:13). These texts emphasize the active presence and gifting of God in the conception and formation of children in the womb.[53]

---

50. Oughton and Peters, *British Medical Association*, 37; Mahdy et al., "Amniotomy."
51. Sailhamer, *Genesis Unbound*, 113.
52. נַחֲלָה, *HALOT*, 1:687–88; נַחֲלָה, BDB, 635.
53. Numerous biblical texts support this (Gen 2:7; 25:23; 29:31; 30:22; 49:25; Deut

Psalm 127:3 also says children are a "reward." This term is translated from שָׂכָר, the Hebrew word that refers to wages, booty, payment, or recompense.[54] God expressed this concept when Joshua gathered the Israelites before him and God claimed he gave descendants to Abraham and Isaac (Josh 24:1–3). God's gift of a child to create a heritage, to establish one's presence, or to maintain the family lineage is similar to God's creation of the world for the benefit of humankind and its continuance. (Isa 45:18). He is the gifting power behind both. God directed the first animals and humans to "be fruitful and multiply" (Gen 1:22, 24, 28). He spoke similar words over the vegetation (Gen 1:11–12). Both the creation of the earth, and the birthing of new human life originate from God's gracious gifting (Isa 45:12, 18). In each case, God's purpose is to provide for life and its propagation. Psalm 127:3 may be a reflection of Gen 15:1, where God promised Abraham a great reward.[55] The context indicates Abraham understood this promise as referring to descendants (those yet to be born), but a portion of the earth was also included, tying together the creation or gifting of new earth (the land promise) and the gifting of children (Gen 15:1–21).

In an eschatological sense, Jesus said the meek or gentle would "inherit the earth," which may reflect the "restoration of all things," and the creation of the "new heavens and earth" (Matt 5:5; Acts 3:21; 2 Pet 3:10–13). This association of God creating a new heavens and earth, and God's birthing or gifting descendants, may be strengthened by Isaiah's claim of a "new heavens and a new earth" that will be inhabited by "my people" (Isa 65:17–19). It is obvious that the people of which Isaiah spoke had not yet been born, but the birthing of these people and the creation of a new dwelling place surely share a nexus. Isaiah strengthens this connection by saying, "For just as the new heavens and the new earth which I make will endure before me, declares the Lord, so your offspring and your name will endure" (Isa 66:22). This verse specifically speaks of the future creation of a new heavens and earth, along with the birthing of children. In the original creation of the heavens and earth God births the earth (humanity's dwelling place) from watery darkness and invisibility, giving it dry land, light, and visibility (Gen 1:1–9; 2 Pet 3:5). In the eschaton, God replaces the heavens and earth that currently lie in spiritual

---

7:13; 28:4, 11; 30:39; Judg 13:5; 1 Sam 1:5–6; Ps 94:9; 139:13–16; Eccl 11:5; Isa 29:16; 44:24; 49:5; Jer 1:5; John 9:1–3).

54. שָׂכָר, *HALOT*, 2:1330–31; שָׂכָר, BDB, 968–69.

55. Goldingay, *Psalms*, 3:503.

darkness, and he creates a new heaven and earth characterized by light. He discards spiritually darkened humanity into "outer darkness," and he births new souls for habitation in the newly created heavens and earth (Isa 9:1; Matt 4:15–16; 8:12; John 1:5; 3:19; 8:12; 12:46; Acts 26:15–18; Eph 6:12; Col 1:12–13; 1 Thess 5:5; 1 Pet 2:9; 2 Pet 2:17; 1 John 2:8; Jude 1:13; Rev 21:24; 22:5).

The physical birth of a person closely resembles the original creation of the heavens and earth in terms of their transitions from water, darkness, and invisibility, into dry ground, light, and visibility. Each has its own specific birthing timetable. Each occurs only as a gift from God. The creation of the eschatological new heavens and earth shares spiritual characteristics paralleling the creation of the original heavens and earth, and human birth.[56] For example, in the eschaton spiritual darkness disappears and only God's light exists, just as the original creation brought the earth from darkness to light, even as childbirth also does. Entrance into the new heavens and earth is reserved for those who have been "born of water and the Spirit," echoing that the original earth was created from water by the work of the Spirit, and that children are born from the hand of God and through water (Gen 1:1–9: 33:5; John 3:3–7; Gal 4:21–31; Titus 3:5–7; 1 Pet 1:3, 23; Rev 22:14). The new heavens and earth are provided as a gift from God, emulating the gifts of the original earth and each newborn child (Gen 1:1–31; Ps 127:3; Isa 45:12, 18; Eph 2:8–9). Like the original creation of the heavens and earth, and as in childbirth, the creation of the new heavens and earth is set within God's timetable (Gen 1:1–13; Prov 3:20; Matt 24:36–39, 42–44). Jesus depicts the ushering in of the end-time with its new heavens and earth as beginning with "birth pains" (Matt 24:8), and likens anticipation of his return (and the unveiling of the new heavens and earth) to a woman giving birth (John 16:16–22). The apostle Paul continues the birthing metaphor in his description of children born of the Spirit, born into freedom, who are part

---

56. Niehaus, *Ancient Near Eastern Themes*, 31–32. The end-time, the parousia, the coming of new Jerusalem, Christian hope, eternal salvation, banishment of the wicked to darkness, the restoration of all things, and the establishment of new heavens and earth are considered interrelated and used collectively, referencing the same general time and the events surrounding the creation of the new heavens and earth. Present possession of these components is advocated in the NT due to the certainty of God's promises, the indwelling of the Holy Spirit, and the present relationship of believers to Christ which is yet to be fully realized with his bodily presence. Detailed discussion arguing such a position is beyond the scope of this presentation, and it is expected readers will find general agreement with this position, even though each component may be presented in some sequential order and not necessarily all at the same exact moment.

of the Jerusalem from above, which is part of the new heavens and earth (Gal 4:21–31; Rev 21:1–2, 10–11). Paul again uses the birthing metaphor to describe the struggle of believers in a dark and corrupt world who await their future hope in the new heavens and earth (Rom 8:18–24).

The intent of this discussion is to propose that God uses water to create physical life, both in his original creation of the earth, and in human reproduction. Based on the evidence presented, it is suggested that this proposal is strengthened by God providing humanity an aide-mémoire, an image of his original creation and purpose, with each new human pregnancy and birth. In both cases, water was, and is, instrumental in initiating life. In both cases, new creation arrives only by God's grace and will. It is also suggested that human creation by water not only looks backward to the original creation of the earth, but also forward to the new heavens and earth. While water is also instrumental in creating the new heavens and earth, the new heavens and earth interestingly results from a renovation of the existing heavens and earth that were created out of water (Jer 33:1–11; Amos 9:11–15; Zech 14:8–11; Acts 3:19–21; Heb 12:27–28; 2 Pet 3:5, 10–13). The inhabitants of the "kingdom of God" included in the new heavens and earth are those "born of water and the Spirit" (John 3:3–7; Rev 1:6–7; 5:10; 11:15–19). This connects birth, albeit spiritual birth, and the creation of a new heavens and earth. The new heavens and earth are also described as the locus for the "water of life" (Ps 46:4; Ezek 47:1–12; Zech 14:8; Rev 22:1, 17).

The connections between human birth and the original creation of the earth are numerous and glaring. The utilization of water in each is clear and unequivocal. Although discussed later, it is noteworthy here that the original creation of the earth and human birth by water mirror both the creation of the new heaven and earth, and the spiritual birth of believers. Throughout these analogies, God has chosen water to play an integral role in accomplishing his purposes of initiating physical life, whether regarding the earth, or humanity.

Creating the Earth

The subject of creation in Genesis captures the mind of even the casual reader. Without it, it is claimed "the rest of the Bible becomes incomprehensible."[57] The creation account is said to be "a highly

---

57. V. Hamilton, "Introduction," 1.

sophisticated presentation, designed to emphasize the sublimity ... of the Creator God."[58] Because of this, "we should take the fact very seriously that creation is the first topic the authors of the Hebrew Bible wanted to present to the reader."[59] But, the topic of creation and the revelation of, and about, the Creator in this first chapter of Genesis is said to be "anything but transparent."[60] How one understands the vagueness about creation, why the text was written, the literary style, the meanings of certain words and their syntactical arrangements, and the theological significance of what is said has generated such conflict, it has been called a "bloodied battleground."[61]

The purpose of this writing is not to advocate for or against a particular theory of cosmology, nor to delve into issues of literary style, genre, or compositional matters. Rather, it is to expose the use of water in the creation process affirming that God chose water as an instrument through which he created life. This refers both to the physical world where life is sustained and propagated, and more narrowly to human life, much of which has already been addressed above. It seems unlikely anyone would deny the presence of water in the creation story of Gen 1–2. What is lacking is the appreciation of the use of water in creation and its repetitive utilization throughout Scripture as a birthing instrument in both the physical sense and also in a spiritual sense. This dissertation argues that water is part of an inclusio existing between Gen 1–2 and Rev 21–22. Between these end points God's use of water unfolds as his mechanism through which life is initiated. In order to see this larger canonical picture, its first boundary marker, Gen 1–2, must be the starting point.

Genesis 1

"In the beginning God created the heavens and the earth" begins the Bible, and along with it heated controversy attends on numerous fronts.[62] Much of the controversy is not relevant to this endeavor, but what is important is that God is clearly named as the sole Creator of what is called "the heavens and the earth." This first sentence "is to be understood as a

---

58. Waltke with Fredricks, *Genesis*, 56.
59. Rendtorff, "Creation and Redemption," 312.
60. Walton, *Lost World*, 5.
61. Walton, *Lost World*, 5.
62. Sailhamer, *Genesis Unbound*, 23; Wenham, *Genesis*, 1:11–15.

principal sentence . . . and . . . it acquires monumental importance which distinguishes it from other creation stories. . . . The narrative unfolds everything that it contains."[63] For those favoring polemic theology, this may provide a clear contrast between monotheism and polytheism. The Egyptians, for example, saw "no distinction between the gods and the universe" as they were essentially the same.[64] Genesis 1:1 offers a very clear distinction of God who is separate and transcendent from the heavens and earth he created. "Heavens and earth" is also inclusive, not just of the literal heaven and earth, but of all that entails, including humanity that dwells therein.[65] It may be viewed as the totality of creation, but also as an infant state which has much more to be realized.[66]

The Hebrew term בָּרָא is translated "created," which has engendered considerable comment. It is an overstatement that the term refers to original creation only, and that only by God, as opposed to things created or formed from that which already exists, or made by another instead of God.[67] The correct understanding is that בָּרָא refers to creation by only God, but not necessarily original creation.[68] That בָּרָא is used three times in Gen 1:27 for God creating humanity from existing matter provides a warrant for this amended use of the term. The significance of this clarification for this work is that God's ability to create life from things that already exist is not an impediment to God's use of water to initiate life. It is completely inconsequential whether water preexisted the earth, or whether water and earth were created at the same moment. That God used water to initiate life is what this work advocates, and *barah* does not encumber this position.

The "heavens and earth" is a merism describing the universe.[69] The world that God created was intended as the habitation for humanity.[70] God declared what he had made "good" (1:4, 10, 12, 18, 21, 25), but it was

---

63. Westermann, *Genesis*, 1:97.

64. A. Morris, "Lost Truth of Genesis," 50.

65. Wenham, *Genesis*, 1:15; Westermann, *Genesis*, 1:101; Waltke with Fredricks, *Genesis*, 59; Steinmann, *Genesis*, 50; Rad, *Genesis*, 48.

66. Poythress, "Genesis 1:1," 99.

67. Westermann, *Genesis*, 1:98–100.

68. Wenham, *Genesis*, 1:14–15; Walton, "Genesis," 1:11; Waltke with Fredricks, *Genesis*, 58–59.

69. Sailhamer, *Genesis Unbound*, 114–15; Westermann, *Genesis*, 1:101; Waltke with Fredricks, *Genesis*, 59; Heidel, *Babylonian Genesis*, 90–91.

70. Sailhamer, *Genesis Unbound*, 117; Waltke with Fredricks, *Genesis*, 59.

declared "very good" only when humanity was made (1:31). The creation of humanity not only completed the created order, but it placed within that world those for whom it was created. Each element of creation was good. When the accumulated components of creation were in place and ready to fulfill their integrated purpose, they were actuated by the addition of those for whom creation was intended, and the process was upgraded to full functionality, or "very good" status.

As part of his creative process, numerous components came into existence by God's spoken word (1:3, 6, 9, 11, 14, 20, 24, 26). Although not specifically stated in the Gen 1 text, there is no reason to think divine directive did not also create the earth and the water in which it was submerged. In Gen 1 Israel's God appears intelligent, self-existent, self-sufficient, and by transcendent fiat created the heavens and earth. Standing in stark contrast are the surrounding polytheistic cultures that have gods who were not necessarily self-existent intelligent beings, but were in some cases composed of "uncreated matter," or in other cases "came into being," frequently needed sustenance, and they were created by divine waters marrying, or by masturbating, or by chaotic conflict.[71] Genesis clearly elevates Israel's God above the gods of competing cultures.

"The earth was formless and void, and darkness was over the surface of the deep, and the Spirit of God was moving over the surface of the waters" (1:2). The phrase תֹהוּ וָבֹהוּ is typically translated "formless and void." It is a merism and an antonym to "heavens and earth."[72] The first word of the phrase, תֹהוּ, means "formless," and can refer to a wilderness, wasteland, emptiness, desert, or nothing.[73] The NRSV translates its nineteen HB appearances as "formless," "waste," "useless," "chaos," "nothing," "confusion," "emptiness," and "empty" (1:2; Deut 32:10, 1 Sam 12:21; Isa 24:10; 29:21; 34:11; 40:17; 41:29). The second word of the phrase, וָבֹהוּ, is often translated "void" and refers to emptiness or wasteness.[74] The phrase references a nonproductive, nonfunctioning wasteland.[75] It is a place where its life-producing purpose is not occurring.[76] Based primarily on etymological

---

71. V. Matthews and Benjamin, *Old Testament Parallels*, 4, 8, 22; Heidel, *Babylonian Genesis*, 88, 96–97.

72. Waltke with Fredricks, *Genesis*, 59.

73. תֹהוּ, *HALOT*, 2:1689–90.

74. תֹהוּ, *HALOT*, 1:111.

75. Walton, "Genesis," 1:11–13.

76. Waltke with Fredricks, *Genesis*, 59–60; Tsumura, *Earth and the Waters*; Westermann, *Genesis*, 1:103.

studies, syntactical arrangement, and use of the terms in the HB, David Tsumura believes the concept of chaos is absent in Gen 1, but rather the idea presented is of a nonproductive womb, a bare state, one that is not functioning in its intended role.[77] Tsumura rejects Gunkel's connection of this text to ancient Near Eastern mythologies, and others agree that such a connection is untenable based upon the actual meaning and usage of *tohu wabohu* in Genesis and in ancient secular usage, as well the lack of ancient texts that actually refer to an unproductive watery wasteland.[78] The two terms תֹהוּ and וָבֹהוּ are considered a hendiadys used as an opposite to creation.[79] John Walton has argued that in the ancient Near East functionality was the key determinant of existence, meaning that during the state of *tohu wabohu* there was no functionality, but when *tohu wabohu* gave way to functionality and productivity, existence, or life, ensued.[80]

From the explicitness of 1 John 1:5, that "God is light and in him is no darkness at all," interpretation from a post-NT perspective may read into Gen 1:2 that the presence of "darkness" insinuates God's absence. Genesis 1:2, however, indicates God was present because "the Spirit of God was moving over the surface of the waters," while at the same time "darkness was over the surface of the deep." God and darkness appear together in this text, but they were not operating in lockstep. Darkness often refers to a spiritual condition that is devoid of light and life (1 John 1:5). In the ancient Near East light, like darkness, was viewed as a condition.[81] Light and life unite spiritually in Jesus, and to have one is to have the other (John 1:4). Light and darkness are antithetical (John 3:19–20; 8:12; 12:46; Acts 26:18). One cannot have both at the same time (John 1:5; 3:19; 8:12; 12:35, 46; 1 John 2:9–10). Spiritual darkness indicates the inability of humanity to properly function, while having light enables life and proper functioning (John 11:9–10; 12:35; Eph 5:8).

The same principle applies to the heavens and earth of which humanity is a part. In its darkness, the water and the earth submerged within it are useless, lacking life, and nonfunctional. While the presence

---

77. Tsumura, *Earth and the Waters*, 30, 41–43.

78. Wenham, *Genesis*, 1:16; Westermann, *Genesis*, 1:103–6; Walton, "Genesis," 1:12–13. Heidel, *Babylonian Genesis*, 97–98. Heidel uses "chaos" to describe the Enuma Elish scene, but agrees the description in Genesis is that of "inanimate matter" rather than one in which living beings existed.

79. Westermann, *Genesis*, 1:103; Wenham, *Genesis*, 1:15–16.

80. Walton, *Lost World*, 1–52.

81. Walton, *Lost World*, 53.

of darkness may seem to bolster both the *Chaoskampf* theory and polemic theology, the presence of darkness in Gen 1:2 positively affirms the inability of existence to function in such a condition.[82] Darkness is an inherent characteristic in the ancient Greek concept of chaos, and here it is the opposite of creation, indicating that what existed was unable to fulfill its intended purpose.[83] Something had to change for this existence to become functional.

Darkness was over the surface of תְהוֹם (1:2). "The deep" is the typical translation of the Hebrew term, תְהוֹם, an etymological equivalent of *Ti'amat*, one of the prime characters in Enuma Elish who represented saltwater.[84] Gunkel claimed this similarity linked the two and helped lend credence to his association of Enuma Elish to Genesis.[85] Upon further investigation this view has been rejected by many who note that coming from the same root word does not make the two terms identical or even related in usage, and the differences within the terms have forced many to sever any mythological connection.[86] The meaning of תְהוֹם, or "the deep," is ocean, sea, or even flood or deluge.[87] The deep appears to be the same "waters" (הַמַיִם) over which the Spirit moved (1:2). In another effort to link Enuma Elish to the Genesis creation account, it is suggested by some that מַיִם (waters) is a dual noun meaning that it is part of a pair, as is שָׁמַיִם (heavens or skies), and that this duality sufficiently links the Genesis story to Enuma Elish. But even some suggesting similarities also post precautions.[88] The significance of "the deep" in Gen 1:2 is that it is water, it is deep or massive, it is hidden in darkness, it is nonfunctional, and it is soon to be revealed that earth is housed within it (1:6–10). "Let there be an expanse in the midst of the waters, and let it separate the waters from the water. . . . God made the expanse, and separated the waters which were below the expanse from the waters which were above the expanse. . . . God called the expanse heaven" (1:6–8). The term translated "expanse" in this text, רָקִיעַ, is used fifteen times in the HB and translated

---

82. Waltke with Fredricks, *Genesis*, 60.

83. Westermann, *Genesis*, 1:104–5; Walton, *Lost World*, 52.

84. V. Matthews and Benjamin, *Old Testament Parallels*, 22; Heidel, *Babylonian Genesis*, 98–99; Wenham, *Genesis*, 1:16; Westermann, *Genesis*, 1:105–6.

85. Gunkel, "Influence of Babylonian Mythology."

86. Tsumura, *Earth and the Waters*, 45–65; Heidel, *Babylonian Genesis*, 98–99; Westermann, *Genesis*, 1:105–6; Wenham, *Genesis*, 1:16; Walton, "Genesis," 1:13, 15.

87. תְהוֹם, *HALOT*, 2:1690–91; Walton, "Genesis," 1:13, 15.

88. Kee, "Study on Dual Form."

as "expanse" each time by the NASB, and as "firmament" each time by the ASV. The NRSV translates the term as "firmament" in Pss 19:2 and 150:1, as "skies" in Dan 12:3, but as "dome" in all other passages. The NIV uses "skies" in Ps 19:1 and Dan 12:3, "heavens" in Ps 150:1, but "vault" in all other texts. What God called "expanse" also presents some translation inconsistency with the expanse also being called "heaven" by the NASB, ASV, and ESV, but called "sky" by the NRSV, NIV, and CEB.

What Gen 1 presents is an expanse, also called heaven or sky, that separated the water into two components, the waters above the expanse and the waters below the expanse (1:6–7). It was God who called this expanse into existence (1:6–7). The only water known to exist at this point is "the deep" (1:2). Following this separation of the deep into two regions, the lower water, "the waters below the heavens, were gathered into one place in order to let dry land appear" (1:9). The dry land was called "earth" and the waters that had been gathered together God called "seas" (1:10). Prior to this separation, God created light (1:3–5). In this process a very clear and orderly birthing process unfolds. God systematically assembles one element after another, taking the raw products that were formless and void, shrouded in darkness, and as the ultimate artisan God provides light, form, and organizes each component to function for his intended purposes.

The end product, the earth ("the heavens and earth"), began in darkness and lacked form or usefulness, being unseen and encased in water. At the time selected by God darkness disappeared giving way to light, water broke apart, fluid and solid earth separated, and the result was a functional habitation for humanity. The numerous parallels to human birth seem overwhelming. Liquid-like sperm and egg unite in darkness and remain encased in a watery substance, hidden until the water breaks apart. The once formless, which progresses into a form, emerges. The hidden becomes visible. Functionality and purpose are launched.

Once the earth was formed, God began adding accoutrements to enhance and sustain human existence, much like the mother who even before birth acquires things with which to surround her newborn to demonstrate love, care, warmth, order, protection, nutrition, and entertainment. God added vegetation, animals, luminaries, and order by the separation of night and day; pleasure from husband/wife companionship and sexual encounters; a sense of belonging from the birth of children, naming of animals, and coregency with God; entertainment in the unusual creatures roaming the earth and their newborns; and most of all, companionship with the Creator. All of these accommodations were planned for in advance, many put in place prior to human creation (or birth), with some coming afterward (Gen 1–2). "Thus, the heavens and earth were completed, and all their hosts" (2:1) identifies the heavens and earth as not just the formless and void earth veiled in darkness, but also the heavens and earth that were revealed by light and separated from the waters, including all that was added to it, such as vegetation, animals, and humanity, to bring it to full functionality.[89] "The heavens and earth" functions epexegetically, meaning that embedded within the term is much more that enhances and clarifies what is meant. It was in the water that God planted the dark heavens and earth. It was from the breaking of that water that God birthed the visible heavens and earth, and each of its components including humanity, to make it fully operational. Thus, it is fair to conclude that God created human life from and by water (2 Pet 3:5).

It would be hard to deny that a general polemical message is absent in the Gen 1–2 creation account. But whether one is primary, or geared toward a specific myth, may diminish the brilliance of God's intricate fashioning and the overwhelming magnanimity toward humanity that engulfs the mind and bewilders one's imagination. Generically speaking, all of the ancient Near Eastern creation myths are eclipsed by the Genesis account. The obvious lack of struggle common in mythology is absent in Genesis.[90] No ancient Near Eastern creation myth has the "spirit of God" present.[91] God is a unified whole, not divided into uneven or unequal parts.[92] The created components are made by God, and are not also part of God.[93]

This discussion has been intended to lead to several admissions. The first is that the heavens and earth were created "out of water and by water" (1:1–10; 2 Pet 3:5). The Gen 1 account makes this clear and Peter's statement is a summation of such. The second is that the phrase "the heavens and earth" functions in somewhat an epexegetical fashion, also referencing the life that dwells within it, including humanity. God did not merely create idle water and land, but a functional habitat in which humanity and all that support it could flourish. Third, since the heavens and earth were created from and by water, and since they include all that dwells therein, including humanity, it is just to claim that God birthed humanity

89. Poythress, "Genesis 1:1."
90. Westermann, *Genesis*, 1:106.
91. Walton, "Genesis," 1:15.
92. Walton, "Genesis," 1:16–17.
93. Walton, "Genesis," 1:17.

from and by water. Fourth, the orderliness of the creation event demonstrates a powerful and cogent God who systematically created with forethought and purpose, leaving nothing undone or to chance. While the intricacies of God's rationale remain a mystery, the presence of his reasoning is nonetheless evident.

Genesis 6–9

The biblical story of the flood is well known today, just as a flood story was well known across the ancient world being popularized by the Epic of Gilgamesh, the Stories of Atrahasis, and others.[94] The following excerpts from Gilgamesh speak of a deluge and of the building of an ark, including using pitch in its construction, and loading the ark.

> He who saw the Deep, the country's foundation. . . .
> [Gilgamesh, who] saw the Deep, the country's foundation. . . .
> He brought back a tale of before the Deluge . . .
> Gilgamesh . . . who restored the cult-centers destroyed by the Deluge.
> (Epic of Gilgamesh 1:1–10, 35–50)[95]

> O man . . . build a boat . . . put on board all living things' seed!
> The boat you will build, her dimensions all shall be equal;
> Her length and breadth the same, cover her with a roof, like the Ocean below.
> The rich man was carrying the pitch, the poor man brought the tackle.
> By the fifth day I had set her hull in position,
> One acre was her area, ten rods the height of her sides. . . .
> Six decks I gave her. . . .
> Into nine compartments I divided her interior.
> I struck the bilge plugs into her belly.
> I saw to the punting-pole and put in the tackle.
> Three myriad measures of pitch I poured in a furnace,
> Three myriad of tar [I tipped] inside,
> Three myriad of oil fetched the workforce of porters.
> Everything I owned I loaded aboard. . . .
> All the living creatures I had loaded aboard.
> I sent my kith and my kin, the beasts of the field, the creatures of the wild.
> (Epic of Gilgamesh 11:10–85)[96]

---

94. Wenham, *Genesis*, 1:146, 159–69; Waltke with Fredricks, *Genesis*, 132; Westermann, *Genesis*, 1:395–406.

95. As cited in George, *Epic of Gilgamesh*, 1–2.

96. As cited in George, *Epic of Gilgamesh*, 86–88.

Stories of Atrahasis have been preserved as Sumerian epics on fragments dated to 800–600 BCE.[97] They speak of the flood, an ark or barge, pitch, closing the door of the vessel, and the destruction of mortals.

> I would build a barge. I would abandon all my possessions . . . to save my life.
> Place a roof over the barge. . . . Make the joints strong, caulk the timbers with pitch.
> I will gather flocks of birds for you. Set the time of the flood for seven days.
> He bolts the door, and seals it with pitch.
> The noise in the land ceases, The flood rushes forward.
> There is no sun, only the darkness of the flood.
> Where is he who so thoughtlessly decreed a flood . . . who condemned his own people to destruction?
> (Stories of Atrahasis 3.1.8–48; 2:48–55; 3:10–54)[98]

Certainly more texts could be cited, but these portray the general concept of a divinely ordained flood that has some analogy to the biblical account, along with considerable disparity.[99] Some believe these similar accounts arise from a simple time when people had in common both home and faith.[100] Whether that is an accurate depiction is open for debate, but the presence of such extrabiblical stories plainly enlivens a polemic theology perspective. The biblical flood story, however, may have more in common with the Genesis creation story.

Noah has been called "Adam *redivivus*" because "both 'walk' with God; both are the recipients of the promissory blessing; both are caretakers of the lower creatures . . . both are workers of the soil."[101] Each is said to bear "the image of God" (1:26–28; 9:6); each is told to be fruitful and multiply (1:28–30; 9:1–7); each sinned by partaking of the earth's fruit (3:6–7; 9:21); the result of the sin of each is nakedness and shame (3:7; 9:21), and curses follow both (3:17; 9:25); both were clothed by another as a result of their sins (3:21; 9:23); each has three sons, and one of each set of sons commits a heinous sin for which he is cursed (4:8–11; 9:22–25).[102]

---

97. V. Matthews and Benjamin, *Old Testament Parallels*, 10.
98. As cited in V. Matthews and Benjamin, *Old Testament Parallels*, 17–19.
99. Coogan, *Brief Introduction*, 61; Westermann, *Genesis*, 1:393–406.
100. Niehaus, *Ancient Near Eastern Themes*, 22.
101. K. Matthews, *Genesis 1—11:26*, 349.
102. K. Matthews, *Genesis 1—11:26*, 349; Waltke with Fredricks, *Genesis*, 127–28.

Many other similarities exist, including that just as with creation and human birth, the flood also operated according to God's timetable.[103]

These parallels help paint the broad duplication of the Genesis story of creation in its story of re-creation.[104] More pertinent to this writing, Adam and Noah come to exist after watery chaos is reset to its intended functionality by God who governs each (1:1; 6:13; 7:1; 8:1; 9:1).[105] It is water that God utilized to birth the heavens and earth, including all life residing therein, and it is again water that God uses to reverse his original creation, and reestablish it.[106] "A new world is born of the watery grave of the old."[107] It is by this watery act that "man is given a fresh start. The commands given at creation are renewed."[108]

The waters of the flood are waters of death and of life. Excluding those in the ark, all animals that roamed the earth and all humanity died. The floodwaters were likely a foul-smelling depressing sight, populated with floating dead bodies that had forfeited life by losing all purpose and utility due to their spiritual degeneracy.[109] The floodwaters mirrored the dark chaotic creation waters before they were separated and light and life was ordained, and the heavens and earth emerged to be anointed with all its appurtenances (1:1—2:1).[110] Just as the waters were shrouded in darkness before they were transformed by light, visibility, and separation in creation, the floodwaters are juxtaposed against light and life, what was "good," and what was "very good." Just as the crowning act of creation was humankind who made it all "very good," once again, after cleansing the earth of its depravity, God saw fit to make humankind the centerpiece of his interest and caused the dark waters of death and worthlessness to also become the fountain of life from which humanity again would emerge.

---

103. K. Matthews, *Genesis 1—11:26*, 349-50; Waltke with Fredricks, *Genesis*, 127-30; Westermann, *Genesis*, 1:393. Genesis 1 provides a systematic day-by-day process of creation. Genesis 6-9 provides a detail of Noah's age, length of time of the rain, time in the ark, and time of water recession. God is identified as being in control of both schedules. The birthing process is discussed above and the gestation calendar is common knowledge.

104. Waltke with Fredricks, *Genesis*, 170-71, 187; Wenham, *Genesis*, 1:183; Westermann, *Genesis*, 1:393.

105. Wenham, *Genesis*, 1:183.

106. Wenham, *Genesis*, 1:145, 183; Westermann, *Genesis*, 1:393.

107. Wenham, *Genesis*, 1:188.

108. Wenham, *Genesis*, 1:188.

109. Westermann, *Genesis*, 1:408-9.

110. Waltke with Fredricks, *Genesis*, 132.

In this floodwater was both death and life, and both were initiated by God. Death arose from God's holy inability to tolerate decadence, while life sprung from his love for humanity, and his desire to dwell among it (1:29–30; 2:16–17, 22; 3:8–24; 6:6–7, 11–14, 17–18; 7:1; 8:1—9:1–17; Lev 26:11–12; Ps 11:4–7; Ezek 36:23; Heb 12:10, 14; 1 Pet 3:13–22; 2 Pet 2:5–10; Rev 21:7–8; 22:15).

The strength of the thesis that God used water to initiate life is enhanced by the overwhelming linkage of the flood narrative to the creation story (cited above). The concept that God initiates life by water is extended from creation to Noah and his family in the flood. This sequel episode helps reinforce the original, and vice-versa. It is noteworthy that only Noah, and not any of his family, was said to be righteous (6:8–9). It is reasonable to believe God saved them as a blessing to Noah, and to repopulate the earth as he later instructed (9:1). While Noah was physically birthed by water, he was also saved from death by water, which rendered a life-giving result (1 Pet 3:18–22). Noah and the flood symbolized the death of the old world and the creation of the new way of life.[111] Thus, even in the flood, God used water to initiate life.

Exodus 2

The Nile River was the defining feature of Egypt and the source of livelihood for the Egyptians.[112] It was considered by the Egyptians a gift from their gods and a symbol of fertility.[113] As the river flooded each year it provided water to a desert region enabling the growth of vegetation that sustained the nation.[114] Along the Nile the Egyptians venerated many gods, and oddly, Egyptians also held to the view of one god, and they lived amidst the tension and diversity created by these opposing views.[115] This background becomes important in the coming discussion of Moses turning the Nile into blood.

One of the famous myths of the ancient Near East was the birth legend of Sargon, king of Akkad (2334–2279 BCE), a city founded about

---

111. Waltke with Fredricks, *Genesis*, 143, 152.
112. LeMon, "Egypt and the Egyptians," 169; Wells, "Exodus," 169–70.
113. Wells, "Exodus," 170.
114. LeMon, "Egypt and the Egyptians," 169–70.
115. LeMon, "Egypt and the Egyptians," 169–71.

3000 BCE that later became an empire based near modern Bagdad, Iraq.[116] Copies of the birth legend of Sargon in different dialects have been dated from 2000–1500 BCE.[117] The parallels with the birth story of Moses are numerous making it difficult to deny the polemical nature of the biblical story, even though significant differences also exist.[118] Excerpts from the myth include the following.

> I am the one and only Great King of Akkad.
> My mother was a priest.
> My mother gave birth to me in secret.
> She hid me in a basket woven from rushes and sealed with tar.
> My mother abandoned me on the bank of the Euphrates River.
> Aqqi lifted me out of the water.
> This good gardener reared me as his own son.
> Aqqi trained me to care for the royal orchards;
> Because Istar, my godmother, watched over me.
> I became a Great King.
> (Birth Story of Sargon 1)[119]

It has been suggested that an "abandoned child" motif was common throughout the ancient world, and this may be the general backdrop for the Moses birth story.[120] Such a motif also seems to fit well with reference to Israel at this time, being supported by the narrative of God remembering and taking notice of Israel who was in bondage (2:24–25).[121] The typology of the Moses birth story with various facets of the Jesus birth story is also evident. For example, both Moses and Jesus were saved in Egypt from murderous kings (2:1–10; Matt 2:13–22); both came up out of the water, Moses by the hand of Pharaoh's daughter, and Jesus at his baptism by the hand of John (2:5; Matt 3:16); both were sent from Egypt into the same land, Israel or what became Israel (Exod 3:8; Matt 2:21); both came from priestly families and functioned as high priests (Gen 46:11; Exod 6:18–20; 28:41; 29:21; Ps 99:6; Heb 5:10; 6:20); each had a complex identity in that Moses was a Hebrew raised as an Egyptian, and Jesus was

---

116. V. Matthews and Benjamin, *Old Testament Parallels*, 91; Hays and Machinist, "Assyria and the Assyrians," 98–100.

117. V. Matthews and Benjamin, *Old Testament Parallels*, 91.

118. Meyers, *Exodus*, 43; V. Hamilton, *Exodus*, 50.

119. As cited in V. Matthews and Benjamin, *Old Testament Parallels*, 91–92.

120. Meyers, *Exodus*, 43; V. Hamilton, *Exodus*, 50; LeMon, "Egypt and the Egyptians," 171.

121. Fretheim, *Exodus*, 42.

thought to be from Nazareth, but was born in Bethlehem, while he was at the same time both God and man (Matt 2:1; John 1:34, 46; 7:42); each fulfilled the role of the deliverer of others, Moses for Israel, and Jesus for the world (Exod 15:22; John 3:16; Eph 4:8; 1 John 2:2).[122]

The importance of this background material increases in significance with future references back to this text. As it pertains to the immediate initiation of life by water, Moses was placed in the water to provide him life, then retrieved from the water and given an abundant life with his own mother's nurturing, with newfound freedom including education and affluence from his stepmother, and by access to the most powerful person in the region, Pharaoh (2:7–10; Acts 7:22). Water was truly a significant instrument in giving Moses life literally and qualitatively.

The ironies in this story are many.[123] Much like the flood in Noah's day that was the symbol of both death and life, the Nile was intended as a place of death to Hebrew children, but became the source of life for Moses, a Hebrew child (1:22; 2:1–10).[124] The intent of killing Hebrew babies in the Nile was a result of Pharaoh's wickedness, through which he intended to thwart God's purpose for his chosen people. Yet, the very water intended to prevent God's desires for his people saved and enabled God's instrument of Israel's deliverance (Moses), thereby advancing God's goals. Parallel is the flood story in which wickedness challenged God's creative purpose for humanity to live in righteous abundance (Gen 1:30—2:3). God let wickedness take its destructive course in the flood, saving only the one through whom he chose to initiate life anew, Noah (Gen 6:13; 9:11). Moses, also a chosen one, survives to lead God's chosen people to new life, while the wickedness of Pharaoh ends in death by water. In each case, Noah and Moses, water was the instrument of both death and life, and in each case God prevailed over wickedness and its purveyors by the use of water.

The Hebrew word for Noah's ark is *tevah*. The only other place in the OT the term is used is for the "basket" to hold Moses (2:3; Gen 6:14).[125] Like the ark of Noah that was covered with "pitch," so the ark of Moses was also covered with "pitch" (2:3; Gen 6:14). While these terms connect Moses to Noah and the flood, Moses is also connected to creation, just

---

122. Fretheim, *Exodus*, 40–41.
123. Johnstone, *Exodus*, 30; Meyers, *Exodus*, 42.
124. Meyers, *Exodus*, 42.
125. Meyers, *Exodus*, 43.

as it has been shown above that the flood was connected to creation.[126] Moses's mother saw him at birth and declared him "beautiful," which is the same Hebrew word used when God saw his creation and repeatedly declared it "good" (2:2; Gen 1:4, 10, 12, 18, 21, 25). In each case this term signaled "a new era."[127]

Exodus 7

Another irony is that the Nile, so revered by Egypt as a source of life, was the springboard for Egypt's nemesis, Moses.[128] Moses transposed this source of life for the powerful nation into blood, rendering death to the aquatic life therein, making it, and all water in Egypt, useless for any purpose (Exod 4:9; 7:14–24).[129] In this act, the Nile that had been intended as a place of death for the male Hebrew infants, instead became a place of death to the Egyptians, and it became such at the hand of the Hebrew infant who had been rescued from the Nile.[130] This act by Moses demonstrated the power of God over the Nile, an icon of Egyptian deity.[131] The fact that the Egyptian magicians were able to replicate this miracle implies that it was short-lived, and may have merely been used by Moses to get the attention of Pharaoh, for surely God knew in advance what the magicians were capable of doing.[132] In this act of turning water to blood, God reverts this portion of his creation back to its chaotic or dysfunctional status to portend the ultimate end of Pharaoh's wicked behavior.[133] It is as if Pharaoh is being chided to remember creation, and the re-creation via the flood with its death to those opposing God, as the consequence for behavior intended to wreck God's creative purposes.[134] The repetition of many water-related terms in this text, such as "Nile," "rivers,"

---

126. Najman and Schmid, "Reading the Blood Plague," 37–40.
127. Meyers, *Exodus*, 43.
128. Najman and Schmid, "Reading the Blood Plague," 40.
129. Wells, "Exodus," 190.
130. Najman and Schmid, "Reading the Blood Plague," 40.
131. Najman and Schmid, "Reading the Blood Plague," 23–42; Keel, *Symbolism of Biblical World*, 73–76.
132. V. Hamilton, *Exodus*, 142; Fretheim, *Exodus*, 115.
133. Fretheim, *Exodus*, 110–11; Najman and Schmid, "Reading the Blood Plague," 37–40.
134. Fretheim, *Exodus*, 110–11; Meyers, *Exodus*, 81; Najman and Schmid, "Reading the Blood Plague," 37–40.

"streams," "ponds," "canals," "pools," "reservoirs," and even vessels holding water, foreshadow Pharaoh's final destruction by water.[135] Moses as the prototype of Jesus has been noted, and this first "plague" adds to that analogy. Moses's first plague of turning water to blood corresponds to Jesus's first miracle of turning water to wine, a substance resembling blood in appearance, and one to be used as a reminder of the blood of Jesus (Matt 26:28; John 2).[136] The typology here is palpable.

Exodus 14–15

The parting of the sea for Israel's escape from the Egyptians shares many similarities with prior water texts. Just as God divided the waters at creation, he divided the waters of the Red Sea (Gen 1:6–10; Exod 14:21); as Moses was saved in the river and Noah in the midst of the sea, so was Israel saved by water (Gen 6–9; Exod 2:1–10; 14:21–22, 29); the wicked inhabitants of the earth were drowned in the flood, while the wicked Egyptians drowned in the sea (Gen 6–9; Exod 14:23–28; 15:2, 4–10, 19); the floodwaters receded and a new era began without the clutter of sin for Noah's family, just as the sea returned to its normal level and Israel began life as a new family and nation, bondage free (Gen 8–9; Exod 14:28; 15:19). In creation, in the flood, at Moses's birth, and for Israel's redemption, the recurring theme from Genesis through Exodus is that water is an instrument of both death and life.

In the song of Moses and Israel God is praised for the victory over the Egyptians using water, and the song calls God "a warrior" (15:2–3). This reflects the divine warrior motif found throughout ancient literature, such as in Enuma Elish and Annals of Tiglath-Pileser I.[137] The concept of a divine war in Israel's song is a shared concept with the ancient Hymns to Enheduanna, while the Israelite women singing and playing musical instruments occurred in the ancient Stories of Sinuhe (15:1–21).[138] It seems that even though having been in captivity, the Israelites may have had some awareness of these concepts and themes common throughout their surrounding world, and used them to declare God's ultimate

---

135. Meyers, *Exodus*, 81; Najman and Schmid, "Reading the Blood Plague," 37–40.

136. Van der Loos, *Miracles of Jesus*, 601; J. Hamilton, *God's Indwelling Presence*, 142; Robert Smith, "Exodus Typology."

137. V. Matthews and Benjamin, *Old Testament Parallels*, 22, 180–81; Fretheim, *Exodus*, 157.

138. V. Matthews and Benjamin, *Old Testament Parallels*, 144–45, 284–86.

power over the enemy using water.[139] It is interesting that the Hebrew term יְשׁוּעָה, translated "salvation," is used in the song, and it is always attributed to the work of God and denotes his assistance.[140] This song boldly declares that it was God, not Israel, who triumphed over the forces of evil that were leading to chaos.[141]

The unproductive waters prior to God dividing the waters at creation, the noxious sea filled with floating carcasses during the flood, the Nile intended to drown Hebrew baby boys, and the Nile turning to toxic blood, portray vivid pictures of chaotic, hopeless, nonfunctioning water prior to God's transforming use of it. These scenes foreshadow the death of the Egyptians in the Red Sea in which death overtakes those unrepentant of their abuse of God's people, and those steeped in wickedness which was antithetical to God's purpose for his creation.[142]

The apostle Paul described this sea crossing as being εἰς τὸν Μωϋσῆν ἐβαπτίσθησαν, or "baptized into Moses" (1 Cor 10:1–2). It seems noteworthy that they διὰ τῆς θαλάσσης διῆλθον, or "passed through the sea" (active voice), but they all "were baptized into Moses" (passive voice) as they were immersed amidst the land below, the sea to their sides, and the cloud overhead (1 Cor 10:1–4). Regarding this baptism, it has been suggested that the middle voice of self-interest might be preferred over the passive voice, or if passive, the term could carry a reflexive meaning, as in "they had themselves baptized."[143] To the contrary, it seems unlikely that amidst the life-threatening fear gripping Israel there was any opportunity for Israel to conceive of a baptism, or to expect to have something done to itself as a reflexive meaning might imply, other than escaping certain death from the Egyptians. This was a moment of terrifying crisis where Israel was at the brink of slaughter, filled with anxiety, and doubtful of survival (14:10–12). It was not a respite for deep theological considerations, but a time for urgent action (14:13–15). The text makes it clear that Israel entered the sea of its own volition, but the spiritual effect Paul specified, baptism, with all its embedded meanings, was the separate work of Christ (14:22; 1 Cor 10:3–4). Israel acted on the pleadings of Moses for its physical survival, but behind Moses was the enabling power

---

139. Wells, "Exodus," 216.
140. Meyers, *Exodus*, 115.
141. Meyers, *Exodus*, 115; Wells, "Exodus," 216–17; Fretheim, *Exodus*, 159–60.
142. Meyers, *Exodus*, 112–17.
143. Thiselton, *First Epistle to Corinthians*, 722; Oropeza, *1 Corinthians*, 127.

of God that provided physical rescue, and also gave Israel hope, blessing, and guidance (14:30—15:27).

This sea crossing by Israel is twice claimed to be an example (Greek *tupos*, or "type") for the Corinthian believers' benefit, and by extension, for believers of all ages (1 Cor 10:6, 11). How God worked among Israel typifies God's continuity in working among believers today.[144] There is a sacramental nature to Israel's baptism which continues in baptism today.[145]

It has been rightly noted that along with Israel's baptism came their redemption, and the ongoing blessings from God. Although some disagree, the text teaches that receiving redemption and blessings was not a guarantee of entering the promised land, a metaphor for eternal salvation, and that the promise could be lost through covenant breaking and rebellion against God.[146] While Israel's crossing of the Red Sea looks backward to creation, the flood, the birth of Moses, and turning the Nile to blood, all obviously abounding in water language, it also looks forward to the crossing of the Jordan, and to Christian baptism, both having in common the presence of water as the instrumentality for change.[147]

Joshua 3–6

After forty years in the desert, the entry into the promised land would mimic the Red Sea crossing, and also creation (4:23; Ps 66:6; 114:3).[148] The departure from Egypt came by passing through the sea on dry ground, and the arrival came by entering Canaan through a river on dry ground. It is as if the journey out of Egypt and into Canaan was a single act bookended with these two crossings, one initiating and the other completing the journey by traversing dry ground through walls of water.[149] In creation, Adam was birthed into a sin-free environment following the transformation of chaotic waters into organized and functional waters operating according to God's purposes. In the flood, the deadly waters subsided and returned to their usual intended state, providing life to Noah in a freshly re-created world, where sin seemed momentarily

---

144. Oropeza, *1 Corinthians*, 128; Schreiner, *1 Corinthians*, 198.

145. Schreiner, *1 Corinthians*, 199–201; Hicks, *Enter the Water*, 11–18, 81–98.

146. Schreiner, *1 Corinthians*, 198–201; L. Morris, *1 Corinthians*, 138–40.

147. Fretheim, *Exodus*, 158; Schreiner, *1 Corinthians*, 198–201; Hicks, *Enter the Water*, 81–82.

148. McConville, *Joshua*, 7; Beal, *Joshua*, 93–95; Woudstra, *Book of Joshua*, 76.

149. McConville, *Joshua*, 7; Beal, *Joshua*, 94.

nonexistent. In crossing the Red Sea, Israel's escape from the oppression of wicked people culminated in the destruction of the wicked in water, transferring Israel into a bondage-free condition in a barren environment where God would be its provider with water, manna, and quail on the journey to taste the milk and honey of the promised land.

It was in this harsh environment that God tested Israel (Exod 15:25; 16:4; Deut 8:1–20). God's purpose in testing Israel was to gauge its obedience and acceptance of his leadership whereby Israel would depend upon him, refrain from sin, and receive his blessing (Exod 15:25–26; 20:20; Deut 8:1–20). Israel had the benefit of the prior examples of Adam and Noah, both given life and placed into sinless worlds after miraculous transformative water events. Yet, sin soon followed each. Now, Israel has just experienced a similar miraculous water event, oppression has been lifted, and God wants it known whether Israel has apprised itself of the past examples of Adam and Noah, and wants to live according to his creative intent in which trust in God, and reverence of God, would permit a blessed existence in that special promised land where righteousness was to reign (Deut 8:1–20; 11:1–17).[150] God's testing was not for his own benefit, as if he was not omniscient. It was for the benefit of Israel. God wanted Israel to apprehend the prior cataclysmic water events of Adam and Noah and decide how it would respond to its own spectacular water event. Jesus may have echoed this text when he cautioned to first count the cost to calculate whether losing family and personal comforts while enduring public ridicule was an acceptable exchange for the rewards of discipleship (Luke 14:26–35). Placing this forty-year intermission between the release from bondage (crossing the Red Sea) and the reception of the glorious promise (crossing the Jordan River), enabled a generation of people time to be tested during which each could consider evidence of the past, as well as current conditions, including God's favor and one's own heart, to determine whether to go forward into a relationship with God. Crossing the Jordan symbolized a step into new life much like Noah and Adam before.

---

150. Fretheim, *Exodus*, 178–79, 216–17.

2 Kings 2

This crossing of the Jordan River also looks forward to the other two crossings of the Jordan, one by Elijah and one by Elisha (2:6–14).[151] In each case, the water parted as it had for Joshua. Both prophets were heavily opposed by prophets of Baal (1 Kgs 18; 2 Kgs 3–13). Their two water crossings, along with Elijah's confrontation on Mount Carmel, clearly portray water, over which mythology had made Baal the mighty warrior and god, as under the control of Israel's God and his servants (1 Kgs 18).[152] Such humiliation of Baal may also reflect back polemically to the ancient creation myths previously discussed.[153]

What is key for this presentation is that God, and no other, has ultimate control over water, and he repeatedly uses water to initiate new life as he did with Adam, Noah, Israel on two occasions, and now a double portion of Elijah's spirit is passed to Elisha, confirmed by God twice parting the water of the Jordan River, once for each prophet (2:1–14). The parting of the Jordan River for Elijah is followed by him being swept into heaven, which is patently a life transformation, while for Elisha the water parted demonstrating his reception of Elijah's spirit, announcing his new way of life (2:9–14). Both men received new life and each was associated with a water event, the parting and crossing of the Jordan River, once for Elijah and once for Elisha. In this text the water metaphor is used in conjunction with "inheritance language" to express the continuity of God's presence with his people, and it specifically endorses the new life of both prophets, and the new role of Elisha.[154]

Jonah

The story of Jonah begins with a chaotic stormy sea, and the prophet Jonah in a boat attempting to sail to Tarshish to avoid his missional call by God to go to Nineveh (Jon 1). The great fish God prepared to swallow Jonah has been linked by some to the violent sea creatures of ancient mythology.[155] The stormy sea was also connected to ancient Near Eastern

---

151. Beal, *Joshua*, 94; McConville and Williams, *Joshua*, 26; Provan, "2 Kings," 121.

152. Beal, *Joshua*, 94; McConville and Williams, *Joshua*, 25–27.

153. Beal, *Joshua*, 94; Provan, "2 Kings," 122–23. Examples are the Epic of Gilgamesh, Enuma Elish, and Stories of Atrahasis.

154. Provan, "2 Kings," 121–22; Fritz, *1 and 2 Kings*, 234–35.

155. Walton, "Jonah," 5:103–4.

mythology as each person on the boat cried out to his own god to calm the sea, and Jonah was also awakened to do the same (1:5–6).[156] Although Jonah left order, and by disobedience spiraled into the chaos of the storm, when the evidence points to Jonah as the cause of the storm he explains that his God is the "God of heaven who made the sea and the dry land" (1:9). While Jonah had abandoned God's call, he had not forgotten God entirely.[157] In this statement, Jonah links his experience to the Genesis creation story.[158] His selfless sacrifice, asking to be thrown into the sea to save the ship's crew, typified Christ and his sacrifice, just as Jonah's three days inside the fish correspond to Jesus's three days in the tomb (Matt 12:39–41; 16:4).[159]

It is clear that the sea represented potential death to Jonah and to the ship's crew. It is also true that the sea represented life, similar to the dark useless waters at creation also becoming fruitful or life giving when separated. The floodwaters during Noah's life killed all but gave life to those in the ark, and Jonah was similarly saved from the stormy sea by his ark, a great fish.[160] The Nile was intended for death, but for Moses it became a source of life. Later the Nile became death to the Egyptians, much like when Israel crossed the Jordan which promised death to the Canaanites, but life to Israel. The sea heralded death to Jonah and his shipmates, but it calmed to save their lives, and the great fish became a saving ark for Jonah.[161] The Jonah story obviously mirrors the prior water episodes in which life was initiated or re-created. Jonah being spit out of the fish was his rebirth.[162] Jonah linked his God to the God of creation, and Jesus linked the Jonah story to his own act of redemption for humanity which was a personal transformation from death to life in order to render life to all.[163] The analogies are glaring even though some categorize the book of Jonah as a parody or satire.[164] One even compares

---

156. Walton, "Jonah," 5:106–7, 109.
157. Coetzee, "And Jonah Swam," 521.
158. Kelsey, "Book of Jonah."
159. Erickson, *Jonah*, 210–12.
160. Kelsey, "Book of Jonah."
161. Kelsey, "Book of Jonah"; Anderson, "Jonah's Peculiar Re-Creation."
162. Coetzee, "And Jonah Swam," 524; Kelsey, "Book of Jonah," 128–29; Anderson, "Jonah's Peculiar Re-Creation"; Erickson, *Jonah*, 246–58, 267–69.
163. Erickson, *Jonah*, 246–58.
164. Walton, "Jonah," 5:103–9; Miles, "Laughing at the Bible"; Coetzee, "And Jonah Swam," 521.

the prophet Jonah to Charlie Chaplin, although other comparisons are better founded.[165] In spite of what may be considered shallow or at least nontraditional views, the initiation of life by the instrumentality of water in Jonah demonstrates the continuity of this theological chord from Genesis to the prophets. In the NT Jesus continues the theme.

John 2

It has been noted herein that Moses was a type of Christ, and his first plague of turning water to blood corresponds to Jesus's first miracle of turning water to wine (2:1–11). For Moses, the plague was an announcement of a new day wherein the pagan powers of Egypt would be challenged by the powerful God of Israel. For Jesus, turning water into wine also symbolized a new day. What had been hidden from the beginning is now being revealed.[166] It announced the activation of Jesus's ministry as well as the outpouring of blessing, both now and in the eschaton (2:11).[167] The prompting by his mother also begins Jesus's journey that culminated in his death, burial, and resurrection, initiating new life to all who will receive it (2:4, 11).[168]

To the Jews wine was a symbol of joy, frequent and plentiful at special events and celebrations.[169] Running out of wine may have also been a symbol, that of "the barrenness of Judaism."[170] Considering Jewish numerology, the presence of six jars of water supports the ineffective nature of Judaism at that time.[171] In this miracle Jesus contrasts the emptiness of what Judaism had become with the vibrancy of himself, and what he was ushering in (2:11).[172] The sheer volume of the wine Jesus created may speak to the overflowing blessing of his new era.[173]

---

165. Miles, "Laughing at the Bible," 179; Erickson, *Jonah*, 215.

166. Haenchen, *John 1*, 179; O'Day, *Revelation in Fourth Gospel*, 244–51; Von Wahlde, *Gospel and Letters*, 90–91.

167. Haenchen, *John 1*, 177; Klink, *John*, 172; O'Day, *Revelation in Fourth Gospel*, 244–51.

168. Keener, *Gospel of John*, 1:506–7; O'Day, *Revelation in Fourth Gospel*, 247.

169. Köstenberger, "John," 431; Köstenberger, *Theology of John's Gospel*, 162–63.

170. Köstenberger, "John," 431; Von Wahlde, *Gospel and Letters*, 91.

171. Ebert, "John 2:1–11," 115–17.

172. Ebert, "John 2:1–11," 115–17; Köstenberger, *Theology of John's Gospel*, 162–63; O'Day, *Revelation in Fourth Gospel*, 249; Koester, *Symbolism in Fourth Gospel*, 82–86.

173. O'Day, *Revelation in Fourth Gospel*, 248; Michaels, *Gospel of John*, 149;

The opening phrase of the Gospel of John mirrors the opening phrase of Gen 1, "in the beginning." Relying on this, and the seemingly patterned use of the term "day," an argument can be made that the Gospel of John is designed to mirror creation with certain things occurring on certain days.[174] "In the beginning" was the first day where Jesus is presented as the light of the world comparable to God ordering light on the first day of creation (Gen 1:3–5; John 1:1–4). "The next day" would be the second day, where John parted waters by baptizing Jesus as a dove descended out of heaven, correlating to the second day of creation where the waters were separated by the newly created heaven (Gen 1:6–8; John 1:29–34).[175] "On the third day" is the wedding feast in Cana of Galilee.

In this water experience Jesus transformed water to wine implying both that the water in the jars was useless for a joyous celebration, symbolizing the present useless status of Judaism, and the new day arriving with its fruitfulness and joy, denoted by the quality and abundance of the wine.[176] This compares to the third day of creation where the ineffectual seas are gathered, dry land appears, and vegetation begins growing, demonstrating a change from fruitlessness to prosperity (Gen 1:9–13; 2:1–11). The three days may also look forward to the transformation of the three days between Jesus's crucifixion where water flowed (John 19:34), and to his resurrection in which the world that lacked hope was given assurance of eternal life. John's second and third days each contain water scenes just as the second and third days of creation, and in each case there occurs transformation from old to new, from void to functionality, and from nonexistence to life. Admittedly, not everyone counts these days exactly the same, but even without agreement as to specific timing, the topical connection to the Genesis creation account is strong.[177]

Haenchen, *John 1*, 173; Von Wahlde, *Gospel and Letters*, 91; Keener, *Gospel of John*, 1:512.

174. Klink, *John*, 83–162; Haenchen, *John 1*, 152; Keener, *Gospel of John*, 1:496–98; Ebert, "John 2:1–11," 92–95.

175. John does not actually record the baptism of Jesus by John the Baptist, but alludes to it. The record of it is attested in the Synoptics (Matt 3:13–17; Mark 1:9–11; Luke 3:21–22).

176. Köstenberger, "John," 431; Köstenberger, *Theology of John's Gospel*, 162–63; O'Day, *Revelation in Fourth Gospel*, 248–49; Koester, *Symbolism in Fourth Gospel*, 82–86; Michaels, *Gospel of John*, 149; Haenchen, *John 1*, 173; Von Wahlde, *Gospel and Letters*, 91; Ebert, "John 2:1–11," 88, 117.

177. Klink, *John*, 83–162; Haenchen, *John 1*, 152; Michaels, *Gospel of John*, 139–41; Keener, *Gospel of John*, 1:496–98; Von Wahlde, *Gospel and Letters*, 80–81; Ebert, "John 2:1–11," 92–95, 131–41.

In this parallel with creation, John connects the literal creation of the physical earth, with the spiritual creation in Jesus. John assigns to Jesus the embodiment of God's creative purposes from Genesis.[178] The water is idle and unproductive until Jesus gathers it, and transforms it, enabling a joyous experience. The water of John 2 continues the OT stories of water-related transformation into new life. It ends by including the revelation of Christ's glory through the process of exchanging water into wine at that moment, while also pointing to more blessing and joy to come as the revelatory process continues (2:11).[179]

John 3

John records Nicodemus, a Pharisee and ruler of the Jews, coming to Jesus by night making a statement, not asking a question (3:1). Nicodemus said, "Rabbi, we know that you have come from God as a teacher; for no one can do these signs you do unless God is with him" (3:2). While Nicodemus thinks he knows something about Jesus and his heavenly origin, Jesus informs Nicodemus about heavenly things of which Nicodemus knows nothing.[180] It is possible that Nicodemus was actually challenging Jesus's legitimacy as a teacher, and spoke as a representative of the Pharisees who felt threatened by Jesus's obvious display of authority.[181] That Jesus "answered" (ἀπεκρίθη) him does not imply Nicodemus asked a question, as ἀπεκρίθη can also refer to a mere response or reply to ongoing conversation, not exclusively the answer to a question.[182] Nicodemus had obviously detected the extraordinary signs of Jesus, but his statement betrayed his incapacity to comprehend the full identity of Jesus and the purpose behind his actions (2:23). Because Jesus's response seems disconnected from Nicodemus's statement, it suggests that Nicodemus said much more than John records. John records what is pertinent to the story, which is that Nicodemus detected that Jesus was sent from God, but apparently little or no more. By contrast, Jesus "knew all men and knew what was in man" (2:24–25). The seemingly unusual response of Jesus appears to be based on the statement of Nicodemus that Jesus is sent

---

178. Klink, *John*, 171.

179. Klink, *John*, 168; Michaels, *Gospel of John*, 152–53; Keener, *Gospel of John*, 1:494; Von Wahlde, *Gospel and Letters*, 88–89, 91; Ebert, "John 2:1–11," 111–13.

180. Keener, *Gospel of John*, 1:534–35.

181. Klink, *John*, 192–97.

182. ἀπεκρίθη, BDAG, 114; Michaels, *Gospel of John*, 179–80.

by God, and it supplies the rationale for Jesus's actions that have brought Nicodemus to him. Jesus is likely speaking to the heart of Nicodemus's motives, whether sincere or not, as much as to the sound of his words.[183]

"Unless one is born again he cannot see the kingdom of God" is Jesus's reply (3:3). Being "born again" (γεννηθῇ ἄνωθεν) was as confusing to Nicodemus as it is for many today. Nicodemus replies by asking, "How can a man be born when he is old?" (3:4). He then asks, "He cannot enter a second time into his mother's womb and be born, can he?" In his questions Nicodemus reveals his shallow insight regarding biblical truth leading Jesus to explain in more detail by saying, "Unless one is born of water and the Spirit he cannot enter the kingdom of God. That which is born of flesh is flesh and that which is born of the Spirit is spirit" (3:5–6). When Nicodemus asks, "How can these things be?," Jesus asks, "Are you a teacher of Israel and do not understand these things?" (3:9–10). This final reply by Jesus indicates that as a teacher of Israel, Nicodemus was expected to have mastered Israel's Scriptures, and the theological truths therein, but he plainly had not. "The one who thought he was the teacher has become the student."[184] The question of exactly what HB principles had escaped Nicodemus's grasp is the question John leaves unasked. The reader has to sift through the ambiguity to find the answer.

What slipped by Nicodemus was the HB teaching on being born again (3:3, 5). He needed new birth himself, but did not know it.[185] It is obvious from his two questions that Nicodemus did not comprehend any sort of birth except natural or physical birth (John 3:4).[186] Strong disagreement exists with the view that nothing in the HB prepares Nicodemus or others to be born from above.[187] Nor is there agreement with the improved version that admits that the ingredients are present in the HB, but that the full construction is lacking.[188] Others see an HB foundation, but it appears limited to prophecies suggesting a new birth and the presence of water, a perspective that is much improved, but this view does not go far enough to include the numerous HB texts that portray birth by

---

183. Klink, *John*, 192–98; Von Wahlde, *Gospel and Letters*, 123; Thompson, *John*, 80.

184. Klink, *John*, 201.

185. Keener, *Gospel of John*, 1:542–44.

186. Keener, *Gospel of John*, 1:545–46; Köstenberger, *Theology of John's Gospel*, 474; Haenchen, *John 1*, 200; Von Wahlde, *Gospel and Letters*, 116.

187. Michaels, *Gospel of John*, 189–90; Thompson, *John*, 81.

188. Carson, *Gospel According to John*, 173; Von Wahlde, *Gospel and Letters*, 116.

water and spirit this research has unveiled.[189] Some find a foundation in non-biblical sources and in the Jewish practice of proselyte baptism, but that is inconsistent with what Nicodemus is expected to know.[190]

The meaning of being born again should fit within the HB context upon which Jesus based his discrediting of Nicodemus.[191] Jesus's response implies the HB was instructional on being born from above and questions Nicodemus about his shameful shallowness by asking piercingly, "Are you a teacher of Israel and do not understand these things?" (3:10).[192] The HB texts related to spiritual birth, or rebirth, that Nicodemus did not comprehend were the very texts already discussed in this research: the creation account, the flood story, the birth story of Moses, the crossing of the Red Sea by Israel, Israel crossing the Jordan, the crossings of the Jordan by Elijah and Elisha, and the Jonah story. In each of these narratives what had previously existed was transformed, or rebirthed, into a new existence as previously detailed.

The same blinders that had been on Nicodemus have found their way onto many others, and have prompted this research. G. R. Beasley-Murray describes this birth by saying, "A man became physically a new creature when God healed him; and he became a new creature in a sense of living in a different environment when his tribulations and dangers were removed, or when his sins were forgiven, bringing thereby renewal in health and circumstances and a changed relationship with God."[193]

Being born "again" (ἄνωθεν) has been variously rendered by English translations.[194] The term carries several potential meanings which may account for part of the difficulty Nicodemus had in understanding what Jesus meant.[195] The term can mean again, from above, from the begin-

---

189. Klink, *John*, 198; Köstenberger, *Theology of John's Gospel*, 474–75; McHugh *John 1–4*, 228; Thompson, *John*, 81.

190. Keener, *Gospel of John*, 1:542–43.

191. Ng, "Johannine Water Symbolism," 100–101.

192. Ng, "Johannine Water Symbolism," 100–101; Keener, *Gospel of John*, 1:558–59; Klink, *John*, 200–201; Haenchen, *John 1*, 202.

193. Beasley-Murray, *Baptism in New Testament*, 227; Köstenberger, *Theology of John's Gospel*, 474–75.

194. "Again" is used by the NIV, KJV, NKJV, HCSB, NASB, ESV, CSB, with the AMP using "again" but "reborn from above" in brackets. "Anew" is used by the ASV, CEB, and RSV. "From above" is used by the CEV, NRSVUE, MSG, NET, WEB. "Again from above" is used by the CJB.

195. Köstenberger, *Theology of John's Gospel*, 474–75; Von Wahlde, *Gospel and Letters*, 116.

ning, for a long time, or anew, and all of these varied translations are used in the NT.[196] Exactly what Jesus meant by this term when spoken to Nicodemus is likely not bound up in the term itself, but rather in the overall context of the encounter.[197] It is not that "born again" is the wrong translation, or that "born from above" is the right translation, or vice-versa. Instead, Jesus points Nicodemus to the HB as being instructional in this matter.

In each of the foregoing HB texts, it was the power of God that created life or rebirthed it. God initiated life for Adam, Eve, Noah, Moses, Israel, Elijah, Elisha, and Jonah. In these examples, either term (born from above or born again) is appropriate. God births, or births again, and the procedure comes from above. For this study, the emphasis is on water being used as God's instrument to initiate life in each of the foregoing HB examples. It is believed that these HB examples of life transformations by water are the ones about which Jesus exclaimed, "are you a teacher of Israel and do not understand these things."

When Jesus spoke of being "born of water and the Spirit," the Greek definite article is absent, making the reading "water and spirit" (ὕδατος καὶ πνεύματος), not water and *the* Spirit. Reference to the Holy Spirit is not indicated, but rather the inner spirit of the individual. It seems Jesus was referencing all of these HB texts in which water was present as part of the spiritual birthing process. For those who may fear slighting the Spirit of God by omitting him from this text, it should be noted that he was present at these spiritually transforming births. Genesis is vocal that "the Spirit of God was moving over the surface of the waters" at creation (Gen 1:2). The Holy Spirit is not said to have disappeared after hovering over the waters, and his presence enabled him to be included in the "us" who created humankind (Gen 1:26).

In each case God, which includes Father, Son, and Holy Spirit, was active in the birthing or rebirthing process.[198] In each case, a spiritual transformation occurred. Adam was changed from dust to humanity to co-reign with God (Gen 1:28). Noah, already a righteous man, was reborn into a new world due to the elimination of spiritual corruptness that surrounded him, and he received God's covenant (Gen 6:5; 9:1–12). Moses's life was preserved (reborn) to become God's spokesman and Israel's spiritual leader (Exod 3:10). Israel was given new life to become a

196. ἄνωθεν, BDAG, 92; Keener, *Gospel of John*, 1:538–39.
197. Klink, *John*, 196.
198. Kunder, "Many Waters," 74; Klink, *John*, 198.

kingdom of priests and a holy nation (Exod 19:6). Elijah was a prophet of God and upon fulfilling his mission ascended into the heavens to live with God (2 Kgs 2:11). Elisha was renewed in the spirit of Elijah (2 Kgs 2:13–14). Jonah, near death, was revived to become God's spiritual emissary to Nineveh (Jon 1–2). It has been suggested that this concept of spiritual transformation may not have been common among Judaism and Hellenistic syncretism before Christianity, and if it had, the expectation Jesus had for Nicodemus might appear somewhat greater.[199] But the words of Jesus to Nicodemus were sufficiently poignant, and rightly so since the evidence that should have directed his theology was obviously present in the HB, irrespective of current cultural or religious practices.

J. Ramsey Michaels asserts that being born of water and spirit in the Gospel of John refers to "the beginning of new life . . . or what this Gospel calls 'eternal life,'" which is an accurate claim.[200] Being born of spirit has to do with the inner change that occurs when God transforms.[201] If God does the transforming then the Holy Spirit is part of that process, even if Jesus does not fully elaborate on that relationship in this text.[202] This point is raised here so as not to eliminate the Holy Spirit from the process, but at the same time not to diminish the fact that the change to the human spirit is the result of God birthing anew or from above. There is no biblical example of it being accomplished by human effort alone, but only by the power of God.[203] Speaking of God, Paul said, "He rescued us from the domain of darkness and transferred us to the kingdom of his beloved Son" (Col 1:13). This contextual emphasis is on the work of God, as opposed to the work of humanity, to accomplish this transformation (Col 1:11–12).

Jesus is plainspoken about the two births, fleshly and spiritual, which are in contrast (3:6).[204] Fleshly birth needed no explanation, but spiritual birth is somewhat elusive, like the wind (3:8).[205] Nicodemus could envision only a physical birth and that only from a mother's womb,

---

199. Beasley-Murray, *Baptism in New Testament*, 227.
200. Michaels, *Gospel of John*, 185.
201. Köstenberger, *Theology of John's Gospel*, 475.
202. Koester, *Symbolism in Fourth Gospel*, 185.
203. Köstenberger, *Theology of John's Gospel*, 476.
204. Keener, *Gospel of John*, 1:552; Koester, *Symbolism in Fourth Gospel*, 184; Klink, *John*, 199.
205. Keener, *Gospel of John*, 1:555–58; Von Wahlde, *Gospel and Letters*, 129.

not "the act of begetting, as from a father, whether human or divine."[206] When Jesus said, "We speak of what we know and testify of what we have seen," the "we" is Jesus and his disciples (2:2, 11, 17, 22). What "we know" and "what we have seen" apparently refers to those people Jesus and his disciples witnessed becoming spiritually transformed by faith in Jesus (1: 45, 49; 2: 11, 22–23). For Jesus, it included his firsthand knowledge and involvement in all of the spiritual births of the HB, and those unmentioned.[207] It may also allude to additional sightings by the disciples included in the promise that "you will see greater things than these" (1:50). What "we" know experientially is contrasted with what Nicodemus thinks he knows from rumor, observation, and consensus (3:2, 11–12).[208]

One of the long-standing questions of John 3:5 is whether being born of water and spirit refers to Christian water baptism. There are at least three aspects to the answer to that question. The first is that it refers to the prior HB examples of spiritual birth, or rebirth, in which one underwent spiritual transformation by the power of God. It was these examples (previously discussed herein) that Nicodemus should have been apprised of, but was not. If this is the totality of what Jesus expected Nicodemus to know, then water baptism may not have been intimated in Jesus's response. The reference to water birth would have had reference only to the foregoing HB examples, even though Paul later called at least one of these episodes a baptism (1 Cor 10:1–4).

The second consideration is that if Nicodemus was expected to know about the baptism of John the Baptist, then water baptism was intended by Jesus's comments about water birth in John 3:5. Very little about the baptism of John is expressed in the Gospel of John, and what is expressed appears to be brief with nothing said as to its purpose. Luke records John's baptism as being a "baptism of repentance for the forgiveness of sins" (Luke 3:3). That is unmistakably a rebirth. If Nicodemus was expected to know about John's baptism, then the water of John 3:5 would seem to include water baptism, but not necessarily Christian water baptism, which had not yet become a practice. We do know Jesus and his disciples also baptized during the same time period of John the Baptist (3:22–23; 4:1–2). How that baptism was similar or different from John's baptism is not exactly stated, other than it was not a baptism into Jesus which gifted the Holy Spirit, and therefore, necessitated baptism into

---

206. Michaels, *Gospel of John*, 181–82.
207. Klink, *John*, 201.
208. Keener, *Gospel of John*, 1:560–61.

Jesus (Acts 19:1–7).[209] The contemporaneous nature of John's baptism to Jesus's encounter with Nicodemus, and even more so the baptism of Jesus, may tend to eliminate them both from the conversation with Nicodemus, but some believe just the reverse, that it makes them more likely a part of the discussion.[210]

A third matter involves a prophetic element. Knowing that John would write his gospel, and knowing Christian baptism would soon be established in terms similar to John's baptism ("repent, and ... be baptized ... for the forgiveness of your sins"), the John 3:5 water rebirth would include reference to Christian baptism (Acts 2:38).[211] Strictly speaking, Christian water baptism was likely not in purview in the conversation between Jesus and Nicodemus.[212] But since Jesus was prone to speak prophetically and use terminology that had multiple meanings, water baptism may be included in the reference to water rebirth for the benefit of those who would later read John's gospel, or hear the apostles as they made disciples (Matt 28:19; Acts 2:38).[213] Thus, the question of whether Jesus spoke of water baptism in the Christian context when speaking of rebirth by water may turn on the vantage point from which one is asking. For the immediate context of Nicodemus, the answer is likely no, water baptism was not suggested. From the perspective of the modern reader making a present day application, the answer is probably yes, water baptism probably was included particularly since Christian water baptism symbolizes the internal spiritual change that occurs by the work of God (Acts 2:38; Rom 6:1–11; Gal 3:26–27; 1 Pet 3:18–22). The ambiguity here may be somewhat frustrating for those who demand absolute answers, but unless better evidence is presented, certainty will have to wait.[214]

The significance of this text to this presentation is that in this pericope Jesus ties his birth message to the HB births and rebirths, demonstrating a seamless theological continuity between the canonical OT and

---

209. Marshall, *Acts*, 325–26.

210. Beasley-Murray, *Baptism in New Testament*, 229–30; Michaels, *Gospel of John*, 183; Carson, *Gospel According to John*, 172; McHugh, *John 1–4*, 228–29.

211. Keener, *Gospel of John*, 1:548.

212. Keener, *Gospel of John*, 1:549.

213. One example, of many, is Jesus explaining his authority for cleansing the temple as "destroy this temple, and in three days I will raise it up," which was not understood until after his resurrection (John 2:19–22).

214. Keener, *Gospel of John*, 1:550; Michaels, *Gospel of John*, 190–91.

NT. The birth Jesus spoke of was no different than the numerous spiritual births of the HB because people have not changed and have the same needs, while the same God is doing the birthing. Water was repeatedly used by God in the HB as the instrument through which spiritual birth occurred. In the NT water consistently remains God's instrument in the spiritual birth process (Luke 3:3; Acts 2:38; Rom 6:1–11; 1 Pet 3:18–22). This consistency is evident throughout the Protestant canon.

John 4 and John 7

The provocative nature of Jesus's interaction with a Samaritan woman in John 4 is stimulating, but complete analysis must be largely bypassed to stay on point of proving this first portion of the underlying thesis.[215] The historical background of the Samaritan/Jew relationship, the geographical setting, and numerous OT allusions add considerable color to the exegesis of the text, but will be omitted since they are not essential to gleaning the requisite textual information for this presentation.[216] A similar position must be taken regarding Jesus's encounter in John 7 while at the Feast of Booths.[217] The background of Jewish feasts, traditions and customs, and the political setting all bear on the exegesis, but comprehensive exegesis is not required for our purposes, so will not be attempted in order to focus more directly on how this text supports the thesis.

In this thought-provoking and interesting pericope Jesus used the occasion of drawing water from a well to contrast ordinary drinking water with spiritual water he labeled "living water" (4:10). The scene also contrasts the water from the well of Jacob, an esteemed ancestor of Samaritans and Jews, with Jesus's own living water, to highlight Jesus's gift as surpassing both Samaritan and Jewish views of acceptable relations with God, and worship to him.[218] Living water may also be termed "flowing" water, and is contrasted with stagnant water or water from a cistern.[219] Inherent is a distinction between what is distasteful and what is life giving. Drinking physical water requires repeated application to quench

---

215. Köstenberger, *Encountering John*, 73–75; Köstenberger, "John," 437–40, 451–55; Haenchen, *John 2*, 227.

216. Keener, *Gospel of John*, 1:586–601; Köstenberger, *Encountering John*, 73–75; Köstenberger, "John," 437–40, 451–55.

217. Köstenberger, *Encountering John*, 90–96.

218. Keener, *Gospel of John*, 1:602–5.

219. Koester, *Symbolism in Fourth Gospel*, 188; Michaels, *Gospel of John*, 240.

thirst, but living water perpetually quenches spiritual thirst and leads to eternal life (4:13–14). The Samaritan may have initially interpreted this living water ambiguously, much like Nicodemus struggled with what being born again meant (3:3–11; 4:11).[220] That Jesus demonstrated himself to be greater than Jacob, the originator of the earthly well of water, distinguished Jesus and his living water as superior, a triumph of the spiritual over the physical.[221]

Jeremiah identified living water with God, while Jesus is said to be the guide to living water (Jer 2:13; 17:13; Rev 7:17). Just as Jesus offered living water to the Samaritan woman at the well, and to those at the feast, so the Spirit, Jesus, and the bride unite to offer "the spring of the water of life," or living water, to all who willingly seek it (4:10; 7:37–38; Rev 21:6; 22:17). Ezekiel spoke of this water that gave life to all who contacted it in a lengthy description of the eschaton that sounds similar to the description of the "river of the water of life" in the new Jerusalem (Ezek 47:1–12; Rev 22:1–5). Zechariah claims the living water will flow out of new Jerusalem (Zech 14:8), while Ezekiel isolates that flowing to come from the temple (Ezek 47:1–12), and with even more granularity John says it would flow from the throne of God, which would be in the temple in the new Jerusalem (Rev 22:1).

Jesus said he could give the gift of living water, but the gift and the giver are inseparable such that receiving one includes the other (4:14).[222] In this Jesus alludes to the gift of himself. According to John, this gift of living water refers to the Holy Spirit (4:10, 14; 7:38–39), but Jeremiah equates it to Yahweh (Jer 2:13; 17:13). Rather than these texts being in conflict, they actually demonstrate the unity of the Father, Son, and Spirit.[223] This same unity is expressed in Paul's prayer for the Ephesians church where he prays for spiritual enrichment through the simultaneous indwelling of Father, Son, and Spirit (Eph 3:14–21). Similar unity is found in Jesus's command to be baptized in the name of the Father, Son, and Holy Spirit (Matt 28:19).

Jesus said that for the one receiving living water, it "will become a well of water springing up in him" (4:14). Later, he described it as "from his innermost being will flow rivers of living waters" (7:38). It seems that

---

220. Von Wahlde, *Gospel and Letters*, 179; Haenchen, *John 2*, 226, 230.
221. Klink, *John*, 240; Ng, "Johannine Water Symbolism," 89.
222. Ng, "Johannine Water Symbolism," 106.
223. Klink, *John*, 238.

Jesus's gift sounds like being "baptized with the Holy Spirit," and being "born of water and spirit," and receiving the "gift of the Holy Spirit," all of which appear largely undifferentiated (1:33; 3:5; 4:14; 7:38–39; Acts 1:5; 2:38; 10:44–48). The common connecting points for each are the Holy Spirit, inner change, and water.

John 4 necessarily is connected to this handful of other biblical texts (cited above) that also speak of living water or water of life.[224] These texts together enlarge our understanding of living water. For this research, it seems obvious from these texts that water is used by God to initiate new spiritual life in Jeremiah, Ezekiel, Zechariah, John, and Revelation.[225] When added to the examples from Genesis, Exodus, Joshua, 2 Kings, and Jonah previously proffered, the Protestant canon is well represented by numerous books either demonstrating or claiming that through the instrumentality of water God initiates life. Other texts could be included such as spiritual transformations in Acts where faith is combined with baptismal water and reception of the Holy Spirit (Acts 8:4–17; 10:44–48; 19:1–7). Epistles such as Romans, 1 Corinthians, and Galatians also speak of the convergence of inner transformation, receiving the Spirit, and baptismal waters. The irresistible conclusion is that there is a biblical theology of water consistent throughout Scripture in which God uses water to initiate life. As the pericope of the interchange with Samaritan woman nears its end, Jesus states that it is the reception of this living water that enables acceptable worship to God (4:23–24).[226] Such is the "heart of the story," that God seeks spiritually transformed people to worship him in truth with their spirits.[227]

The seventh chapter of John complements the fourth chapter by Jesus also offering living water to those who were thirsty (7:37). Jesus includes the requirement of faith as a prerequisite of receiving "rivers of living waters" that flow from one's "innermost being" (7:37–38). The Holy Spirit is defined as the living water in this text, and for the second time the prerequisite of faith is asserted (John 7:39). Other than the two mentions of faith as a prerequisite for receiving living water, the primary difference in John 7 and John 4 is the contrasting backdrop of the well in John 4, versus the context of the feast, and its final-day water ceremony

---

224. Ng, "Johannine Water Symbolism," 106.
225. Michaels, *Gospel of John*, 243–45.
226. Köstenberger, *Theology of John's Gospel*, 439–40.
227. Keener, *Gospel of John*, 1:585, 615.

in John 7.²²⁸ Otherwise, the two episodes each show Jesus offering living water, a symbol of perpetual life.

John 9

A man blind from birth received sight by Jesus putting clay made from his own spit on the man's eyes, and sending him to the pool of Siloam to wash (9:1–7). The significance of this story for this presentation is threefold. First, the reception of sight by someone blind from birth is a rough equivalency of receiving new life. The fact that the text states the man was "blind from birth" intimates this is a story about birth (9:1).²²⁹ In using clay to provide this new life, Jesus mirrors the creation of the first human who received life after being formed from the dust of the ground (9:5–6; Gen 1:3; 2:7).²³⁰ Jesus announcing that he is "the light of the world" also alludes to creation (9:5–6; Gen 1:3).²³¹ Such links the life-giving ability of Jesus in John with the life-giving ability of God in Genesis, demonstrating a continuity of concept through the OT and NT, and that concept is that life is created only by God, not superstition or human effort.²³² In this case life came by God the Son.²³³

Second, just as God used water in the Genesis creation story, and in numerous additional cases already discussed, so Jesus uses water to heal this man providing him new life (9:7, 11, 15).²³⁴ This again speaks to canonical continuity and the use of water to initiate life. Third, the text does not use the terms "faith" or "believe" until after the rebirthing event, but the blind man obviously demonstrates his faith by following Jesus's directions and washing in the pool of water (9:35–38). While faith was not required in birthing the first humans, it was evident in all the other births or rebirths previously discussed. Noah was considered righteous and demonstrated his faith by building the ark (Heb 11:7). Moses was given life as an infant because of his mother's faith in building his ark

---

228. Klink, *John*, 374. Kunder, "Many Waters," 143–46. John 4 does not specify faith as a prerequisite to receive living water, but it is implied by Jesus suggesting the woman ask him for it, which she later does (John 4:10, 15).

229. Michaels, *Gospel of John*, 540.

230. Klink, *John*, 438–39.

231. Klink, *John*, 438–39.

232. Michaels, *Gospel of John*, 545.

233. Michaels, *Gospel of John*, 541; Koester, *Symbolism in Fourth Gospel*, 200.

234. Michaels, *Gospel of John*, 547–48.

and posting a guard (Exod 2: 2–4). Israel following Moses across the Red Sea, and then following Joshua across the Jordan, were demonstrations of faith. Elijah demonstrated faith by following God's command to cross the Jordan, by striking the Jordan with his mantle, and by expecting God to provide Elisha with a double portion of his spirit as requested and promised (2 Kgs 2:6–10). Elisha also demonstrated faith by accompanying Elijah, expecting to receive the double portion of his spirit, and by using his mantle to part the Jordan (2 Kgs 2:6–14). Jonah prayed from within the fish and recommitted himself to God (Jon 2:2–4, 7, 9). Jesus's mother had faith Jesus would handle the wine shortage (John 2:3–5). The Samaritan woman demonstrated faith by asking for living water, and by telling others about Jesus resulting in their belief in Jesus (John 4:15, 28–29, 39–42). Jesus promised living water to those who had faith (John 7:37–39). While this discussion is focused on water and not faith, it is important to note that the two appear to work conjointly to facilitate life.[235]

It is true that blindness was often associated with sin which provides a spiritual application of the life-giving event (9:24–25, 31, 34, 39–41).[236] If blindness represented sin, then the transformation of the blind man, by faith, water, and the power of Jesus, heralds the availability of new life free from sin, a transformation which was an earmark of messiahship.[237] Based on this it seems that the focus of initiating life has somewhat shifted from the OT examples, becoming more Christocentric.[238]

John 19

The heartbreaking story of Jesus on the cross reaches a pivot point when the soldier pierces his side and from it flows water and blood (19:34). The shedding of blood has arguably been the primary focus of this text for most with parallels typically being drawn to the Passover, the atonement, or the Lord's Supper.[239] It is common for the scene to provide the warrant for the OT prophetic statements regarding the suffering servant, the defeat of sin, or the typological sacrificial lamb, while Jesus's own

---

235. Köstenberger, *Theology of John's Gospel*, 225.

236. Keener, *Gospel of John*, 2:777–79; Von Wahlde, *Gospel and Letters*, 424; Klink, *John*, 436–37; Haenchen, *John 2*, 37.

237. Köstenberger, "John," 459.

238. Köstenberger, *Theology of John's Gospel*, 223–24.

239. Haenchen, *John 2*, 195; Köstenberger, "John," 502–6; Von Wahlde, *Gospel and Letters*, 820, 824–25; Keener, *Gospel of John*, 2:1148–53.

statements about his death are validated.[240] It is not that these correlations are inappropriate; they do exist. But, too often the other liquid that flowed from Jesus's side disappears in the theological fervor surrounding blood. If there is meaning to one of the fluids there must also be meaning to the other.[241]

Jesus's final statement, "It is finished," is typically explained as his declaration of the completion of his earthly ministry of seeking and saving the lost by atoning for sin (19:30).[242] The blood becomes of primary interest because it intimates the end of life and is easily connected to the concept of the work of Jesus being finished by spilling his own blood, dying on the cross. But John 19:34 speaks of blood *and* water with seeming equal emphasis, terms that are full of symbolism.[243] Craig Keener calls the presence of water an "anomaly" and the "primary emphasis" of this text.[244]

Blood reflects death such as with the Passover lamb, or the sacrificial lamb of a sin offering, and there are obvious intertextual connections with Jesus being called the "lamb of God who takes away the sin of the world," or "the Lamb unblemished," and "a lamb that is led to slaughter" (Exod 12:1–13; Lev 4:32; Isa 53:7; John 1:29; 1 Pet 1:19). Paradoxically, blood also symbolizes life as shown in the statement that "the life of flesh is in the blood," and "unless you . . . drink His blood, you have no life in yourselves . . . the one who . . . drinks My blood has eternal life" (Lev 17:11; John 6:53–54).[245] Blood, symbolized by wine, is to be drunk by believers to remember Jesus and as a covenantal sign (Matt 26:26–29; 1 Cor 11:23–33).

Water too, has been shown as an instrument of both death and of life for Noah, Moses, Israel, Jonah, and the Samaritan woman. When blood and water emerged from the side of Jesus, each represented the paradox of symbolizing both death and life.[246] In the immediate context blood represented Jesus's physical death, but that was the entrée to new life in

---

240. Klink, *John*, 811–12, 821; Von Wahlde, *Gospel and Letters*, 822–25; Köstenberger, *Theology of John's Gospel*, 419–20; Keener, *Gospel of John*, 2:1148–49.

241. Klink, *John*, 814–15; Carnazzo, "Seeing Blood and Water," 96.

242. Klink, *John*, 814–15; Carnazzo, "Seeing Blood and Water," 96; Stibbs, *Finished Work of Christ*; Jensen, "Does τετέλεσται Mean 'Paid.'"

243. Von Wahlde, *Gospel and Letters*, 818–19; Klink, *John*, 814–15; Keener, *Gospel of John*, 2:1153.

244. Keener, *Gospel of John*, 2:1153.

245. Thompson, *John*, 404; Carnazzo, "Seeing Blood and Water," 3, 5–39.

246. Koester, *Symbolism in Fourth Gospel*, 1:201–3.

a new spiritual body (1 Cor 15:20–49).[247] Thus, the immediate context of blood representing Jesus's physical death possesses spiritual ramifications.[248] It is believed that the presence of water not only makes strong allusion to the numerous foregoing OT and NT examples of life being initiated by water, but that Jesus himself adds one more final and powerful example of water's presence in his own transformation. The blood and water representing death on Friday afternoon at the cross, doubles as the blood and water representing life on Sunday morning at the tomb. It was here where Jesus donned a transformed body, a spiritual body, making the same available for all who would accept him (1 Cor 15).[249] But the message deepens.

When Jesus raised Lazarus he said, "Lazarus has fallen asleep" and that he would "awaken him out of sleep" (John 11:11). The disciples did not understand so Jesus explained that he meant Lazarus being asleep meant that he had died, but Jesus used the term "asleep" because he knew Lazarus being dead in the tomb was temporary (John 11:11–14). Jesus used the occasion to declare, "I am the resurrection and the life; he who believes in me will live even if he dies" (John 11:25). The parallels with Jesus's death and resurrection are obvious. Of particular interest to this study is that when Jesus died on the cross, the outflow of blood and water proved he was physically dead such that the soldiers did not break his legs. But Jesus was only temporarily dead and came back to life like Lazarus. Unlike Lazarus, Jesus lived never to die again (19:33; 20:17; Acts 1:11; Rom 6:23; Heb 7:25). During the process of Jesus being "asleep" and then coming back to life, Jesus birthed his bride, the church (Acts 20:28; Eph 5:25–26; Rev 21:9). Such is reminiscent of Adam giving birth to Eve, his bride (Gen 2:21–22).[250] Jesus went "to sleep" and from his side flowed blood and water, birthing the church. Adam was put "to sleep" and from his side his bride was birthed. As part of the creation of the heavens and earth from water, Adam was created from the dust that arose from that earth, as previously discussed. From his side his bride was created, making her also a product of the creation of the heavens and earth by water. From his mother, Jesus was birthed by water as Mary's amniotic sac broke and "water" rushed out, birthing Jesus. Later in his death, blood and water flowed out of Jesus's side, birthing his bride, the church. The parallels

247. Klink, *John*, 814–15.
248. Thompson, *John*, 404.
249. Martin and Wright, *Gospel of John*, 327.
250. Klink, *John*, 815; Keener, *Gospel of John*, 2:1154; Thompson, *John*, 404.

between Jesus and Adam are numerous, which likely led Paul to call Jesus the second Adam (Rom 5:14; 1 Cor 15:22, 45).

The outflow of blood and water from Jesus's side powerfully mirrors death giving way to life by the power of God, just as God has repeatedly demonstrated in scene after scene starting in Genesis and continuing throughout the NT. Jesus's death and resurrection functions somewhat as a capstone demonstrating vividly what this chapter has been advocating, that God uses water as an instrument to initiate life. The difference with Jesus is that he makes it personal by his own physical death, and by his resurrected new life he makes it universal.

In chapter 1, Eckhard Schnabel was quoted as saying, "It seems provocative that . . . among evangelicals, systems of theological thought have been more important than the biblical text."[251] The John 19 text does plainly speak of water, but somehow a biblical theology of water does not seem to have evolved. Andreas Köstenberger has astutely noted that the text of John 19 does not dwell on the sacrificial nature of this scene, nor on the condescension of Christ or related matters, but moves hastily from the crucifixion to the resurrection.[252] It is believed that the reason little interruption occurs is that the death of Jesus was ineffectual without his resurrection. The death and resurrection are theologically viewed as sequential parts of a whole which are necessary to completing the transformation process, much like Gen 1 leads the reader step by step through elements of creation, enumerating specific days, until creation was completed and the final product was called "very good" (Gen 1:31).

The scene of the cross is an exemplar for all believers (1 Pet 2:21–24; 4:1). As Schnabel suggests, perhaps theological systems have drowned out (no water pun intended) what appears to this writer as abundant textual evidence supporting a coherent theology in which God initiates life through the instrumentality of water. That this piercing (again, no pun intended) reality is evident within Jesus's death and resurrection, and is also evident in creation, cannot be passed off as sheer coincidence.[253] That the image of this transformation is threaded throughout the OT and NT by ample and clear-cut examples, supports the presence of a biblical theology of water. Rather than classify the many examples from Genesis to Revelation as isolated and unrelated stories, together they form

---

251. Schnabel, "Viability of Premillennialism," 785.
252. Köstenberger, *Theology of John's Gospel*, 255–57.
253. Klink, *John*, 815.

a biblical theology of water, the existence of which validates canonical solidarity within the traditional Protestant canon.

1 Peter 3

Peter's reference to Noah and the flood requires only limited comment here since the flood was discussed in detail in the prior subsection on Gen 6–9, and since this text will be examined in more detail later. Suffice it to say here that Peter recognizes the transformative nature of the flood, removing death and initiating new life, by means of water, from which he speaks of an "appeal to God of a good conscience" (1 Pet 3:21). He further associates this transformative water scene of Noah to water baptism, salvation, the resurrection of Christ, and eternal life (1 Pet 3:21).[254] This reference by Peter authenticates the position taken in this research regarding the flood as the instrument of death and of life, which Peter maintains continues as a modern example.

1 John 5

The concept of being born of God is frequently addressed in 1 John. First John says being born by God is evidenced by being righteous (2:29), by the absence of sin (3:9; 5:18), by loving (4:7), by faith in Jesus (5:1), and by overcoming the world and believing that Jesus is the Son of God (5:4). These are the traits of one who has passed from death unto life, or has undergone spiritual transformation (John 5:24; 1 John 3:14).

Jesus is said to be the one who "came by water and blood . . . not with water only, but with the water and with the blood. . . . For there are three that testify: the Spirit and the water and the blood; and the three are in agreement" (5:6–8). The "coming" by water and blood of this text is viewed by Howard Marshall as the baptism (water) and death (blood) of Jesus.[255] He makes an interesting and accurate observation when he says, "It is hard to see why past events cannot continue to bear witness, in the same way as the Old Testament Scriptures can still bear witness to Jesus."[256] He then provides the example of Abel continuing to bear wit-

---

254. Eternal life is not specifically stated, but is implied by the presence of Jesus in heaven, angels and authorities subjected to him, and being at the right hand of God.
255. Marshall, *Epistles of John*, 237–38.
256. Marshall, *Epistles of John*, 237–38.

ness (Heb 11:4).[257] Marshall is correct in his assertion that past events, including the OT, continue to bear witness, but Marshall regresses only to the baptism of Jesus to find meaning for the witness of water, and not farther back to the proliferation of evidence from the OT already presented herein that demonstrates water as part of the life-giving process. Robert Yarbrough takes a near-identical position as Marshall and similarly stops short of looking farther back than Jesus's baptism for the water and blood testimony.[258]

John Painter agrees that "blood and water" imply singularity, or functional simultaneity, and he believes Jesus's "coming" refers to a specific or singular event that may have two components, a starting point which he seems forced to accept as possibly the baptism of Jesus, and the end point of Jesus's death.[259] Others agree and hold a similar uncertain position linking the water and Jesus's baptism.[260] Painter further argues the preposition διά (by or through) indicates instrumentality or agency, supporting the conclusion that water and blood were the single united instrumentality through which Jesus "came."[261]

It is respectfully believed that coming by water has been inadequately identified by Marshall, Yarbrough, Painter, and others who refer it to the baptism of Jesus, when additional and better possibilities exist. Without denying Jesus's baptism is one announcement of his coming, or that this may be referenced in the text, this text most likely has reference first to Jesus's physical birth in which Mary's water broke. That would be a scene of both water and blood, and would constitute his first "coming." Another obvious coming would be Jesus's death, where water and blood issued from his side (John 19:34). Only these two events are marked by both water and blood. Finding blood in Jesus's baptism seems a difficult task and perhaps the only way to do that is by the reasoning of those just noted.

A better explanation is that Jesus's coming by water and blood is used in a tripartite fashion that includes his physical birth, his baptism, and his death where he underwent transformation from a physical body to new life in a spiritual body. A tripartite interpretation parallels the three witnesses, the Spirit, the water, and the blood (5:7). All three were involved in Jesus's physical birth (Luke 1:35). The Spirit and the water, but not the

---

257. Marshall, *Epistles of John*, 237–38.
258. Yarbrough, *1–3 John*, 282–83.
259. Painter, *1, 2, 3 John*, 322–26.
260. Crowe, *Message of General Epistles*, 128.
261. Painter, *1, 2, 3 John*, 323.

blood, were present at Jesus's baptism (Luke 3:21–22). Blood and water were present at his death (John 19:34), but the Spirit is not mentioned.

The weakest possible explanation of Jesus's coming referenced in this text would seem to be his baptism, due to the absence of blood. Stressing that his coming was "not with the water only" (5:6), John may have entirely dismissed the baptism as a coming. Andreas J. Köstenberger admits that "John is scrupulous to deny an understanding of Jesus that views him as having come 'by water only' and not also 'by blood.'"[262] Assigning "came by water" exclusively to the baptism of Jesus is foreign to the context of 1 John 5, but interpreting it as the embodiment of God's creation transformed by water (and blood) fits extremely well within 1 John and within the context of 1 John 5:1–12, particularly since the subjects of birth and rebirth have been a consistent motif in 1 John as noted above.

Birth is specifically stated in this text (5:1, 4). First John 5:1–12 begins by speaking of being born of God (5:1,4) and ends with the admonition "he who has the Son has life" (1 John 5:12). The text calls Jesus "the Son" numerous times (5:5, 9, 10, 11, 12), which indicates a begetting or birthing. The Spirit, water, and blood referencing Jesus's physical birth may at first seem peculiar, but it is a messianic reference, a reference to Jesus's divinity, which is at the heart of the argument in 1 John 5, and why John stresses Jesus's sonship.[263] Jesus was born of the virgin Mary by the power of the Spirit and his first appearance (physical birth) was by water and blood. All three (Spirit, water, and blood) testified to this event. It has been argued earlier in this chapter that there is a parallel between physical birth and spiritual birth. In this text, the two are intertwined.

The explanation of coming by water and blood as a metaphor for living a transformed life is the most direct explanation of this text because it harmonizes with the context, and it reflects what is possible based on John 19:34 and the resurrection that follows. As advocated when discussing John 19, on the cross Jesus embodied the numerous teachings of the OT and NT about being born again, or born anew. The water and blood of John 19:34 are surely referenced by the "water and blood" of 1 John 5:6–8.[264] The focus of 1 John 5:1–12 is on being born anew and living a transformed life to overcome the world (5:4 twice), with the goal of sharing the same eternal life Jesus has, which was received by his overcoming

---

262. Köstenberger, *Theology of John's Gospel*, 96.

263. Köstenberger, *Theology of John's Gospel*, 270; Yarbrough, *1–3 John*, 281–82.

264. Köstenberger, *Theology of John's Gospel*, 164; Klink, *John*, 814.

the world (5:11–12). Such was exhibited by the water and blood flowing from his side followed by his resurrection.

The testimony of the Spirit who agrees with the testimony of the water and blood acknowledges the power of God behind spiritual transformation, and he agrees with it because he is truth (1 John 5:6).[265] That "the three are in agreement" is to be expected since they share a common source.

Revelation 21–22

This research began by asserting that Gen 1–2 and Rev 21–22 create an inclusio, bookending the subject of water, with many threads in between connecting these two canonical ends. The setting for these two chapters (Rev 21–22) is obviously the arrival of the new heaven and earth, and a new Jerusalem (21:1–6, 22; 22:1–5, 17). In this environment life has been transformed from the prior earthly conditions with illness, death, and pain, which were exchanged for the peaceful and glorious presence of God (21:1–4, 22).[266] Of note is the disappearance of the sea, which as noted earlier was a symbol of chaos, darkness, and death (21:1).[267] The sun and moon become irrelevant because the light of God perpetually shines to light this new heaven and earth (21:23). Those who are spiritually thirsty will be given the "spring of the water of life" which separates them from the wicked (21:6–8; 22:14–15). These wicked will be thrown into "the lake that burns with fire and brimstone, which is the second death" (21:8). The contrast between "water of life" and "the lake that burns with fire and brimstone," is a contrast that is also possible between the "water of life" and the "sea" (20:13–14; 21:1, 8).[268] The one is living and gives life while the other is a place of darkness and death, and such has been contrasted since Gen 1.

In this new habitation, there exists a "river of the water of life" that proceeds "from the throne of God and of the Lamb" (22:1; Ezek 47:1–12; Zech 14:8). On either side of the river is the "tree of life" perpetually bearing fruit (22:2). Those present in the new Jerusalem are "those who wash their robes," as opposed to those who remain morally filthy (22:14–15).

---

265. Crowe, *Message of General Epistles*, 128.
266. Koester, *Revelation*, 802–3.
267. Koester, *Revelation*, 803–4.
268. Koester, *Revelation*, 807.

"The Spirit and the bride" invite any who is "thirsty" to come and "take of the water of life" (22:17).

Several truths seem evident from this text. First, this reassuring invitation and promise to believers paints a picture of water as an eternal life-giving source.[269] It concludes the story of life from Gen 1 when the heavens and earth were created by water. But concluding that story does not complete it, for God has made this water of life available to all who thirst for it, and it lasts forever. Like Jesus, it is the alpha and omega. Second, throughout the OT and until Jesus's ascension, life was initiated by water at the will of God, or by the pleadings of his prophets and priests, or those who somehow found the way to righteousness, such as Noah. The text explains that this transformation now is offered, and even urged by both the Spirit and bride, the church (22:17), reflecting how it has been since Pentecost (Acts 2:36–47). There is some debate over the grammatical construction as to whether John records the Spirit and bride asking Jesus to come, or whether the thirsty are being asked to come, or whether both Jesus and the thirsty are being asked to come.[270] This debate is somewhat irrelevant because the Spirit and the bride are working together in each case.[271] This is both a foreboding responsibility and a blessed honor. If the reference is to calling those thirsty, as appears to be the case, this is a monumental undertaking.[272] To be responsible for calling others to the living water can be downright scary, just as building the ark for Noah must have been, or as Elijah confronting Ahab or the prophets of Baal seemingly was. But, that is counterbalanced with being in lockstep with the Spirit who is also calling sinners to the transformation of living water. Whether the Spirit's work is considered prevenient grace is not our concern. What matters is that the church has a missional responsibility and the Spirit joins with the church in that.[273] Exactly how that works appears to be shrouded in a level of mystery that remains largely unsolved.

Third, this invitation ends the NT and the Protestant canon with a glimpse into a new world that sounds much like the world when it was originally created and called "very good" (Gen 1:31). Adam was without sin, without illness, without death, in the presence of God and in

---

269. Koester, *Revelation*, 857.

270. Koester, *Revelation*, 856–57; Smalley, *Revelation of John*, 577–78; Osborne, *Revelation*, 793–94; Beale, *Book of Revelation*, 1148–50.

271. Osborne, *Revelation*, 793–94.

272. Smalley, *Revelation of John*, 578.

273. Roloff, *Revelation*, 739–94.

a magnificent safe and opulent place (Gen 1–2). The same is offered in new Jerusalem (Rev 21–22). The water of life available here is the same the prophets mentioned and that Jesus offered, which has already been discussed. Bookends normally match, and the Bible's bookends do match. They help frame a repetitious story that is part of the backbone of Scripture from start to finish. That interrelation of many texts from many different biblical books unifies the Bible, and supports it as a single corpus. The primary purpose of this subsection is not to engage in detailed exegesis, but to note the numerous mentions of water and water-related terms, and to summarize their impact.

CHAPTER SUMMARY

This chapter has endeavored to demonstrate that God has used water as an instrument to initiate life. It started with examples that stretch from Gen 1 and continue throughout the OT and into the NT, even to its last book, Revelation. The water is not magic, but God has for some reason seen fit to use it as a symbol and mechanism by which he creates life, or announces change from an old way or circumstance to a new way or circumstance, from an old person to a new one. He created the heavens and earth this way which included the first humans. He did it with Noah, Moses, Israel, Elijah, Elisha, Jonah, the Samaritan woman, the blind man at the pool of Siloam, and it happened to Jesus himself. The apostles preached about transformation throughout Acts and the Epistles, urging hearers to change from their old way of living to a new way through faith in Christ, repentance, and the water of baptism, by the grace and power of the Holy Spirit. The message is consistent and coherent from Genesis to Revelation, revealing a portion of a biblical theology of water in which God uses water to initiate life. This consistent message also helps undergird canonical unity.

3

Water and Cleansing

THE FIRST ELEMENT OF the thesis is that God uses water to initiate life as part of a biblical theology of water. The second element of this thesis is that God also uses water to cleanse or purify, which is also a part of a biblical theology of water. The cleansing that is portrayed in the Bible is presented in varied forms which will be discussed. It will also be noted that in some texts, the initiation of life by water and purification by water seem to occur concurrently. The biblical texts also point to different types of cleansing, both physical and spiritual.

PHYSICAL CLEANSING

Physical cleansing with water is so universally common that the mention of it is almost unnecessary. The Bible does speak about physical cleansing with water, such as when David bathed after grieving for his dead son (2 Sam 12:20) and the chariot of the dead king of Israel was washed by the pool of Samaria (1 Kgs 22:38). A second usage is when literal washing is used in a figurative sense to portray a spiritual message or meaning. Examples would include Jesus washing the feet of the disciples to demonstrate humility and service to others (John 13:14) and Pilate washing his hands to absolve himself of the crucifixion of Jesus (Matt 27:24).[1] A

---

1. Kruger, "Symbolic Acts," 164.

third biblical use of washing with water is its use in a purely literary manner, or as a figure of speech, and the washing is not literal or physical, but metaphorical, referring to spiritual cleansing. Examples of this include a reference to washing hands for a pure heart and for innocence (Ps 73:13) and God washing Israel to cleanse and prepare it for fellowship with him (Ezek 16:9). While the Bible offers many examples of washing merely for physical cleansing, a practice that is obviously universal and without debate, it also mentions literal washing that is designed to represent something spiritual, typically spiritual cleansing, and it is also used completely in a metaphorical manner. It is the second usage, literal washing to represent something spiritual, that is primarily in focus in this chapter.

SPIRITUAL CLEANSING

Starting in Genesis and continuing throughout the Bible, numerous episodes of spiritual cleansing provide insight into this second use of water, and become part of an overall biblical theology of water. Many of the same "water texts" used in the last chapter in which the focus was on the initiation of life, will be explored again to include the cleansing aspect. Adding this second perspective may broaden one's understanding of a given text, while also helping to authenticate the presence of a biblical theology of water.

Genesis 1–2

In the previous chapter the heavens and earth existing in submerged waters, followed by the separation of the waters, was discussed in some detail where it was noted that this birthing process involved water (1:1–10). It was also suggested that the birth of a human baby mirrored the birth of the earth. Imagining that this separation of the earth from the deep at creation is an act of cleansing may not be immediately evident (1:6–10). Claus Westermann believes the act of separation itself is essential to creation and "gives rise to something new" bringing "light to what was originally there."[2] What was originally there was God (1:1). "The Spirit of God was moving over the surface of the waters," but God was not in the waters (1:2). What Westermann referred to as "new" is that the chaotic darkness of the deep was lighted, and then separated (1:1–6). Because "God is light

2. Westermann, *Genesis*, 1:122.

and in him is no darkness at all" we know God was not in the waters, but that when he ordered, "Let there be light," it was his first step of several in transforming what existed into something new (1 John 1:5). The separation of the waters, and the earth from the water that followed the arrival of light was a next step in bringing about that new something (1:1–10).

God is holy (Lev 11:44). For God to dwell in, or on, the earth it must also be holy. By each act of bringing light and separation to the dark *formless and void* God systematically cleansed the earth, making it habitable for his own dwelling with humanity.[3] It was not because of sin that the heavens and earth were cleansed. James D. G. Dunn points out that in Jewish culture sin does not have to be present for impurity or a lack of holiness to exist, and that washing can be for cleansing apart from any involvement in sin (Lev 13–15).[4] It was not sin, but the primeval chaos, darkness, and uselessness that were washed away so that order, light, and purpose might replace them. This cleansing announced the transformation that old things had passed away, and a new purpose and existence had arrived.

Jesus similarly was baptized by John not to wash away any personal sin, but to mirror this washing in creation while the Father, John the Baptist, the Holy Spirit, and Jesus himself proclaimed Jesus's readiness to make available the good news so that what presently existed could be transformed into something new, eternal, and holy (Matt 3:1–17; Mark 1:4–11; Luke 3:21; John 1:31). The washing of creation and the baptismal washing of Jesus both announced existence on new terms.[5] The effect of this cleansing at creation is identified by Graham Cole as "divine concomitance," or "alongsidedness," meaning "God with us," as a nuance of God in relation to his creation.[6] The holy God wants to dwell with us. "His holiness, more than any other attribute, determines his interaction with humanity."[7]

As God added each element of "the heavens and the earth" during each sequential day of creation, he continued his systematic preparation of the holy habitat in which he and his holy creation would dwell. It was the first sanctuary, the place in which God would dwell with those made

3. Firmage, "Genesis 1."
4. Dunn, "Jesus and Purity."
5. Keating, "Baptism of Jesus"; Bockmuehl, "Baptism of Jesus"; Gruenwald, "Baptism of Jesus."
6. G. Cole, *God Who Became Human*, 33.
7. G. Cole, *God Who Became Human*, 103.

in his likeness.[8] When he created humankind in his own likeness and image, God's holiness was included in that likeness and image, and such is the highest potential afforded humanity (1:26-27).[9] With regard to Eden, humanity was charged to "cultivate it and keep it" which is a term meaning to serve and guard what God has decreed.[10] Included in that, humanity was to guard and protect itself against infringements on its own holiness.[11] Humanity's failure to assume one of its first responsibilities ruptured Eden's holiness resulting in humanity's expulsion from the presence of God and his holy habitat (Gen 3:22-24).

What is advocated here is that humanity was made holy just as God is holy, and the garden was created holy as the dwelling place for both God and humanity. In the preparatory steps of creation of the heavens and earth, the separation of the waters was part of God's purification of not only his dwelling place, but also of humanity's. God used literal water to accomplish a spiritual function, for himself and for humanity.

Genesis 6-9

It may seem obvious that the world was full of wickedness and the flood was designed to eradicate that contamination, leaving righteous Noah in an unadulterated world (6:6-13). That alone should make the case that God used water in the flood to purify the earth and humanity. The flood was essentially a re-creation of the earth with Noah being charged much the same as Adam. For example, God said to Noah, "Be fruitful and multiply and fill the earth," exactly as he directed Adam (Gen 1:28; 9:1,7). God said to Noah, "The terror of you will be on every beast of the field and every bird of the sky" which is not exactly the same, but similar to what Adam was told (Gen 1:26-28; 2:19; 9:2). Noah was told, "Every moving thing that is alive shall be food for you," while Adam was pointed to every tree (Gen 1:29, 16; 9:3). When Noah left the ark, God directed that human life was to be honored because it was made in his likeness (Gen 1:26-28; 9:4-6). It seems clear by these supporting examples that

---

8. Beale, "Eden, the Temple," 7.
9. Firmage, "Genesis 1," 103.
10. Beale, "Eden, the Temple," 8.
11. Firmage, "Genesis 1."

allude to creation, that God was using the waters of the flood to reestablish holiness as was originally intended.[12]

Exodus, Numbers, and Joshua

Seeing Israel's Red Sea crossing as the entrée into new life, or joining Paul and calling it a baptism, may seem a more obvious metaphor than identifying the sea crossing with cleansing or purification, but purification is a significant part of the event (Exod 12:14–22). The preparation prior to crossing included what became known as the Feast of Unleavened Bread, which appears concomitant with the observance of Passover (Exod 12:14–17, 23–27). Terence Fretheim says, "It is a sacramental vehicle for making the exodus redemption real and effective for both present and subsequent generations."[13]

This feast included seven days of eating without leaven in the bread, and the first and seventh days were each called a "holy assembly" (Exod 12:16, 18). Those who failed to comply by eating leaven were to be "cut off" (Exod 12:15, 19). When Israel departed Egypt, they carried with them bread without leaven (Exod 12:34, 39). The Passover meal, which at least in this context appears to include the Feast of Unleavened Bread, was only for Israel and any circumcised non-Israelite who had joined them (Exod 12:42–49). The prohibition of leaven extended beyond what was eaten to the presence of leaven anywhere within Israel's borders (Exod 13:6–7). Leaven may have been prohibited because it represents a human invention or addition to what God had created. The flour was crushed grain, and when water was added it became dough. Both the water and the grain came directly from God without any human interference, but adding yeast changed the God-given elements into a God/human blend that diminished God's presence.[14] The apostle Paul related the unleavened bread to "sincerity and truth," both qualities inherent in God's holiness (1 Cor 5:6–8).[15] Others have noted Israel was intended to be a holy nation of priests, making this feast a declaration of that hallowed status.[16]

---

12. Beale, "Eden, the Temple," 8.
13. Fretheim, *Exodus*, 139.
14. Ko, "Significance of the Omission."
15. Langston, *Exodus through the Centuries*, 110–11.
16. Langston, *Exodus through the Centuries*, 109–10.

The purpose of the leaven prohibition is stated as "because of what the Lord did for me when I came out of Egypt. And it shall serve as a sign . . . that the law of the Lord may be in your mouth, for with a powerful hand the Lord brought you out of Egypt" (Exod 13:8–9). Thus, the preparatory consecration for crossing the Red Sea is directly related to the presence of God within Israel and his saving power (Exod 13:21–22). After the crossing, this sanctification ritual also served as a memorial of God's presence, deliverance, and power (Exod 13:8–9).[17] This biblical purpose fits well with the aforementioned rationale of holiness in the leaven restriction.[18] Carol Meyers believes the remembrance is closely linked to the activity of the ritual, which in turn "creates and maintains identity" as God's chosen and sanctified people.[19]

During the excursion to Canaan, those "numbered men" who rebelled against God died and did not enter Canaan (Num 14:29), and the spies who acted in fear succumbed to plague (Num 14:36–37). When Korah rebelled, he and his comrades were called "wicked" and they were destroyed for their wickedness and lack of devotion (Num 16:25–26, 30–33). Their failure to become holy and maintain sanctity was an affront to God who dwelled among them. Their sinfulness proved them unholy, and prevented their entrance into Canaan where God would continue to dwell among them. Even Moses and Aaron were refused admission into Canaan because they, too, failed to treat God as holy before the people of Israel, even though by contrast, God consistently proved himself holy (Num 20:12–13).

Just before crossing the Jordan into Canaan the ark of the covenant, a symbol of God's presence and his covenant relationship with Israel, was readied to cross the river and the Israelites were warned to keep sufficient distance from the ark (Josh 3:2–4). Israel was to consecrate itself prior to following the ark across the Jordan into Canaan because it was in God's presence, which would be verified by a demonstration of his power (Josh 3:5–7, 10–13). Upon entering the promised land all Israelite males were circumcised as a sign of their dedication to holy living under the covenant relationship with God (Gen 17:13–14; Josh 5:2–7). Just as Moses was said to be standing on holy ground because God was present, so Joshua was told the same (Exod 3:5; Josh 5:15). While the Red Sea crossing is called a "baptism" (1 Cor 10:2), the crossing of the Jordan was not so labeled,

---

17. Meyers, *Exodus*, 101.
18. Fretheim, *Exodus*, 148–49.
19. Meyers, *Exodus*, 101–2; see also Fretheim, *Exodus*, 139.

but the two events are strikingly similar. In both cases water is parted or walled up; God is present, whether in the cloud or in the ark; Israel's faith in God propelled it across the temporarily dry ground; water and purification combine resulting in Israel living in a new location geographically, and in a new spiritual existence in the presence of holy God.

What all of this history intimates is that God demanded holiness of his people, Israel, because he is holy (Lev 11:44). Being made in the likeness of God means replicating God's character which centers on his holiness (Gen 1:26–28; Lev 11:44). In preparing to cross the Red Sea, leaven was not to be eaten, nor was it taken along in the exodus, because eating without it symbolized eating only what came from God and that Israel depended totally upon God. Leaven was also sometimes a metaphor for corruption and its prohibition reflected the purity with which Israel was to be identified.[20] Israel prepared itself and passed through water, emerging cleansed in a new land and in a new relationship with God.

After the crossing of the sea Israel's song praised God's holiness (Exod 15:11), and stated that God was guiding Israel into his holy habitation (Exod 15:13). It called the journey's end in Canaan the place of God's dwelling and sanctuary where he would reign in victory (Exod 15:17–18), and the song spoke of new land which was to be a place where God's presence eliminated diseases that plagued the Egyptians (Exod 15:26). Fretheim calls it "a kind of 'realized eschatology.'"[21] Some see this as a polemic against Baal, the Canaanite god, and if it is, it still takes nothing away from what is affirmed about God and his holiness.[22] It does seem that the exodus event transcends both Israel and Egypt and has a more spiritual message.[23] Upon entry into the land of Canaan a sin offering acknowledged Israel's marred spiritual condition, and a priest atoned for its sins, rendering Israel in a condition of holiness, a people properly prepared for God's presence in their midst (Num 15:18–25).

Before leaving Egypt and crossing the Red Sea, during the forty-year desert wandering, just before crossing the Jordan, and immediately after crossing the Jordan, Israel was called to purge itself of all moral and spiritual contamination to ready itself for the presence of God. Israel's miraculous crossing of both bodies of water is closely linked with its purification prior to, and after, the crossings. The waters that Israel passed

---

20. Kaiser, "Exodus," 511.
21. Fretheim, *Exodus*, 168. See also Kaiser, "Exodus," 539.
22. Meyers, *Exodus*, 121.
23. Langston, *Exodus through the Centuries*, 169.

through represent God's spiritual washing based upon Israel's adherence to the specified cleansing rituals, and it was God's invitation to join into his presence by allowing him to lead Israel through the waters (1 Cor 10:1–4). "Be holy, for I am holy" is the guiding principle (Lev 11:44). Israel readied itself, so its own holiness provided the appropriate habitat for holy God. When God appeared to this cleansed people, his power had already been demonstrated with the two partings of the waters, so all would know and fear him (Josh 4:23–24). Just as God used water to cleanse the earth in creation and in the flood, water again symbolized the leadership of God directing purified people to their destination by crossing the Red Sea and the Jordan River.

Israel's Ritual Cleansings

Soon after the Israelites' leaving Egypt, God used the wilderness wandering as a time to establish his covenant and the ancillary rites and duties expected under it (Exod 19–30). As the emergent mass of Israelites began transformation into a nation, and God through Moses provided laws by which its citizens should be governed, water appears as the mechanism of purification for priests and for the populace. At the doorway to the tent of meeting water was literally applied to priests for spiritual or moral purification prior to their service at the tent of meeting (Exod 29:4; 40:12). A bronze laver of water was set between the tent of meeting and the altar for priests to cleanse themselves a second time prior to placing offerings on the altar, with failure to do so met by penalty of death (Exod 30:17–21; 40:30–32).

Leviticus is rife with instances where the citizenry of Israel was enjoined to use water for cleansing to prevent Israel from becoming unholy. Water purification was used for cleansing various sacrifices made to God (Lev 1:9, 13; 8:21); for purifying anything touched by any unclean "swarming things" (11:29–32); for cleansing contaminated vessels (6:28); for purifying a person and his house from leprosy (14:6–52); for purifying people from bodily discharges, including cleansing the bed on which such may have occurred, as well as anything touched by the discharging person, such as a saddle, or another person (15:1–18); for purification after a menstrual cycle, including anything upon which the woman sat, or anyone who touched things upon which she sat (15:19–30); for cleansing body and clothing of one touching a dead animal or an animal killed by beasts (17:15–16); and for the consecrating of priests (8:6; 16:1–28).

Leviticus and Numbers introduce the concept of "running water" or living water for purification (Lev 14:5, 6, 50, 51, 52; 15:13; Num 19:17). While the Hebrew term underlying the translation "running water" is actually "living water" (*mym hyym*), the term is used in the context as literal running water, and not in the metaphorical sense found in some of the OT prophets and in the NT (Song 4:15; Jer 2:13; Zech 14:8; John 4:10; 7:38; Rev 7:17; 21:6; 22:17).[24] Running water is used in Leviticus and Numbers for purification from corpses, from leprosy, and from unusual bodily discharges.[25] In each case the washing is by running or pouring water.[26]

When the red heifer was slaughtered outside the camp, the priests who killed it were to wash their clothes and their bodies with water as a cleansing act, and cleansing water was retained by Israel to remove impurity and purify it from sin (Num 19:6–9). Spiritual cleansing from the literal application of water was also to occur for those touching the dead (Num 19:11–21). Failure to purify oneself was considered defilement of God's dwelling place (Num 19:13). Both Leviticus and Numbers are replete with water-cleansing directives, which helps establish that the concepts of water and holiness are closely related. Purification by water that was seen in creation, in the flood, in the crossing of the Red Sea, and in what would be seen in later events, was unmistakably established by the ritual cleansings directed by God through Moses for all Israel. This literal application of water to accomplish a spiritual purpose, that of moral purity or holiness, continues throughout the Bible.

2 Kings 5

The story of Naaman being cleansed of leprosy by dipping seven times in the Jordan River at the directive of Elisha demonstrates an example of literal water cleansing a physical ailment. The ritual of washing in running water for cleansing leprosy is here applied to one outside Israel, but one in whom there was a believing heart (Lev 14:6–52; Num 19:10; 2

---

24. Katz, "He Shall Bathe," 378.

25. Katz, "He Shall Bathe," 378–79; Gane, "Leviticus," 1:302. See also Gen 26:19 where the same Hebrew term is used.

26. Katz, "He Shall Bathe," 378–79.

Kgs 5:14–19).[27] What is also evident is the spiritual application because Naaman became a believer in the God of Israel, and even asked forgiveness for the times he would be required to accompany his master into the pagan temple of Rimmon (2 Kgs 5:15–19).[28] He was reborn a new man. There was thus both a physical and a spiritual cleansing.

This story can arguably be relied upon as an example of water initiating new life, or used to emphasize the importance of water baptism.[29] But the cleansing aspect of the story seems predominant based upon Naaman's interest in physical cleansing (2 Kgs 5:12–14), not spiritual cleansing, even though Naaman appears to have undergone a conversion to a new life of faith in God (2 Kgs 5:15–19).[30] There are some parallels with the healing of the blind man who was healed at the pool of Siloam (John 9). In each case there was physical healing by water as God's agent of cleansing. In each case faith led to washing in water, and in each case after the cleansing there was a newfound devotion toward God.[31] To some there is an obvious similarity to Christian baptism, as just suggested, but in his work on baptism, G. R. Beasley-Murray omits any mention of the Naaman story.[32] This text will be considered in a discussion of water baptism in chapter 6.

Ezekiel 36

Ezekiel 36:25 says, "Then I will sprinkle clean water on you, and you will be clean; I will cleanse you from all your filthiness and from all your idols." This biblical text, perhaps more than any other, clearly associates water and spiritual cleansing. The context speaks of the nations knowing God and God proving himself holy in their sight (36:23), gathering nations from across the world and bringing them to Israel (36:24), Israel being given a new heart and the Spirit of God (36:26–27), and Israel living in the promised land with agricultural abundance (36:28–30). The immediate context makes it plain that the referenced time of Israel's cleansing by

27. R. Cole, "Numbers," 1:369; Provan, "2 Kings," 134.

28. Patrasescu, "Naaman and the Jordan."

29. Van Dorn, *Waters of Creation*, 22–23; E. Ferguson, "Baptism According to Origen."

30. Barrick, "Living A New Life," 30–31.

31. Gallagher, "Elijah and Elisha," 10–11.

32. Jang, "Water Rite and Conversion," 161–72; Beasley-Murray, *Baptism in New Testament*, 9.

water is yet future.³³ It is a time that takes Israel out of the ordinariness of daily life surrounded by corruption, and plants the nation in a new environment characterized by holiness.³⁴ It speaks to a cleansing that will present Israel holy so it is equipped to dwell in the presence of God.³⁵

This text has oft been used to reference Christian baptism, and sometimes to promote sprinkling, rather than immersion, as a mode of that baptism.³⁶ What seems evident in this text is that it does not directly relate to water baptism in this age, but instead refers primarily to the eschaton.³⁷ Beasley-Murray interprets the text as pointing to "the last day," and attributes the language of sprinkling to the conjoining of ceremonial washing to spiritual cleansing which had spiritualized washing in the minds of many Israelites.³⁸ Commentators also frequently cite this text as the prophetic backdrop of John 3:3–5 where Nicodemus is instructed about birth from above, or being born again, yet not all agree whether such is the case, and if it is, to what degree it is.³⁹

What is important to this study is that the idea of cleansing is enumerated three times in this text (Ezek 36:25).⁴⁰ This cleansing comes by God's use of water, and likely echoes the ritual cleansings previously discussed in Exodus, Leviticus, and Numbers.⁴¹ Yet, the cleansing by water refers to a time in the future, which demonstrates God's use of water to cleanse across time, from creation, to the flood, to the Red Sea and Jordan River crossings, to the Israelite ritual washings, and here it is foretold in the eschaton. Cleansing by water is also frequent throughout the NT, which will be a forthcoming discussion. It does seem that God has established water cleansing as his means of purification of his people for all ages.

---

33. Beasley-Murray, *Baptism in New Testament*, 9; R. Alexander, *Ezekiel*, 255.
34. Goldingay, *Ezekiel*, 34.
35. Kelle, *Ezekiel*, 297.
36. Zimmerli, *Ezekiel 2*, 248–49; Nettles, "Baptist Response," 74; Castelein, "Believers' Baptism," 136; Kulbacki, "Memory of Baptism"; Godbey, *Buried by Baptism*; Michaels, *Gospel of John*, 184–85.
37. R. Alexander, *Ezekiel*, 255; Keener, *Gospel of John*, 1:551–55.
38. Beasley-Murray, *Baptism in New Testament*, 9.
39. Keener, *Gospel of John*, 1:551–55; Klink, *John*, 198; Köstenberger, *Theology of John's Gospel*, 163, 350, 474–75; Von Wahlde, *Gospel and Letters*, 115–17.
40. Bodi, "Ezekiel," 4:480.
41. Bodi, "Ezekiel," 4:480; Zimmerli, *Ezekiel 2*, 249.

Jonah

The obvious earmarks of the beginning of the Jonah story include Jonah running away from the presence of the Lord (1:3, 10), the struggling ship on the stormy sea (1:3–4, 13–15), and the great fish (1:17). The story turns, however, on Jonah's repentance while in the sea. While the term "repentance" is not voiced in the text, the concept is very clear, and in response to that repentance God's grace is applied.[42] While surrounded by water, inside the great fish (Jonah's ark) Jonah prays to God and God answers (2:1–2). Jonah acknowledges he was separated from God, but wants to return to God's "holy temple" (2:4).

Fred Blumenthal has interpreted this episode as Jonah attempting to extinguish God's prophetic voice echoing in his head, and realizing that even in running away, even though sleeping through a storm, and even in the belly of a fish in the depths of the sea, the voice of God will have an impact (Isa 55:11).[43] Jonah's prayer to "look again toward your holy temple" was an acknowledgement that he would again listen to God's voice, after having attempted to suppress it or ignore it (2:4).[44] It was not that Jonah was running away from God as he readily admitted he feared God (1:9). Instead, Jonah was running from his responsibility as a prophet.[45] Jonah readily admits his unfaithfulness, and renews his vow to the Lord, acknowledging that God is worthy of his sacrifice and is the provider of salvation (2:8–9). The fact that God immediately answers his prayer (2:2), and removes Jonah from death in the sea (2:10), implies that Jonah's sin has been removed and he has returned to a state of holiness, again listening to, and walking with, the Lord (3:3). It is interesting that Jonah did not ask for deliverance from the sea, but instead cried out regarding his separation from God, and his desire to again listen to God's voice and acknowledge him as holy (2:4, 7, 9).[46] With Jonah, God used water to provide new life, but he also used water to cleanse Jonah of his sin, based on Jonah's repentance.

---

42. Kaltner et al., "Jonah in the Book," 171.
43. Blumenthal, "Jonah."
44. Blumenthal, "Jonah," 104.
45. Shulman, "Jonah."
46. Blumenthal, "Jonah," 105–6.

Zechariah 13

"In that day a fountain will be opened for the house of David and for the inhabitants of Jerusalem, for sin and impurity" (13:1). In the closing chapters of Zechariah, the prophet paints a picture of the end-time when God reestablishes Israel, vanquishes its foes, and blesses his people while his name is exalted (Zech 12–14). The fountain to be opened is an echo of the ritual cleansings with water from the Torah, and a forward looking visualization of the living water to flow out of Jerusalem (Zech 14:8).[47] The purpose of the fountain of water is stated as "for sin and for impurity," which means the water is designed to spiritually purify (13:1).[48] The water is to cleanse just as it has throughout Israel's past and throughout the OT. Here its focus is on Jerusalem, as opposed to all people, and to the priesthood in particular.[49]

The text is thematically connected to Ezek 36:25, in which God cleanses all his people by the use of water, and appears also linked to Ezek 47.[50] The text is complemented by Zech 14:8 where living water is to flow from Jerusalem, which Mark Boda identifies as possibly the Gihon Spring lying "just south of the Temple Mount."[51] He suggests the water flow shifts dependence on water from the uncertainty of rain to direct dependence on God, and links this spring to the Gihon that watered Eden (Gen 2:10–14).[52] Like Ezek 36, the focus is on a future time when God will act "in one day" (Zech 3:9–10).[53]

---

47. Boda, *Zechariah*, 722–24; Baron, *Zechariah*, 442; David L. Petersen, *Zechariah 9–14*, 123.

48. Baron, *Zechariah*, 441; David L. Petersen, *Zechariah 9–14*, 123; Redditt, *Zechariah 9–14*, 107.

49. Boda, *Zechariah*, 722–24; David L. Petersen, *Zechariah 9–14*, 123; Redditt, *Zechariah 9–14*, 112–13; Goldingay and Scalise, *Minor Prophets II*, 300; Klein, *Zechariah*, 478.

50. Boda, *Zechariah*, 724–25; David L. Petersen, *Zechariah 9–14*, 123–24; Goldingay and Scalise, *Minor Prophets II*, 301.

51. Boda, *Zechariah*, 763–64.

52. Boda, *Zechariah*, 764–65.

53. Baron, *Zechariah*, 444–46; Klein, *Zechariah*, 476; Ralph Smith, *Micah-Malachi*, 280.

John 1

The question of the Pharisees to John the Baptist, "Why then are you baptizing if you are not the Christ, nor Elijah, nor the Prophet," raises the question as to which OT text or tradition gave the expectation that any of those three named would baptize (1:25). There seems to be no trace of a baptizing tradition for any of the three.[54] This expectation may arise from an errant interpretation of Ezek 36:25, which states God will sprinkle clean water to cleanse Israel in the eschaton.[55] Some suggest the Pharisees presupposed a messianic baptism.[56] Several have noted Jewish proselyte baptism as the foundation for John's baptism, which was used to initiate a non-Jew into Judaism, and was well known throughout the diaspora.[57] If this undergirded John's baptism, he was essentially declaring all people, Jew and non-Jew alike, outside fellowship with God and in need of cleansing so that new life with God might ensue.[58] John's cleansing came by repentance and baptism in which sins were forgiven (Luke 3:3, John 1:29), but it looked forward to the Messiah who would remove the sins of the world and baptize in the Holy Spirit (1:29–31).[59]

The point of interest in this discussion is the cleansing that came by water. It clearly was not the water itself that cleansed, but the water symbolized the cleansing from the Messiah who would remove sin and baptize in the Holy Spirit those prepared by their show of repentance and faith in the efficacy of John's baptism.[60] This baptism anticipated the coming One who was not presently known by John's inquisitors (1:26–31).[61] Just as the water was not an end in itself in creation, in the flood, in Israel's crossings of the Red Sea and the Jordan, in Naaman's cleansing, in Jonah's purification, or in Ezekiel's or Zechariah's water cleansings, the same is true with John's baptism.[62] John's water symbolized cleansing by its demand for repentance and faith that looked forward to forgiveness

---

54. Haenchen, *John 1*, 145; Klink, *John*, 131.
55. Haenchen, *John 1*, 145–46; Michaels, *Gospel of John*, 102.
56. Keener, *Gospel of John*, 1:440.
57. Keener, *Gospel of John*, 1:446; Michaels, *Gospel of John*, 102.
58. Keener, *Gospel of John*, 1:446–48; Michaels, *Gospel of John*, 102; Klink, *John*, 131.
59. Keener, *Gospel of John*, 1:440; Köstenberger, *Theology of John's Gospel*, 189.
60. Köstenberger, *Theology of John's Gospel*, 189; Klink, *John*, 131.
61. Köstenberger, *Theology of John's Gospel*, 189; Klink, *John*, 131.
62. Klink, *John*, 131–32; Köstenberger, *Theology of John's Gospel*, 164.

of sins in the Messiah.[63] John's baptism of Jesus was a cleansing, but not a cleansing from sin, as previously discussed. This cleansing was a washing away of the old system, and the announcement of a new era derived through Jesus.[64]

John 19

The water that flowed from the side of Jesus while on the cross has been addressed herein in terms of its initiation of new life (19:34). The unity between blood and water has also been addressed and that comingling is evident in this flow from Jesus's side (19:34). New life for the heavens and earth, which included the first humans, was "very good" and points to a pure and sinless condition (Gen 1:31). After the earth was cleansed by the flood, Noah exited the ark a righteous man into a world where no sin existed since all earthly wickedness had been destroyed (Gen 6:5–7, 11–13; 7:21–23). When Israel crossed the Red Sea and Jordan River it was cleansed and began its new life in a cleansed condition, having engaged in ritual acts of sanctification that permitted God's presence to lead it through water and into the new purified existence. The same was true for Naaman and Jonah. Even though the cleansing was typically soon marred by sin, it does not negate that cleansing occurred. In these examples new life occurred only when cleansing also occurred. The two are inseparable.

The blood and water emerging from Jesus on the cross, both symbols of purification, together make it obvious that cleansing occurred along with the initiation of new life.[65] Added to those symbols sour wine was given Jesus via a hyssop branch (19:29). Hyssop was reminiscent of the smearing of blood on the lintel and doorposts marking the death of the firstborn, and with it, Israel's cleansing, both of which protected it from that death (19:29; Exod 12:1–22).[66] The text also echoes the use of hyssop for the cleansing of leprosy (Lev 14), and the removal of sin in the red heifer ritual (Num 19). David recalled the cleansing associated hyssop and with water when he said, "Purify me with hyssop, and I shall be clean; wash me, and I shall be whiter than snow" (Ps 51:7). The hyssop,

---

63. Klink, *John*, 131–32.
64. Dunn, "Jesus and Purity."
65. Klink, *John*, 815.
66. Klink, *John*, 811; Keener, *Gospel of John*, 2:1147; Köstenberger notes additional echoes of the Passover may be found in Jesus's unbroken bones (John 19:33, 36; *Theology of John's Gospel*, 164).

along with the blood and the water, looks backward to cleansing and new life in Israel's history and before, but also looks forward to new life and cleansing for all being initiated by Christ on the cross.[67]

Acts

Prior to Peter's direction to receive forgiveness of sins and the gift of the Holy Spirit by repentance and water baptism, Peter preached that "God has made him both Lord and Christ—this Jesus whom you crucified" (2:36). "When they heard this they were pierced to the heart, and said ... Brethren, what shall we do?" (2:37). There is no doubt that such a message was taken personally, shocking the hearers, breaking their hearts and convicting them of sin.[68] The goal of Peter's sermon was to proclaim the risen Jesus as the Christ, and he forcefully preached intending to convict his audience to repent and believe his message.[69] The audience's question was essentially "How do we cleanse ourselves of this sin guilt?"[70] Peter's solution was to "repent and be baptized" (2:38). They obviously already believed Peter's message that Jesus was the risen Christ or their question would not have been asked. Based upon that belief, repentance and baptism was intended to lead them to forgiveness of sins (2:38).[71]

The message sounds like a continuation of what John the Baptist had been preaching, but while John looked forward to Christ who would forgive, Peter is now looking backward to what had just occurred a few days prior, Jesus's crucifixion, resurrection, ascension, and the outpouring of the Spirit (1:1–11; 2:1–4; Luke 24:1–51).[72] Joel B. Green has identified two sets of pairs that are common in the messages of John the Baptist and Peter: repentance and baptism, and baptism and forgiveness.[73] It was the inward act of repentance coupled with the outward ritual of baptism in water that provided cleansing by God that enabled the Spirit to dwell

---

67. Klink, *John*, 815.
68. Marshall, *Acts*, 85.
69. Padilla, *Acts of the Apostles*, 152–56; Crowe, *Hope of Israel*, 111–14.
70. J. Green, *Conversion in Luke–Acts*, 125.
71. Crowe, *Hope of Israel*, 112, 120, 140–44; Padilla, *Acts of the Apostles*, 197; Marshall, *Acts*, 85–87.
72. Marshall, *Acts*, 86; J. Green, *Conversion in Luke–Acts*, 125–26: A. Collins, "Origin."
73. J. Green, *Conversion in Luke–Acts*, 125.

Water and Cleansing

within (2:38).[74] Just as John expected behavioral evidence of repentance from those being baptized (Luke 3:8), Peter's audience who repented and were baptized changed their behaviors (2:42–47).[75]

The phrase "for the forgiveness of sins" (Acts 2:38) has traditionally been problematic for some who struggle to accept spiritual purification by water baptism. The debate may center on the force of the word "for" (*eis*), and Daniel Wallace has rendered a clarifying perspective by citing this usage as a "causal/permissive passive," which "implies consent, permission, or cause of the action of the verb on the part of the subject."[76] Thus, baptism is not something one actively does to receive forgiveness, but something acquiesced to that is passively received. Wallace goes on to ask if a causal force of the term is not the proper use, then "what are we to make of Acts 2:38?"[77] In other words, the cause of forgiveness comes by the water (preceded by faith and repentance) which is passively received, not actively worked for or earned. Wallace continues by suggesting "the idea of baptism might incorporate both the spiritual reality and the physical symbol. In other words, when one spoke of baptism, he usually meant both ideas—the reality and the ritual."[78] He illustrates this by reference to Cornelius who had already received the Holy Spirit when Peter directed water baptism to follow (10:44–48).[79] It is not the water itself that forgives, but the sacramental nature of it.[80] Similarly, it was not the water that purified Israel, their priests, or their offerings, but the physical ritual unleashed the unseen spiritual cleansing.

It seems simple enough to review John's baptism which was "of repentance for the forgiveness of sins," and uses the same terms as Acts 2:38 (Luke 3:3). John baptized in water pointing forward (as has already been discussed herein) to the coming Messiah who would take away the sins of the world (John 1: 29). It was the Messiah and the completion of his mission that forgave sins, but access to that forgiveness was by means of repentance and baptism according to John and Peter. If John's baptism was not essential then why he advocated it must be explained. The same is true of Peter's instructions. If baptism did not remove sins, then Peter's

---

74. J. Green, *Conversion in Luke-Acts*, 125.
75. J. Green, *Conversion in Luke-Acts*, 125–26.
76. Wallace, *Greek Grammar*, 440–41.
77. Wallace, *Greek Grammar*, 370.
78. Wallace, *Greek Grammar*, 370–71.
79. Wallace, *Greek Grammar*, 371.
80. Hicks, *Enter the Water*, 10–169; Allison and Köstenberger, *Holy Spirit*, 448.

rationale for advocating it when asked for a solution to sin guilt by his audience seems bizarre. Undergirding the cleansing by water, there is a water-cleansing typology forecast in the numerous water cleansings of the OT.[81] That being the case, a NT realization (the anti-type) of the OT type must be uncovered, and if that is not accomplished in baptism, then such appears nonexistent and the type becomes illusory.

Wallace notes the ritual and the forgiveness are closely intertwined.[82] So is repentance and baptism.[83] Bifurcating each element of the conversion or cleansing process to designate one part as effectual for forgiveness and other parts ineffectual seems exegetically unjustified. Peter strongly connects repentance and baptism by the conjunction "and" (*kai*) which leaves no room for claiming one or the other is either primary or unnecessary (2:38).[84] Howard Marshall correctly says Peter's instruction "contained two requirements, which are in effect one."[85] Green agrees by saying "when one or another aspect of this response is mentioned in the narrative, the others can be assumed as well."[86]

This presentation unpacks many biblical texts regarding cleansing by water with the evidence consistently indicating that God uses water to cleanse, irrespective of the various components associated with that cleansing.[87] For example, along with cleansing water Noah had to build an ark; Israel had to eat unleavened bread; Naaman had to wash in a specific river. It is not that the water itself holds efficacy, but it is an outward and physical application that expresses spiritual significance, and that may include or be associated with other physical or material elements.[88]

About three decades after Pentecost Peter issued a written message that was consistent with his instructions in Acts 2:38. He said, "Baptism now saves you—not the removal of dirt from the flesh, but an appeal to God for a good conscience—through the resurrection of Jesus Christ" (1 Pet 3:21). Peter used the example of Noah being saved by water to demonstrate the redemptive aspect of water, which in Noah's time also involved

---

81. A. Collins, "Origin," 40.
82. Wallace, *Greek Grammar*, 371.
83. Kellum, *Acts*, 41–42; J. Green, *Conversion in Luke–Acts*, 125; Marshall, *Acts*, 86.
84. Kellum, *Acts*, 41–42.
85. Marshall, *Acts*, 86.
86. J. Green, *Conversion in Luke–Acts*, 127.
87. Beasley-Murray, *Baptism in New Testament*, 99–104.
88. Allison and Köstenberger, *Holy Spirit*, 448–49; Hicks, *Enter the Water*, 10–169.

a cleansing of sin from the earth.[89] He linked this salvation and cleansing by water to the resurrection of Jesus, just as he did in Acts 2. Early Christian interest in typology identified the flood and baptism typology as an "overarching pattern" which continues today.[90] This pattern is of water initiating new life and cleansing concurrently within the same event.[91]

In another text from Acts, Ananias told Saul, "Get up and be baptized, and wash away your sins, calling on His name" (22:16). Saul had already proven his faith by allowing his companions to lead him to Damascus where Ananias located him (9:3–9). Ananias laid hands on Saul healing his blindness, imparted to him the Holy Spirit, and baptized him (9:1–19; 22: 6–16). Like the scene at Pentecost, faith, repentance, baptism, forgiveness, and reception of the Holy Spirit coalesce in the conversion process.[92] This ritual act of baptism in water was symbolic of the unseen spiritual cleansing that occurred. Green says this episode is "the clearest evidence" portraying this purification or sanctifying phenomenon.[93]

Romans 6

Romans describes baptism as a burial in which believers are "buried with him through baptism into death, so that as Christ was raised from the dead through the glory of the Father, so we too might walk in newness of life" (6:4). The imagery of Jesus dying and being raised in a new body is the paradigm for believers baptism in which the "body of sin might be done away with" (6:6), and "newness of life" (6:4) might follow. The believer is signifying the burial of an old way of life, and the adornment of a new one. The believers old way of life ends or dies, and the believer is raised a new creature (6:4, 6, 8, 11, 13). This death is not because of any magic in the water, but outward physical water burial symbolizes inward spiritual rebirth. Those having been baptized are considered as "having been freed from sin," and "become slaves of righteousness" (6:18).

That cleansing has occurred in the transformation inherent in baptism seems evident by these statements, and Paul confirms such when from this baptismal transformation he says, you "derive your benefit,

---

89. J. Green, *1 Peter*, 137–38.
90. J. Green, *1 Peter*, 256.
91. J. Green, *Conversion in Luke-Acts*, 72.
92. J. Green, *Conversion in Luke-Acts*, 50, 124–25; Allison and Köstenberger, *Holy Spirit*, 390–91, 448–49.
93. J. Green, *Conversion in Luke-Acts*, 72.

resulting in sanctification" (6:22). Historically, water baptism has been considered a cleansing, and Paul considers it such here.[94] It is the place where spiritual circumcision takes place, where one's identity is changed, and new life begins.[95] This result cannot be earned, but is a gift from God that is passively received from the Holy Spirit working through the instrumentality of the water.[96]

1 Corinthians

After a listing of sinful lifestyles, Paul says, "Such were some of you; but you were washed, but you were sanctified, but you were justified in the name of the Lord Jesus Christ and in the Spirit of our God" (6:11). The term "washed" (ἀπελούσασθε) is strengthened by its compound preposition (ἀπο) making it translated as "washed clean" by several English translations.[97] This has been called a "'baptismal aorist,' especially since the notion of having one's sins washed away fits a baptismal context in conjunction with the (probably) punctiliar aorist of event."[98]

The proximity of the terms "washed" and "sanctified," along with the common context, would seem to unite them at the same time or event, but the addition of "justified," which means being in right standing with God, strengthens the unity of these three terms.[99] Hans Conzelmann describes this baptismal washing as a "bath of purification."[100] One is sanctified and placed in right standing when washed, or baptized. Anthony Thiselton says, "This *washing clean* is not just the *forgiveness* for which the believer asks day-by-day renewal. It is a *wiping clean of the slate once-for-all* which is associated (as here) with justification by grace which is independent of renewed pardon."[101] The verbal action here is passive, or perhaps middle, making the nature of this transformation something that comes not by individual effort, but by acquiescing to the work of the Spirit of God.[102]

94. Kolb, "God's Baptismal Act," 101.

95. Kolb, "God's Baptismal Act," 101; Yarbrough, *Romans-Galatians*, 98–100.

96. Kolb, "God's Baptismal Act," 98–102; Yarbrough, *Romans-Galatians*, 98–100.

97. Thiselton, *First Epistle to Corinthians*, 453. See the AMPC, CEB, ERV, EXB, ICB, NCB, NCV, and NJB.

98. Thiselton, *First Epistle to Corinthians*, 453; Conzelmann, *1 Corinthians*, 107.

99. Ciampa and Rosner, *First Letter to Corinthians*, 241.

100. Conzelmann, *1 Corinthians*, 107.

101. Thiselton, *First Epistle to Corinthians*, 454.

102. Thiselton, *First Epistle to Corinthians*, 454–55; Conzelmann, *1 Corinthians*,

Ephesians 5

Speaking of the church, Paul said Christ "gave himself up for her, so that he might sanctify her, having cleansed her by the washing of water with the word, that he might present to himself the church in all her glory, having no spot or wrinkle or any such thing; but that she would be holy and blameless" (5:25–27). The text indicates that Jesus lived and died to sanctify the church, and to present her to himself holy and blameless. He cleansed her by the washing of water with the word to accomplish this, although the meaning of "washing" is not readily clear to modern readers.[103] Paul here may be alluding to the washing of Ezek 16, where God speaks of his cleansing of Israel.[104] Others, see this cleansing as baptism.[105] Connecting this text to Titus 3:5 is common.[106] The similarity of language is apparent as Paul speaks of "washing of regeneration and renewing by the Holy Spirit" (Titus 3:5). Ephesians 5 has been viewed by some as referring to the corporate church, while others see the individual aspect within the community of the church in Titus 3.[107]

While more in-depth discussion of the exact meanings of the washings in Ephesians and Titus would be interesting, they are beyond the scope of this presentation. The important point is that both texts use water, either metaphorically, in physical baptism, or in some other sense, to cleanse believers who make up the church. The imagery points to the second leg of the thesis that God uses water to cleanse or purify throughout the Bible.

Hebrews 10

The writer of Hebrews has progressed in his sermon on Jesus to discussing the blood and water, which has been reviewed, leading to the pleading to "draw near . . . having our hearts sprinkled clean from an evil conscience and our bodies washed with pure water" (10:22). "Sprinkling" is reminiscent of the OT ritual of sprinkling blood from Lev 16 and other

---

107; L. Morris, *1 Corinthians*, 97.
   103. Liefeld, *Ephesians*, 146.
   104. Bock, *Ephesians*, 178.
   105. Rollock, *Commentary on Ephesians*, 194–95.
   106. Bock, *Ephesians*, 178; Rollock, *Commentary on Ephesians*, 194–95.
   107. Bock, *Ephesians*, 178; Wall, *1 & 2 Timothy*, 360–67.

texts.¹⁰⁸ F. F. Bruce suggests having "our bodies washed with pure water" likely refers to baptism which is the present "outward application of water as the visible sign of the inward and spiritual cleansing wrought by God in those who come to him through Christ." Bruce makes the connection already discussed of an outward physical application functioning in consort with an inward spiritual cleansing.¹⁰⁹ There is not complete agreement on Bruce's position that baptism is referenced, but finding a meaning that had current relevance to the first readers, as well as those since, seems lacking if it does not reference baptism.¹¹⁰ David Petersen also believes the washing refers to baptism, and like Bruce, notes the outward expression of baptism, joined by the inward cleansing.¹¹¹ Again, water and cleansing are difficult to separate as the water is the instrumentality, whether literal or figurative, that results in cleansing.

1 Peter 3:21

Using Noah's salvation by water as his point of comparison, Peter says, "Corresponding to that, baptism now saves you—not the removal of dirt from the flesh, but an appeal to God for a good conscience through the resurrection of Jesus Christ" (3:21). While Peter's statement may seem to lend strong support to the salvific efficacy of baptism, he is clear that it is not the physical act of baptism that abrogates or cleanses sin ("not the removal of dirt from the flesh"), but it is "the appeal to God for a good conscience." The term "appeal" (ἐπερώτημα) can mean "the content of asking, question, a formal request, appeal."¹¹² Some prefer the word "pledge."¹¹³ First Peter 2:19 speaks of bearing up under suffering "for the sake of conscience" (συνείδησιν). First Peter 3:16 admonishes to keep a "good conscience" (συνείδησιν). First Peter 3:21 again uses the same term regarding baptism and the "appeal to God for a good conscience." The appeal of these texts are all linked by conscience (συνείδησιν). All three usages are bound up in the eternal reward that comes to those who have maintained their faith, like Noah, in the face of threatening circumstances. All three

---

108. Cockerill, *Epistle to the Hebrews*, 473–74; Bruce, *Epistle to the Hebrews*, 253–55.
109. Bruce, *Epistle to the Hebrews*, 255.
110. Schreiner, *Commentary on Hebrews*, 318–19.
111. David G. Petersen, *Hebrews*, 241–42.
112. ἐπερώτημα, BDAG, 362.
113. Crawford, "Confessing God"; Keener, *1 Peter*, 318–19.

are connected to the resurrection of Christ (3:21), and it is the power of the resurrection of Christ that empowers the salvation or cleansing from sin related to baptism.[114] Appealing to a good conscience by the resurrection of Jesus Christ is to live in faithfulness against surrounding wickedness and ridicule. It is knowing that Christ is the example of such endurance, even unto death that turned into eternal victory, a victory shared by those who have made a faith commitment and remember their baptism as a symbol of that commitment.[115] Water was the agent used by God to save Noah, and Peter claims baptismal water as a similar instrument God uses to save believers. Peter is clear to note it is not the water itself that saves, but it is the outward physical act that reflects an inward appeal to God seeking an inward spiritual cleansing.

1 John 5:6–8

Some background is in order prior to discussing 1 John 5:6–8, which says, "This is the One who came by water and blood, Jesus Christ; not with the water only, but with the water and with the blood. It is the Spirit who testifies, because the Spirit is the truth. For there are three that testify: the Spirit and the water and the blood; and these three are in agreement."

In Israel's purification rites water is said to cleanse, but oil and blood are also given a joint cleansing function.[116] The priest was to be consecrated by being washed with water, followed by an anointment with oil (Exod 29:1–9). The oil appears to reflect one chosen by God and enabled by the Spirit of God.[117] After the priest was cleansed with water and anointed with oil, he took a bull, slaughtered it, and sprinkled its blood on the base of the altar, but burned the remainder of the bull outside the camp as a sin offering (Exod 29:10–14). The priest then slaughtered a ram, sprinkled its blood on the altar, cut it into pieces, washed the entrails and legs with water, and offered them with the remaining ram as a burnt offering on the altar (Exod 29:15–18). Each time the offering was made, the priest washed his own hands in the water of the bronze laver positioned between the tent and the altar (Exod 30:17–21). The practice of using

---

114. Stallard, "Baptism Now Saves Us"; Achtemeier, *1 Peter*, 99; Schreiner, *1–2 Peter, Jude*, 111–12.

115. Achtemeier, *1 Peter*, 104.

116. Kline, "Day of the Lord," 763; Bruce, *Epistle to the Hebrews*, 226.

117. C. Wright, *Knowing the Holy Spirit*, 89; Allison and Köstenberger, *Holy Spirit*, 37.

both water and blood in consort seems to be standard practice for Israel's cleansing, having been preceded by the priest's anointment with oil (Lev 1:1–9, 10–13; 8:1–6, 10–12, 14–21; 14:1–20, 49–53; 16:23–28; Num 19).[118]

Ezekiel describes God's love and care for Israel by combining cleansing with water, washing off blood, and applying oil (Ezek 16:1–9). The NT references the practice of combining blood and water in the purification process (Heb 9:19), but mentions oil only for cleansing or healing without the presence of blood and water (Mark 6:13; Luke 10:34; Jas 5:14).[119] It has been suggested that in this blood and water terminology, there is a remembrance of the ancient ritual, but also an allusion to the "symbolism of baptism for the washing away of sin."[120] J. Bergman Kline finds that "blood" is sometimes used in Hebrews, somewhat as a synecdoche, for the conjoining of blood and water.[121] Others agree that cleansing the flesh and cleansing the spirit are not independent of each other in the OT.[122] It seems certain that texts such as "one may almost say, all things are cleansed with blood, and without the shedding of blood there is no forgiveness" (Heb 9:22) are not intending to extrapolate water from the cleansing process since water is specifically mentioned within the broader text (Heb 9:19–22). In this text water is clearly mentioned as part of the cleansing, but the emphasis happens to be on the blood element as it corresponds to the sacrifice of Christ, laying the foundation for the writer's next discussion (Heb 9:23—10:18).[123] The point is that while water, blood, and oil were all utilized in the OT as part of a purification process, sometimes only one or two of these elements are specified and that specificity may not exclude the other elements.

When blood and water flowed from the side of Jesus on the cross, they symbolized not just the redemption that came by the shedding of blood, but also the blessing of cleansing by water (John 19:34).[124] Jesus is called the one who "came by water and blood," and the testimony of "the Spirit and the water and the blood," are said to be "in agreement" (1 John 5:6–8). This text illustrates the unity in blood, water, and Spirit working

---

118. Parker, "Use of Blood," 21–23; Bruce, *Epistle to the Hebrews*, 226.
119. Kline, "Day of the Lord," 763–64.
120. Marshall, "Soteriology in Hebrews," 264.
121. Kline, "Day of the Lord," 764–65.
122. Kalengyo, "Sacrifice of Christ," 307.
123. Cockerill, *Epistle to the Hebrews*, 408–11.
124. Kline, "Day of the Lord," 764–66.

in tandem, and "their witness stands or falls together."[125] Anointing kings with oil symbolized the Spirit's presence on the king.[126] Jesus was anointed not by symbolic oil, but by what the oil represented, the Holy Spirit (Acts 10:38), or the "oil of joy" (Heb 1:9). Those who believe in Jesus also receive an anointing of the Holy Spirit (Acts 2:38; 1 John 2:20).[127]

In 1 John 5:6-8 oil is not mentioned, but what the oil represented, the Holy Spirit, is. Together, the blood, water, and Spirit, reminiscent of the OT cleansing ritual and when OT kings were anointed with oil, provide a theological foundation for Jesus's crucifixion and resurrection. The blood atoned for sin, the water cleansed, and the oil of the Holy Spirit heralded Jesus's eternal kingship. Water, blood, and oil, are metaphors of purification and the three elements tend to work concurrently. While cleansing by water is the focus of this presentation, in this text cleansing water is accompanied by blood and the Holy Spirit.

Revelation

In the last chapter it was established that "water of life" or "living water" initiated life that had no end. The meaning of the "springs of the water of life" in Rev 7:17 is not found only in the term, but also in the context where it is preceded by the concept of cleansing stated as "washed their robes and made them white in the blood of the Lamb" (7:14). It is these who have been cleansed who serve at the throne of God in his temple, and are guided to the "springs of the water of life" (7:15-17). Because "John's eschatology in Revelation is dynamic, and not linear," the entire context helps define the "water of life" as more than an eternal life-giving source.[128] It reflects an "overall process."[129]

Some believe the cleansing specifically references the forgiveness of sins at baptism.[130] Many link this water of life and the cleansing to various OT references to ritual cleansing (Exod 19:10, 14; 29:10-21; Isa 1:18; 64:6; Dan 11:35; 12:1, 10; Zech 3:3-5).[131] Others point out the cleansing

---

125. Marshall, *Epistles of John*, 237.
126. C. Wright, *Knowing the Holy Spirit*, 87-120.
127. Allison and Köstenberger, *Holy Spirit*, 186-87.
128. Smalley, *Revelation of John*, 196.
129. Beale, *Book of Revelation*, 443.
130. Roloff, *Revelation*, 99; Koester, *Revelation*, 429-30.
131. Beale, *Book of Revelation*, 432-45; Koester, *Revelation*, 429-30; Smalley, *Revelation of John*, 195-201; Osborne, *Revelation*, 325-26.

of the blood of Jesus shed on the cross, for which we have already joined to it the water which also flowed, together providing such cleansing (John 19:34).[132] The presence of these cleansed saints before the throne of God in the temple of God, places them in a location in which one cannot enter and live without cleansing (21:27).[133] Those not included in the new heaven and earth are described as sin ridden (21:8; 22:15), which is contrasted with those who have washed their robes (22:14). The context then, along with the term, portray the "water of life" as providing life, but also as providing cleansing. This same "water of life" is further referenced in Revelation where it is similarly interpreted as giving life and providing continual cleansing, flowing from the presence of God in his temple (21:6; 22:1, 17).[134]

CHAPTER SUMMARY

The second portion of the thesis is that throughout the Bible God uses water to cleanse or purify. Such has been documented in creation, in the flood, with Israel itself, in Israel as a Levitical ritual, with Naaman, by John the Baptist, in water baptism, and in the new heaven and earth. Not every text was explored in depth, but only to the extent sufficient to demonstrate the connection between water and cleansing. The close relation of blood, oil, and water was also discussed, and it was noted the three often unite in cleansing texts. Water cleansing is only symbolic. It is an outward physical ritual that heralds an inward spiritual cleansing. In other words, it functions figuratively.

---

132. Osborne, *Revelation*, 325–26; Smalley, *Revelation of John*, 196–201; Beale, *Book of Revelation*, 432–45; Roloff, *Revelation*, 95.

133. Beale, *Book of Revelation*, 439–45; Beale and Kim, *God Dwells among Us*, 44, 119; Osborne, *Revelation*, 326–29; Smalley, *Revelation of John*, 198–201.

134. Smalley, *Revelation of John*, 541, 562–63; Osborne, *Revelation*, 738–39, 769–71; Beale, *Book of Revelation*, 1055–58, 1103–4, 1149–50.

4

Water and Sustaining Life

As with the cleansing purpose of water, water as a sustainer of physical life is common knowledge. Scientists claim water was essential in the creation of the world, including even in the creation of rocks.[1] Although common knowledge, science also bears out that sustaining life in animals and plants, including in humans, requires adequate amounts of hydration.[2] Although interesting scientific inquiry lies behind what has become conventional wisdom regarding the necessity of water to preserve life, considering the spiritual application is more aligned with the purposes of this writing.

SPIRITUAL SUSTENANCE

The spiritual application of water maintaining life is often portrayed with a physical example, much like the other uses of water already discussed in previous chapters. Some of these may be readily apparent while others appear more obscure. A closer examination will expose several examples of physical water portraying a spiritual message.

---

1. Westall and Brack, "Importance of Water."
2. Chaplin, "Water."

Genesis 2

Terence Fretheim correctly believes creation language is used more in the Bible for God's sustaining work (i.e., his ongoing work as Creator) than it is for his originating work.[3] That being the case, the preponderance of water references in Gen 1 that largely speak to originating work is not diminished in Gen 2 where both originating and sustaining acts abound.[4] The notation that God had not sent rain, and presumably as a consequence there were no shrubs or plants growing, speaks to the necessity of water to enable and support plant life (2:5).[5] The text seems to imply that God is the provider of rain which makes the life emanating after the application of rain a direct consequence of God's work or gift.[6] God thus both initiates life by water, as previously discussed, and upholds that life by water.

"A mist used to rise from the earth and water the whole surface of the ground" (2:6), which was obviously insufficient to support vegetation, and it seems to be a repetitive occurrence.[7] The exact meaning of "mist" (אֵד) is uncertain with various possibilities proposed.[8] Numerous English translations prefer the term "mist."[9] Our purpose is not to find a conclusive definition for the term, but to understand that the water present in this form was insufficient for maintaining life in larger vegetation, and that more water, such as from rain, was required (2:5–6). Larger plant life, such as trees, also received water from a river or stream that continuously flowed out of Eden, and divided into four separate branches (2:10).[10] Each of the first three branches is said to "flow," while the fourth river is merely called "Euphrates," a river so large and well-known that its flowing may need no further explanation (2:11–14).[11]

It is obvious from Gen 2 that vegetative life requires substantial amounts of water to survive, but Genesis is hardly written to tell humanity what it already knows by life experience. Instead, the spiritual message

---

3. Fretheim, *God and World*, 1–13.
4. Fretheim, *God and World*, 1–67.
5. Westermann, *Genesis*, 1:199.
6. Westermann, *Genesis*, 1:199.
7. Gesenius, *Hebrew Grammar*, 331; Wenham, *Genesis*, 1:64.
8. Hasel and Hasel, "Hebrew Term 'ed'"; אֵד, *NIDOTTE*, 3:50–51; Westermann, *Genesis*, 1:200–201.
9. NASB, ASV, AMPC, ESV, JUB, KJV, and RSV.
10. ראש, *HALOT*, 2:1165–67; Westermann, *Genesis*, 1:184; Waltke with Fredricks, *Genesis*, 86–87; Wenham, *Genesis*, 1:64–65.
11. Westermann, *Genesis*, 1:219.

in this physical example is that from God's gift of rain the blessing of life occurs. The description of the garden is that of well-watered lushness that brings to the eye and to the stomach a calming or peaceful effect (2:9–10).[12] From this blessing in the garden of God a continual flow of life-giving water branches into four directions which may serve as a metaphor for the entire world, just as the four winds or the four corners of the earth encompass the entire world.[13] The linkage of Gen 2:10–14 to the continuous water flowing from God's temple in Ezek 47 or Zech 14:8, or the water of life in Rev 22:1, continues the message of God's gift of life, both to initiate it and to sustain it.[14] Such a focus on the physical importance of water to the preservation of life, while well understood by all of humanity, lays the typological foundation for the spiritual application of the principle suggested here in Gen 2, and expressed further elsewhere.[15]

Genesis 6–9

The flood story in Genesis provides an obvious expression of water ending life for most of the world (7:21–23), while at the same time sustaining life through the ark floating on the water for the eight persons and animals aboard (8:1, 15–19). Thomas Schreiner calls the flood a "covenant of preservation" because its intent was the preservation of life.[16] Upon his departure from the ark, since the floodwater that saved and sustained Noah had subsided, Noah became a farmer, and planted a productive vineyard (9:20–21). The presence of water that enabled plant growth is implied (9:20–21), just as it is today when one observes, or partakes of, farm produce. It is universally accepted that water is essential for crop life and growth. Just as water in the flood had destroyed the wicked and initiated new life for the righteous, just as the floodwater cleansed the earth of its filth making it fresh and pristine, upon Noah's exiting the ark, water preserved life in plants and animals, including humanity (9:1–7).[17] Water

---

12. Waltke with Fredricks, *Genesis*, 85–87; Wenham, *Genesis*, 1:61–62.
13. Westermann, *Genesis*, 1:216–19; Sailhamer, *Genesis Unbound*, 75–84.
14. Beale and Kim, *God Dwells among Us*, 8–9, 69–70; Wenham, *Genesis*, 1:65; Waltke with Fredricks, *Genesis*, 86–87; Walton, *Lost World*, 81–82.
15. Walton, *Lost World*, 81–82.
16. Schreiner, *Covenant and God's Purpose*, 36.
17. Waltke with Fredricks, *Genesis*, 143.

is a necessary provision, making possible God's directive to "be fruitful and multiply" (8:17; 9:1).[18]

John Walton notes that God's work of "originating and sustaining can be seen as variations of the work of the Creator, even though they do not entirely merge together."[19] Walton sees the sustaining of life as an extension of the creative process.[20] But it also generated another benefit, that of order and peace, which is seen in the fruitfulness and multiplication of animal and human life (8:17; 9:1), and also in the hierarchical arrangement between animals and humanity (9:2–3).[21] In this flood story, God uses water to initiate new life, to cleanse the earth, and to sustain life, as the thesis of this dissertation asserts.

Genesis 16 and 21

The story of Hagar and Ishmael is surrounded by the presence of water. Hagar is met by "the angel of the Lord" while she was by a spring of water (16:7). A river, or flowing spring, is always a symbol of God's presence, and the flowing spring is where the angel, who some hold to be God himself, appeared.[22] When sent away by Abraham, Hagar and Ishmael were given a skin of water to sustain them (21:14). When the water was gone, death seemed certain until the angel of God called to her and helped Hagar see a nearby well of water that revived her and Ishmael (21:15–19). The sustaining of physical life by water is evident in these two episodes of Hagar, but there is also a spiritual context connected to the physical.

The first pericope follows a covenant making scene in Gen 15 and precedes the covenant of circumcision in Gen 17.[23] Wedged between these two covenant scenes, God, or his messenger, appears at a well of water in the desert, a symbol of life, and promises multiplication of descendants which was in keeping with his covenant with Abraham (12:1–3; 13:14–16; 15:1–21; 16:7–10). Standing alone, the presence of water here might not seem significant. But when the broader picture is revealed, it seems difficult to separate water from the covenantal promise of God made to

18. Waltke with Fredricks, *Genesis*, 143; Walton, *Lost World*, 121–22.
19. Walton, *Lost World*, 122.
20. Walton, *Lost World*, 121–23.
21. Waltke with Fredricks, *Genesis*, 146, 154–56.
22. Wenham, *Genesis*, 1:65; Westermann, *Genesis*, 2:242–44; Waltke with Fredricks, *Genesis*, 253–54; Pao and Schnabel, "Luke," 257.
23. Drey, "Role of Hagar," 180–81.

Hagar, which, incidentally, happens to be the only OT instance of God, or his messenger, addressing a woman by name.[24] In the presence of water, God spoke to Hagar, giving her a blessing and promise, and sent her back to Sarah to be submissive, bringing peace to their broken relationship.[25]

The Hagar settings appear somewhat similar to that of the Samaritan woman at the well where Jesus announces the availability of living water (John 4). Hagar had been given to Abraham by Sarah for childbirth purposes, but enjoyed less than a wifely status and was separated from Abraham, once leaving him on her own (16:1–6), and once being sent away from him (21:9–14).[26] The Samaritan woman was said to have no husband, yet lived with a man as though his wife (John 4:17–18). Both women lived in what may be called a wifely role, yet neither fully occupied the position of wife, or was accepted as a wife. As Hagar was approached by an angel announcing new life within her, so Jesus announced new life that could spring up within the Samaritan woman. It is also noteworthy that neither woman was an Israelite, but each received a promise of life from within her. Water was the backdrop at both announcements. Physical life was to flow from Hagar, but living water from within was directed to the Samaritan.

The language in the first Hagar narrative sounds a lot like the announcements of the birth of Jesus (Matt 1:19–21; Luke 1:5–80).[27] "You will bear a son" (16:11) corresponds to "She will bear a son" (Matt 1:21). "You shall call his name" is an identical directive in each announcement (16:11; Matt 1:21). The announcement of prosperity and blessing occurs with each (21:18; Matt 1:21: Luke 1:32–33). God was with each child as they grew (21:20; Luke 1:80). In each case, a covenant was involved. For Hagar, her promise came because Abraham was the father of her baby and God had previously promised that from Abraham's seed countless descendants would emerge (12:1–3; 13:14–16; 15:1–21).[28] For the announcement of the birth of Jesus, God was his Father and numerous OT prophecies foretold a coming new covenant associated with this new deliverer who would bless many (Jer 31:27–34; Hos 2;18; Ezek 16:60). The copious similarities of these scenes cannot be ignored, particularly

---

24. Waltke with Fredricks, *Genesis*, 254.
25. Waltke with Fredricks, *Genesis*, 254–57, 297.
26. Waltke with Fredricks, *Genesis*, 252.
27. Westermann, *Genesis*, 2:246.
28. Drey, "Role of Hagar"; Block, *Covenant*, 92, 109.

the linkage of water to covenantal promises.[29] Water is associated with an implied covenant at creation, with the Noahic covenant, and now to the remembrance of the Abrahamic covenant with Hagar. In all three of these episodes a covenant is cut in close association with water.[30]

For our purposes, God's promise to Hagar gave her life and sustenance by returning her to Sarah pregnant and with the promise of many descendants (16:9–12). It was here, living with Abraham and Sarah, that Ishmael was born and named by Abraham (16: 15–16). Ishmael was then circumcised by Abraham (17:23), and elevated and supported as a son above servants (17:23). The sustenance provided by Abraham was presumably available to both Hagar and Ishmael. Hagar's first encounter with God was beside a spring of water (16:7). Her second encounter with God follows the absence of water and near death from dehydration, but ends with a well of water, a full skin of water, and God blessing Ishmael (21:15–21). The presence of water to revive and undergird life is twice noted with Hagar. God's supply of life-sustaining water is connected to his promise, or his covenant, and to his blessing. This physical application of water to sustain has spiritual overtones and helps demonstrate the spiritual sense that accompanies the physical presence and utilization of water. With Hagar and Ishmael, God used water to provide life in their immediate moment, which enabled life and sustained it for generations to come.[31]

Genesis 24

The servant of Abraham was instructed to find a wife for Isaac from within the family in his home country (24:3–4). The servant found a place of rest next to a well of water near the city of Nahor (24:10–11). It was here that the servant found a wife for Isaac, Rebekah, by asking her for a drink of water (24:12–27). The parallels with Jesus's encounter with the Samaritan woman in John 4 abound.[32] In both stories women were addressed by a man. Both women were unmarried. Neither woman was an Israelite, even though Rebekah was a niece to Abraham (24:15). In

---

29. Block, *Covenant*, 432–34; Richter, *Epic of Eden*, 92–118.
30. Schreiner, *Covenant and God's Purpose*, 20–36; Block, *Covenant*, 15–66.
31. Westermann, *Genesis*, 2:343–44.
32. Klink, *John*, 236; Michaels, *Gospel of John*, 236–39.

each case well water was present. In each case the woman was asked for a drink. In each case the conversation resulted in blessing.

In Gen 24 the Hebrew term *hesed* is used four times and translated "lovingkindness" or "kindly" by the NASB.[33] The term generally denotes faithfulness, loyalty, or graciousness.[34] In this context it describes the blessing of God upon the servant, and upon Jacob, in finding Rebekah for a wife (24:27). It also points backward to the promise of God to Abraham to increase his descendants (12:1–3; 13:14–16; 15:1–21), and in this promise sustain the life of those of his lineage.[35] Water is present and prominent in the chapter, being mentioned nine times (24:11 twice, 13, 14, 17, 32, 43, 46 twice). The related term "well" is mentioned twice (24:11, 20), and the related term "drink" is mentioned twelve times (24:14 twice, 17, 18 twice, 19 twice, 22, 43, 44, 45, 46). These twenty-three water references in thirty-five verses overwhelmingly declare the connection of water to the blessing of God as he advances his promise to Abraham by facilitating and sustaining descendants. It provides an example of physical water providing a material or physical benefit, but with spiritual ramifications that are eventually realized in Christ.

Genesis 26

Genesis 26 describes drought conditions in which Isaac and the Philistines argued over water multiple times (26:14–21). Isaac eventually moved and found water over which there was no quarrel, and he declared it a blessing from God (26: 22). From that place Isaac traveled to Beersheba where God appeared and reiterated to him the same promises that had been made to his father, Abraham, after which Isaac built an altar to the Lord and dug a well that provided water (26: 23–25).

In seventeen verses (26:15–32) water is referenced four times, and its related term, "well," is mentioned eight times. Such repetition captures one's attention not just of the necessity of water to maintain physical life, but to the spiritual events attached to it such as, God extending his promise to Abraham further to Isaac (26:24), Isaac building an altar to God (26:25), and a covenant of peace (*shalom*) being made with his

---

33. Gen 24:12, 14, 27 are translated "lovingkindness." Gen 24:49 is translated "kindly."

34. חֶסֶד, *HALOT*, 1:337; Waltke with Fredricks, *Genesis*, 328.

35. Wenham, *Genesis*, 1:143; Westermann, *Genesis*, 2:387; Waltke with Fredricks, *Genesis*, 328–31; Block, *Covenant*, 112–13.

competitor over water in which Abimelech credited Isaac's blessings as coming from the Lord (26:26–31). This pericope ends with water being found on the same day the covenant of peace with Abimelech was cut (26:29–33).

Like the previous examples from Genesis, this story of Isaac links the presence of water, and the physical necessity of water, to spiritual aspects that include God's covenant and God's blessing. But this pericope additionally states that there was a human covenant of peace or well-being (26:29, 31).[36] The term "peace" may also include the ideas of deliverance and salvation.[37] While peace is specifically stated as part of this event, the rain and rivers of Gen 2 provide imagery of a calm habitation, a garden, full of things pleasing to the sight and appetite (Gen 2:8–9).[38] After the flood, the earth in its re-created state was intended to support fruitfulness and multiplication providing compliance with God's plan (Gen 8:16–17; 9:1).[39] Humanity was empowered over animal life which brought order, a typical accompaniment of peace (Gen 9:2–3). A soothing comfort from a covenant prohibiting another global flooding was made with animal life and humanity (Gen 9:8–11). God's initial instruction to Hagar was to make peace by returning to Sarah in submission, but she also appears to have received solace immediately from God's blessing of childbirth, which was a fulfillment of the covenant promise to Abraham (Gen 16:9–14). In Hagar's second encounter with the Lord she received immediate consolation by the provision of water, and more by the ongoing blessing of God upon her and Ishmael (Gen 21:17–21). In Gen 24, as already noted, God's lovingkindness (*hesed*), an aspect of peace, was upon Abraham's servant and Isaac. This blessing extended to Rebekah as well, bringing peace to all parties (Gen 24:58–67).

God's use of water to sustain life may appear as merely a quantitative benefit, but its qualitative measure is equally appropriate, if not more so. Life in the garden was not intended as mere existence, but as a beautiful, secure, and serene environment with perpetual purpose.[40] The same was desired for Noah, Hagar, Isaac and Rebekah as a couple, and for Isaac amidst hostile Philistines, as previously noted. In the NT Jesus describes

---

36. שָׁלוֹם, *HALOT*, 2:1506–10; Westermann, *Genesis*, 2:429–30.
37. שָׁלוֹם, *HALOT*, 2:1509–10.
38. Waltke with Fredricks, *Genesis*, 85–87.
39. Waltke with Fredricks, *Genesis*, 143.
40. Walton, *Lost World*, 121–23.

this life as more than mere existence, as life flourishing, life of abundance (John 5:40; 10:10).

Genesis presents water as essential for physical life, but water is a metaphor for the presence of God and his blessings.[41] Water is used in connection with God's covenants, with his announcements, with his instruction, and with his provision of peace, as well as with human covenants of peace. The term "well" is "a symbolic meeting place for marriages."[42] Such seems an appropriate metaphor for the spiritual marriage of God's purposes with human life as seen with Hagar, Rebekah, and Isaac. In each case, near the presence of a well of water, life was positively impacted by God's presence, direction, and blessing. The preponderance of water and water-related terms provide a backdrop for spiritual guidance, and blessed life, whether in the garden, during and after the flood, with Hagar, with Rebekah, and with Isaac's encounters with the Philistines. Water is consistently affiliated with sustaining spiritual life.

Exodus 1–2

The story of Moses floating in a basket, or ark, in the Nile has already been discussed as a scene of initiating life. More vividly it portrays the sustaining of life. Due to the edict by Pharaoh to destroy all Hebrew male infants (1:15–17), Miriam placed her son, Moses, in the ark among the reeds at the edge of the Nile River (2:2–4). His life was preserved as Miriam intended, because the daughter of Pharaoh found him and raised him as her son (2:5–10). Through the experience of having his own life preserved by the waters of the Nile, Moses himself became a symbol of life for others, and a symbol of God's presence as he delivered Israel from Egyptian slavery (3:1—14:31; Pss 77:20; 106:23; Isa 63:11–12; Acts 6:11; 7:20–38; 1 Cor 10:2; Rev 15:3).[43] Terence Fretheim says, "God works through persons who have no obvious power. . . . Even more, God's plan for the future of the children of Israel rests squarely on the shoulders of one of its helpless sons, a baby in a fragile basket."[44] God distinguished Moses from others through whom he worked by noting the face-to-face

---

41. Wenham, *Genesis*, 1:65.
42. Waltke with Fredricks, *Genesis*, 332.
43. Fretheim, *Exodus*, 157; Najman and Schmid, "Reading the Blood Plague," 34–36.
44. Fretheim, *Exodus*, 37.

encounters that characterized their special relationship (Num 12:5–8). Around the throne of God, a place of perpetual life, it is the Song of Moses that will be heard along with the Song of the Lamb, as they both represent God's deliverance (Rev 15:3).[45]

This humble beginning in the Nile River, which symbolized preservation of life for Moses, leads to a water well scene where Moses "delivers" the daughters of Reuel from more powerful shepherds, after which he is given a wife by Reuel, whose name means 'friend of God' (2:15–22).[46] This well water was used to maintain the life of the flocks (2:16). But there is a spiritual connection. This well scene is reminiscent of the well scenes of Hagar (Gen 16; 21), Rebekah (Gen 24), and Jacob and Rachel (Gen 29) where life was also sustained and extended through marital unions to subsequent generations.[47] This well scene also points forward to the water sustaining life in the wilderness.[48]

Exodus 7 and 14

When Moses turned the water to blood in Egypt, fish died in the Nile and people could not drink its water (7:18–24). The fact that the water preserved life for the fish and for humans is understated in Exodus likely because such is common knowledge. But when the water becomes blood, and the life-sustaining properties disappear, bringing quick death to the fish with the implication of the imminent death of humans, everyone notices.[49] It was in this act that God declared his power over the water, and its life-giving and life-sustaining qualities (7:17).[50] Also in this act God foretells the coming death of Egyptians in water.[51]

---

45. Koester, *Revelation*, 634–36; Roloff, *Revelation*, 183–85; Beale, *Book of Revelation*, 792–96; Smalley, *Revelation of John*, 383–89. These references discuss whether two songs exist, or whether the two songs are referenced epexegetically. Since the themes of each are near identical, and the source of deliverance is the same, God, the issue is probably irrelevant for purposes of this presentation.

46. Meyers, *Exodus*, 44–45.

47. Meyers, *Exodus*, 45–46.

48. Fretheim, *Exodus*, 43; Wells, "Exodus," 191, 216.

49. Najman and Schmid, "Reading the Blood Plague," 39–40; Noegel, "Moses and Magic," 51.

50. Fretheim, *Exodus*, 115–16; Najman and Schmid, "Reading the Blood Plague," 35.

51. Meyers, *Exodus*, 81–82; Najman and Schmid, "Reading the Blood Plague," 34–35.

As Moses led the Israelites across the parted waters of the Red Sea, the water provided life to Israel in that moment as the Egyptian army was closing in. The water also extended and sustained life for Israel by giving it a new beginning in a new land, with freedom from slavery, and the opportunity to procreate without fear of oppression inflicted upon Israel's progeny. It was a fulfillment and extension of God's creative purposes which include the sustenance of life, which in this case was provided through the parting of water.[52]

The entire plague cycle in Exodus begins and ends with water.[53] Water to blood begins the series, while water engulfing the Egyptians ends it. "The entirety of Exodus 1–15 is framed by the motif of water."[54] It is through this mechanism of water that God expresses his power, his will, and destroys the wicked while delivering and preserving his elect.

Exodus 15 and 17

After three days in the wilderness without water, the Israelites complained (15:22). The water at Marah was bitter and undrinkable (15:23), but when Moses threw a tree in the water it became sweet and potable (15:25). As the Israelites' journey continued, water again was demanded at Rephidim, or Horeb (17:1–6). This time water was provided by Moses striking a rock so that water flowed out (17:5–6). From this rock water "gushed out, and streams were overflowing" (Ps 78:20). It is presumably this rock that is referenced in 1 Cor 10:4 with which Christ is identified, and he is the one who provided "spiritual drink" from the rock.[55] Exactly how this refers to Christ is somewhat puzzling as it may refer to his standing on, or near, the rock (17:6), and it may indicate Christ's preexistent state.[56] It is this same Horeb upon which God would appear and from which Moses would receive the law (Deut 4:10).

52. Fretheim, *Exodus*, 164–70.
53. Najman and Schmid, "Reading the Blood Plague," 39–40.
54. Najman and Schmid, "Reading the Blood Plague," 39.
55. Thiselton, *First Epistle to Corinthians*, 724–30. It has been suggested that Num 20:8–13 may be a reference to the same event of Exod 17:1–7, and referenced in 1 Cor 10, due to their similarities, but this writer does not believe the two events are the same even if joined in 1 Corinthians. Due to this similarity, exploring Num 20 would be redundant so it is omitted herein. For more detailed discussion, see Koning, "Hermeneutic Process"; Kok, *Sin of Moses*; MacDonald, "Anticipations of Horeb"; Anthony-Llorens, "Water From the Rock," 1–24; Pitkänen, *Commentary on Numbers*, 142–45.
56. Thiselton, *First Epistle to Corinthians*, 724–30.

The miraculous manifestation of water just prior to receiving the law from the same location may be reminiscent of the Genesis well scenes in which God appeared and spoke twice to Hagar (Gen 16; 21), located Rebekah for Isaac (Gen 24:27, 48, 50), was declared the provider of blessing to Isaac (Gen 26:29), was sought in going to the well to find a wife (Gen 28:19–22), and followed upon departure after obtaining a wife (Gen 31:3, 5, 13, 16). In each of the well cases God spoke or acted in the presence of water. Similarly, at Horeb water flowed, then God acted by giving the law. A spiritual experience arose from the physical one.[57]

At Marah and at Horeb, Israel complained against Moses's leadership, which was a complaint against God (15:24; 17:2–3).[58] In each case, God used the lack of water as a test of Israel (15:25; 17:2, 7), and from providing water to quench a physical need God proved his ability and desire to provide for all of humanity's needs.[59] Israel's issue was a lack of trust that God would sustain it, which is evidenced by fear (14:10–13), by complaining (15:24–26), and by argument with Moses (17:2–4), which questioned whether God even dwelled with Israel (17:7). As in the Genesis well scenes, at Marah, and again at Horeb, using water God proved his desire and ability to physically sustain Israel, as part of his overall spiritual plan of eternal life for all.

Exodus 29–40

The use of water for purification is well attested in the Pentateuch and was discussed in chapter 3. It was noted in that discussion that Aaron and his sons were to be washed with water at the doorway to the tent of meeting as part of the declaration of their perpetual priesthood (29:4–9; 40:12–15). Upon entry into tent of meeting, Aaron and his sons were also to wash in the bronze laver of water as a perpetual ritual "so that they will not die" (30:17–21: 40:30–32). "So that they will not die" is another way of saying "so that they can continue to live," which means that God's prescriptive use of water as a cleansing ritual also sustained life.[60] Terence Fretheim seems to concur by stating the emphasis here is on "the nature

---

57. Meyers, *Exodus*, 129.
58. Meyers, *Exodus*, 134.
59. Meyers, *Exodus*, 134; Fretheim, *Exodus*, 189–91.
60. Sailhamer, *Meaning of the Pentateuch*, 385.

of divine-human interaction. It stresses process, not end."[61] Fretheim says the tabernacle with its consecratory regulations "is an actual vehicle for divine immanence."[62] In other words, the cleansing rituals that enable one to come into the presence of God, or more correctly, permit God to come into the presence of humanity, were not for a momentary appearance, but for unending interaction and relationship.[63] Similar instruction about washing rituals occurs in the remainder of the Pentateuch, and there it also is designed to avoid death and maintain life so that relationship with God is uninterrupted (Lev 1:9–13; 8:6–21; 14:5–52; 15:5–27; 16:4–28; Num 8:7–21; 19:7–21; Deut 21:6; 23:11). This water purification ritual goes beyond cleansing. It also functions as the sustainer of life in which continual interface with God is enabled.

Joshua 3

Chapter 2 discusses the initiation of life and chapter 3 discusses cleansing related to the crossing of the Red Sea and the Jordan River. As noted above, the crossing of the Red Sea also sustained the life of Israel. So did the crossing of the Jordan. These two crossings share many similarities.[64] Of significant difference is that the Jordan crossing involved entrance directly into the promised land such that life was not only sustained, but substantially upgraded in terms of shelter, food, land possession, variety in landscape, abundance of water, and the promised elimination of Israel's enemies by the hand of God (Exod 23:22–30; Josh 10), all of which amounted to a new social order.[65] Entering the land was a testimony to God's faithfulness.[66] "The parting of the Jordan waters echoes the creation account. The waters part because God rules them in power.... And as at creation, the 'tamed' waters of the Jordan bring Israel into a land that (like original creation) is to be a place of rest, provision, and fellowship with God."[67] The waters of the Jordan crossing are thus intimately connected to sustaining the life of Israel.

---

61. Fretheim, *Exodus*, 272.
62. Fretheim, *Exodus*, 315.
63. Sailhamer, *Meaning of the Pentateuch*, 379; Walton, *Lost World*, 121–23.
64. Beal, *Joshua*, 93–94.
65. Dozeman, *Joshua 1–12*, 251.
66. McKenzie, *Introduction to Historical Books*, 54.
67. McKenzie, *Introduction to Historical Books*, 95.

2 Kings 2

Using inheritance language, Elijah says, "Ask what I shall do for you before I am taken from you" (2:9) to denote the continuation of God's provision for Elisha.[68] Elisha requests a double portion of Elijah's spirit (2:9), and upon receiving the requested gift, Elisha verifies its reception by his question, "Where is the Lord, the God of Elijah," after which the Jordan is parted, confirming that he had received what he requested (2:14).[69] It is this question asked by Elisha that provides insight into the sustaining power of God, passed from one generation to the next, signaled by the parting of the Jordan. God parted the Jordan for Elijah (2:8), and then shortly thereafter parted the water again for Elisha (2:14). God's presence and sustaining power provided over multiple generations is confirmed by these two water partings much like the two crossings of Israel over the Red Sea and the Jordan. In all four cases water is connected to the sustenance of life as part of God's spiritual purposes.

The Psalms

The Psalms contains numerous references to water in which the sustenance of physical or spiritual life is thematic. Psalm 1 is said to "set the tone for the entire hymnic collection" and speaks of being "planted by streams of water" from which fruit is produced and prosperity arises (1:3).[70] Fruit and prosperity are earmarks of life, and in this text that arises from adhering to God's ordained structure, specified here as finding "delight in the law of the Lord" (1:2).[71] Such delight leads to meditation on God's law (1:2), which results in being "planted by streams of water" and thriving perpetually, which is described by the metaphor of a tree leaf that "does not wither" (1:3).[72] Water and life, both physically and spiritually, cohere in this text.

Embedded in a "divine warrior" scene, Ps 18, a near carbon copy of 2 Sam 22, provides powerful imagery of God, and also of water.[73] God himself is said to be enveloped with a "canopy around him, darkness of

---

68. Provan, "2 Kings," 121–22; Sweeney, *I and II Kings*, 273.
69. Provan, "2 Kings," 123; Sweeney, *I and II Kings*, 274.
70. Brueggemann, *Message of the Psalms*, 38; Goldingay, *Psalms*, 1:90–91.
71. Brueggemann, *Praying the Psalms*, 50.
72. Goldingay, *Psalms*, 1:84–86.
73. Longman, *Psalms*, 110–14.

waters, thick clouds of the skies" (18:11), and from him "the channels of water appeared, and the foundations of the world were laid bare" (18:15). Not only does this speak of God's eternal existence being enveloped in water or clouds, he has made water part of the fabric from which the world was made and remains. The two, God and the cosmos, are thus eternally linked by water.

Psalm 23 tells of God's desire to provide both the necessities of life, as well as abundance.[74] God shepherding his followers to "quiet waters" (23:2) describes a key component of the shepherd's work.[75] "Lying down in green pastures" suggests the sheep eats, drinks, then rests near the water so it can get up to eat and drink again at will.[76] Eating, drinking, and resting are recurring endeavors. This constant provision enables one to proclaim "he restores my soul" (23:3), and speaks of the effect of God's provision without which one cannot survive, and with which one enjoys enduring sustenance and inner peace in the presence of God.[77] The use of water in this text is the language of sustenance and peace.

Psalm 42 is a prayer of longing for God.[78] It begins, "As a deer pants for the water brooks, so my soul pants for you, O God" (42:1–2). This text compares the thirst of a deer who needs physical sustenance to the person who thirsts for spiritual provision from God. It is God who refreshes and restores the one thirsting for him, and he is the fountain that can never dry up.[79] Psalm 63 echoes a similar idea by saying, "My soul thirsts for you, my flesh yearns for you, in a dry and weary land where there is no water" (63:1). Both of these psalms use thirsting for water imagery to express the constant spiritual nourishment that is supplied by union with God.

Psalm 46 does not begin with a call to praise God, but it does extoll God as the constant and reliable source of refuge and strength.[80] In this it complements Pss 42 and 63 (referenced above) by stating, "There is a river whose streams make glad the city of God, the holy dwelling places of the Most High. God is in the midst of her, she will not be moved" (46:4–5). This text presents God existing eternally in the presence of a

---

74. Futado, "Psalms 16, 23," 234–36.
75. Goldingay, *Psalms*, 1:347.
76. Goldingay, *Psalms*, 1:350.
77. Goldingay, *Psalms*, 1:350, 353–54.
78. Blaising and Hardin, *Psalms 1–50*, 327.
79. Blaising and Hardin, *Psalms 1–50*, 327–28.
80. Kimmitt, "Psalm 46," 68.

river, a river that cannot be extinguished, a river that is always available for the thirsty to receive, and which merits humanity's trust.[81]

Depicting God's preparation and maintenance of the earth, Ps 65 says,

> You visit the earth and cause it to overflow;
> You greatly enrich it;
> The stream of God is full of water;
> You prepare their grain, for so you prepare the earth.
> You water its furrows abundantly,
> You settle its ridges,
> You soften it with showers,
> You bless its growth.
> You have crowned the year with your goodness,
> And your paths drip with fatness.
> The pastures of the wilderness drip,
> And the hills encircle themselves with rejoicing.
> The meadows are clothed with flocks
> And the valleys are covered with grain;
> They shout for joy, yes, they sing. (Ps 65:9–13)

This is a psalm of praise for God's intervention in Israel's affairs to bless them.[82] It also expresses the unrelenting work of God in the lives of his creation to bless and provide using the metaphor of water that sustains the earth and its inhabitants.[83]

Psalm 104 looks back to God's initial work of creation.[84] After describing the earth's creation by water (104:1–9), God's continual provision that maintains the earth as the habitation for humanity is announced which says God "waters the mountains from his upper chambers; the earth is satisfied with the fruit of his works" (104:13). While God has been involved in the original creation of the world, his creative work in the world is ongoing.[85] As part of this continuing activity God provides water, which causes grass to grow for cattle, and vegetation to grow for humanity (104:14); it provides food from the earth, including wine and oil (104:14–15); and it gives life to trees, which in turn house the birds

---

81. Kimmitt, "Psalm 46," 63–74; Estes, "Transformation of Pain," 161.

82. Brueggemann, *Message of the Psalms*, 135.

83. Brueggemann, *Message of the Psalms*, 136; Chisholm, "Suppressing Myths," 82; Ansberry, "Wisdom and Biblical Theology," 180.

84. Goldingay, *Psalms*, 3:183; Brueggemann, *Message of the Psalms*, 31.

85. Goldingay, *Psalms*, 3:186.

(104:16–17).[86] God's provision of water supplies drink for the various beasts of the field and houses creatures of the sea (104:10–12, 25–28). God's creation of the world was not a singular act, but an ongoing commitment to maintain what he created. John Goldingay says, "But as king, God also constructed a palace to live in, a palace within the cosmos, as if wanting to be in a position to be involved with the world on an ongoing basis."[87] It is this continual provision of life-sustaining water in the form of rain that typifies the spiritual blessings from God, and signifies his eternal purposes.[88]

Taken together, these psalms reflect a consistent message that God created the world by physical water, and he continues to use water to sustain his creation, which often is a metaphor for spiritual life. As humans, animals, and plants require water for survival, and thirst for such, the human spirit also longs for water in the metaphorical sense. Just as God sustains life in the physical, he also does in the spiritual, and these texts further assert that God desires to supply continual water, both physically and spiritually. Furthermore, his water source is unending, suggesting that life from him is unending as well.

Isaiah

Isaiah provides rich usage of the term "water" as he develops the ideas of spurning God, undergoing judgment, and then being restored and blessed by God.[89] He likens the unrepentant Israelites to "an oak who fades away or as a garden that has no water" (1:30), taking the well-known physical necessity of water to emphasize spiritual bankruptcy that leads to certain demise and eventual death.[90] Those who reject God are said to have "rejected the gently flowing waters of Shiloah" (8:6), referencing the ever-diminishing desire for God, which God will replace with "strong and abundant waters of the Euphrates, even the king of Assyria," which will "rise up over all its channels and go over all its banks. Then it will sweep on into Judah" (8:7–8).[91] God here uses water to describe his own

---

86. Goldingay, *Psalms*, 3:187–88.
87. Goldingay, *Psalms*, 3:198.
88. Goldingay, *Psalms*, 3:198–99.
89. Abernathy, *Book of Isaiah*, 25.
90. Williamson, *Isaiah*, 1:161.
91. Balogh, "Historicising," 524–28; Williamson, *Isaiah*, 2:226–31.

provision that sustains, and contrasts it with the "strong and abundant waters" of death at the hands of the Assyrian king.[92] Being satisfied with God's water would have rectified the spiritual dearth Isaiah's audience experienced that led to their downfall.

Isaiah also speaks of restoration in water terms by saying, "Then he will give you rain.... On every lofty mountain and on every high hill there will be streams running with water" (30:23–25). Restoration includes the arrival of justice, which is "like streams of water in a dry country" (32:2). In its context this description is of God's justice, righteousness, and protection as part of his blessing.[93]

That "His water will be sure" describes the ongoing supply of God's blessing to the righteous who "see the King in His beauty" (33:16–17).[94] This event is pictured as "waters will break forth in the wilderness and streams in the Arabah. The scorched land will become a pool and the thirsty ground springs of water" (35:6–7). Isaiah includes an even stronger spiritual application to the water when he says, "For I will pour out water on the thirsty land and streams on the dry ground; I will pour out my Spirit on your offspring and my blessing on your descendants; and they will spring up among the grass, like poplars by streams of water" (44:3–4). Klaus Baltzer finds in this text an analogy to Ezek 37:1–4, where dry bones were given life. In both cases, he asserts, "The subject is the revivification of the people and the return to the land."[95] Baltzer thus sees an eschatological fulfillment, which, when linked to the many previous texts cited beginning in Genesis, demonstrates God consistently, from beginning to end, expressing his sustaining blessings in water terms.[96]

The prophet Isaiah pleads with his hearers by saying, "Everyone who thirsts, come to the waters" (55:1), and he assures that for those who do come, "the Lord will continually guide you, and satisfy your desire in scorched places, and give strength to your bones; and you will be like a watered garden, and like a spring of water whose waters do not fail" (58:11).[97] The invitation is to a feast, and the context is set in covenant

---

92. Baker, "Isaiah," 4:46–48.
93. Roberts, *First Isaiah*, 410.
94. Roberts, *First Isaiah*, 428–29.
95. Baltzer, *Deutero-Isaiah*, 186.
96. Baker, "Isaiah," 4:3.
97. Baker, "Isaiah," 4:79.

language.[98] The gift is satisfying and unending.[99] This means water is the image for covenant blessings that never end.

Jeremiah

The general tone of Jeremiah's use of water imagery resembles that of Isaiah. Isaiah foretells Assyria overtaking Israel, describing it as "strong and abundant waters" (Isa 8:7–8), while Jeremiah's description of the Babylonian invasion is depicted as "Behold, waters are going to rise from the north and become an overflowing torrent, and overflow the land and all its fullness" (47:2).[100] Isaiah portrays those abandoning God as "an oak who fades away or as a garden that has no water" (Isa 1:30), and Jeremiah's choice of words is "They have forsaken me, the fountain of living waters, and hewn for themselves cisterns, broken cisterns that can hold no water" (2:13). By this statement Jeremiah identifies the inability of God's people to function as God intended.[101] This was not a call to repent, but an indictment of Israel's unraveled spiritual condition.[102] Jeremiah describes this abandonment of God's guidance to seek support from Egypt as to "drink the waters of the Nile," and seeking support from Assyria is to "drink the waters of the Euphrates" (2:18).[103] This foreign water is also described as "poisoned water" (8:14; 9:15), and "a deceptive stream" or "water that is unreliable" (15:18). Such metaphor speaks to the inability of foreign gods or leadership to provide the necessities of life.[104] William McKane suggests that a curse is associated with this statement with echoes of the golden calf incident (Exod 32:20).[105]

The restoration of God's people in Jeremiah also reflects some of the same imagery of Isaiah. Jeremiah said, "I will make them walk by streams of water" (31:9), "their life will be like a watered garden and they will never languish again" (31:12), while Isaiah said, "you will be like a watered garden, and like a spring of water whose waters do not fail" (Isa

---

98. Baker, "Isaiah," 4:65–71; Block, *Covenant*, 342–43.
99. Goldingay, *Isaiah 56–66*, 181.
100. Voth, "Jeremiah," 340.
101. Kaiser and Rata, *Walking the Ancient Paths*, 47.
102. McKane, *Jeremiah*, 1:33.
103. McKane, *Jeremiah*, 1:36; Voth, "Jeremiah," 241.
104. Kaiser and Rata, *Walking the Ancient Paths*, 112–13.
105. McKane, *Jeremiah*, 1:190–91.

58:11). Jeremiah endorses Isaiah's idea of continual blessing, or watering, by these texts and by the phrase "a perennially watered pasture" (49:19; 50:44). God's blessing, according to both prophets, is so rich and secure that nothing can stand against it.[106]

While there are many similarities, Jeremiah stands apart from Isaiah by using the term "fountain of living water" (2:13; 17:13), even though the idea of life-giving water, but not the term, is found in Isaiah (41:17–20; 55:1–3). The term is used only here (2:13; 17:13), and in two other places (Song 4:15; Zech 14:8) in the HB with reference to God.[107] The living water is a metaphor for God, and he is contrasted with the empty and broken cisterns that represent dependence on anything or anyone other than him (2:13; 14:3).[108] The focus of Jeremiah's use of water, much like Isaiah's, is that any water from a source other than God does not sustain life. Water from God is living water, and as its name implies, does sustain life. Jeremiah recalls Ps 1:3 when he speaks of being like "a tree planted by the water" (17:8), a vivid image of God's continuous rejuvenation by water.

Ezekiel

Like his prophetic counterparts, Isaiah and Jeremiah, Ezekiel uses the term "water" to describe both the oppression of following voices other than God (26:19; 27:26, 34), and for God and his blessing (1:24; 34:18; 43:2).[109] He also contrasts these two opposing powers (waters) noting God's superiority (31:2–18; 32:2–16). As with Isaiah and Jeremiah, Ezekiel speaks of restoration.[110] In this, Ezekiel mirrors the shepherding motif of Ps 23 where God's sheep are fed and watered with clean water (34:11–18). Through Ezekiel, God promises Israel, "I will "sprinkle clean water on you, and you will be clean.... I will give you a new heart and put a new spirit within you.... I will put my Spirit within you and cause you to walk in my statutes" (36:25–27). This sprinkling of clean water

---

106. McKane, *Jeremiah*, 2:1225–28; McKane, *Jeremiah*, 1:36; Voth, "Jeremiah," 241; G. Smith, *Interpreting the Prophetic Books*, 67–68.

107. The Hebrew term (מַיִם חַיִּים) is also found four other times in the HB (Gen 26:19; Lev 14:5, 50; Lev 19:17) but not in reference to God, a person, or an ideology. Instead, it refers to physical water that is flowing or springing.

108. McKane, *Jeremiah*, 1:47; Voth, "Jeremiah," 275.

109. G. Smith, *Interpreting the Prophetic Books*, 101–2.

110. G. Smith, *Interpreting the Prophetic Books*, 70–71.

not only cleanses, but it continues to function alongside the cleansing to enable a continual walk in unison with God.

In a graphic expression of the outpouring of God's power and blessing, a stream flows out from under the altar of God's temple, which continually flows and rises ever higher, which makes saltwater fresh and enlivens whatever it touches (47:1–12). This abundance of water is reminiscent of the abundance of Gen 2:10–14.[111] But it is not the abundance of water that is the significant focus of the text; instead it is the ever-increasing and consistent flow that pours blessing upon blessing, bringing restoration and life.[112] The flowing of this stream, which starts gently but appears to gain momentum and expand, may also reflect the waters of Shiloah of which Isaiah spoke (Isa 8:6–7).[113] While the term "living water" is not used by Ezekiel, he clearly describes here living water with symbolism that seems similar to that used by John (Rev 22:1–2).[114] The symbolism of the measuring rod in this prophecy (47:3–5) represents the king rebuilding his temple, an obvious allusion to the eschatological reestablishment of God's garden kingdom which is yet future.[115] This imagery is of blessing that cannot be measured.

Through his vivid images, Ezekiel pictures a rebellious people in exile because they have failed to listen to God. He also pictures God who will restore his people, cleansing them and sustaining them as a flowing stream providing life (47:1–12). The life generated by this stream is continuous (47:12).

Zechariah

Zechariah 14:8 describes a day of restoration when "living water will flow out of Jerusalem," which draws upon the previous prophetic messaging, particularly Ezek 47:1–12.[116] The text "focuses on water."[117] This life-giving and life-sustaining water will arrive as the foes of God and Israel are defeated (14:1–7), mirroring the message of other prophets

---

111. Zimmerli, *Ezekiel 2*, 510; Nevader, "Creating *Deus Non Creator.*"
112. Zimmerli, *Ezekiel 2*, 515; Fretheim, *God and World*, 196.
113. Zimmerli, *Ezekiel 2*, 510–11.
114. Zimmerli, *Ezekiel 2*, 515.
115. Bodi, "Ezekiel," 4:497–98; Zimmerli, *Ezekiel 2*, 509.
116. Terblance, "Abundance of Living Waters."
117. Boda, *Zechariah*, 763.

(Hos 4:3; Amos 1:2; Mic 1:3–4; Zeph 1:2–3).[118] This apocalyptic imagery also stresses the absolute power and control of God not to just vanquish the foes, but to bless his people with never-ending superabundance.[119] As the water of Ezek 47:1–12 was linked to the waters of Gen 2:10–14 above, Mark Boda similarly links Zechariah's "living water" to the Gihon spring (Gen 2:10–14) and to Ezek 47.[120] In this transforming event Zechariah envisions God establishing his authority over the earth, and establishing himself as its true king. Part of this includes cleansing and renewal, which the water flowing from Jerusalem symbolizes.[121] The living water in Zechariah arrives as part of a global geographic transformation, as in Ezekiel, and its flow is perpetual, sustaining those who are God's.

Matthew

Jesus directed his apostles to make disciples by baptizing them into the name of the Father, Son, and Holy Spirit, followed by teaching those baptized to observe the teachings of Jesus (28:19–20). While the application of water in baptism was singular and transient, the effect was enduring, the directive being complemented by living according to "all that I commanded you" (28:19–20). There was also a continuing impact of baptism because it was into the name of the Father, Son, and Holy Spirit, who are united beings, and eternal (Rom 16:26; Gal 6:8; Eph 3:11).[122] Being baptized "into" (εἰς) the name of the Father, Son and Holy Spirit, means being in fellowship with them, and fellowship most appropriately exists on an eternal continuum where they exist.[123] Grant Osborne appears to support this eternal co-existence as he sees the statement that Jesus has "all authority" (28:18) stemming from Dan 7:13–14 in which the eternal kingdom of the Messiah is forecast that will never be destroyed.[124] Jesus directed baptism in water as normative for disciple-making and promised his accompaniment of the disciple-makers for the remainder of "the age" and beyond (28:20).

---

118. Floyd, "Habakkuk," 203.
119. Sandy, *Plowshares & Pruning Hooks*, 79, 108–9.
120. Boda, *Zechariah*, 764; Terblance, "Abundance of Living Waters."
121. Boda, *Zechariah*, 766–67.
122. Quarles, *Matthew*, 352; Bauer, *Gospel*, 233.
123. Osborne, *Matthew*, 1081; Bauer, *Gospel*, 241–42.
124. Osborne, *Matthew*, 1078–79.

The work of disciple-making by the apostles is enhanced by the eternal accompaniment of Jesus, and Jesus also accompanies all disciples through the gift of the Holy Spirit who replaces him on the earth while he is away (John 14:17; Acts 2:38). This makes the baptism and instruction that leads to discipleship an uninterrupted experience of accompaniment of Jesus or the Holy Spirit.[125] Disciple-making was designed to spiritually sustain disciples and accomplish the eternal purposes of Jesus's ministry (Luke 19:10; John 3:16; Eph 3:11).[126] The eternal kingdom is accessible in the "here and now," but extends past the measure of time because of Jesus's eternal nature, partly supported by the fact of his resurrection that assures it.[127] The point is that Jesus connects the water of baptism to the Godhead and discipleship, and Jesus connects his ongoing presence with those baptizing and making disciples. There is a continuous divine presence connected to baptism and disciple-making.

Luke

Crowds came to the baptism of John the Baptist, but their apparent willingness to undergo the rite of baptism was not supported by a penitent heart, which prompted John to ask, "Who warned you to flee from the wrath to come?" (3:7). Those who "acknowledged God's justice" were baptized by John, but those who "rejected God's purpose for themselves" were not baptized (7:29–30). The "wrath to come" that was avoided by repentance and baptism speaks to the end-time and to the eternal realm (3:7, 15–17).[128] Joel Green finds in this a covenantal and eschatological context.[129] These texts demonstrate that John's baptism had ongoing effects beyond the immediate, and even beyond this life and into the eschaton as part of "God's purpose."[130] Green calls Luke 7:29–30 a "commentary on 3:1–18."[131] He also notes that "God's purpose" is a motif of Luke and is part of the "ongoing story of God's engagement with his people."[132] In these

---

125. Osborne, *Matthew*, 1082–83; Bauer, *Gospel*, 293–94.
126. Osborne, *Matthew*, 1081; Bauer, *Gospel*, 318, 26.
127. Osborne, *Matthew*, 1079, 1083; Bauer, *Gospel*, 154, 321–22.
128. J. Green, *Gospel of Luke*, 173–74; Chen, *Luke*, 49.
129. J. Green, *Gospel of Luke*, 173–74.
130. J. Green, *Gospel of Luke*, 299–300.
131. J. Green, *Gospel of Luke*, 300.
132. J. Green, *Gospel of Luke*, 300–301.

texts, Luke describes repentance and water baptism as a declaration and commitment of loyalty to God's purpose of eternal cohabitation, which necessitates continuous efficacy of the water rite in sustaining spiritual life until the eschatological redemption occurs, and beyond.[133]

John

While chapter 2 discussed the initiation of life by water in John 3:3-5, it is important to emphasize here that this new life was not fleeting, but permanent. Life began again (or anew) for the purpose of entering the "kingdom of God" (3:5) which is eternal (2 Pet 1:11).[134] Andreas J. Köstenberger notes that John's frequent references to water in the early chapters gradually build to his more important "theological themes such as eternal life or the Holy Spirit."[135] John 3:3-5 is a good example of what Köstenberger means as the purpose of rebirth is related to eternal life with Christ, and it is achieved through the power of the Holy Spirit (1:32-33; 3:6).[136] It is a life that is "born of spirit" which is contrasted to being "born of flesh" (3:6), and is "heavenly" contrasted with "earthly" (3:12).[137] Jesus states this new birth is about eternal life (3:15, 16) which means its sustainability is endless.[138]

The "living water" Jesus offered the Samaritan woman at the well is contrasted with physical water, with which thirst reappears (4:10-13). The living water differs because it is a constantly flowing spring that leads to eternal life (4:14).[139] It is this same ceaselessly flowing living water that Jesus promised at the feast (7:38).[140] Jesus's living water, as was similarly spoken of by Jeremiah and Zechariah, extends into the eschaton (Jer 2:13; 17:13; Zech 14:8; John 4:14; Rev 22:1-2), which assures its perpetual effect.[141]

---

133. J. Green, *Theology of the Gospel*, 36–37.

134. Köstenberger, *Theology of John's Gospel*, 348; Michaels, *Gospel of John*, 185.

135. Köstenberger, *Theology of John's Gospel*, 162.

136. Köstenberger, *Theology of John's Gospel*, 163–64; Koester, *Symbolism in Fourth Gospel*, 14.

137. Michaels, *Gospel of John*, 185–87.

138. Köstenberger, *Theology of John's Gospel*, 348.

139. Köstenberger, "John," 438.

140. Koester, *Symbolism in Fourth Gospel*, 14.

141. Köstenberger, *Theology of John's Gospel*, 165; Michaels, *Gospel of John*, 185; Koester, *Symbolism in Fourth Gospel*, 228.

The gift of the Holy Spirit was symbolized by the "living water" Jesus promised to those who believe (7:38–39). This gift, which was to come after Jesus's glorification (7:39), was reminiscent of the Spirit anointing Israel's kings (Saul, David) and prophets (Moses, Elijah, Elisha).[142] In this case, as prophet and king, in the full power of his eternal enthronement Jesus anoints with the Spirit all who believe.[143] It was the glorification of Jesus (7:39), something that obviously had not occurred up to the point of his ascension (Acts 1:4–8), that triggered the bestowal of the Spirit to all believers after his ascension (Act 1:9—2:4, 38). This is not merely an idle gift, but the presence of the living God with whom believers finally have fellowship.[144] This Holy Spirit presence and fellowship is as unending as the one who enables and maintains it.

In John 13 Jesus washed the disciples feet and stated to Peter that if he did not wash his feet, "you have no part with me" (13:8). It was this act of washing that Jesus presented as the permanent model for believers' relationships, first with Jesus (13:8), and then with others (13:14). Associated with the water application is blessing (13:17).[145] Craig R. Koester suggests that Jesus's statement "if I do not wash you, you have no part with me" (13:8) carries the meaning of "if I do not love and die for you, you have no part in me," which amounts to being rejected for eternal salvation.[146] Others agree with Koester's sentiment that humbling oneself, and loving others, is the example and call of Christ intended by this text.[147] The rejection for being unwashed is permanent, but the participation in Christ is equally permanent. The washing with water portrays this ceaseless coexistence with Christ.

The water that accompanied the blood that flowed from the side of Jesus while on the cross identified Jesus as human (19:34).[148] The water was the focal point of the text (19:34), and a vivid reminder of Jesus's words that "whoever drinks of the water that I will give him shall never thirst" (John 4:14).[149] This "symbol-laden term 'water' does not express

---

142. Koester, *Symbolism in Fourth Gospel*, 228.
143. Koester, *Symbolism in Fourth Gospel*, 228.
144. Klink, *John*, 376; Michaels, *Gospel of John*, 468–69.
145. Köstenberger, *Theology of John's Gospel*, 236–37.
146. Koester, *Symbolism in Fourth Gospel*, 134; see also Michaels, *Gospel of John*, 728.
147. Michaels, *Gospel of John*, 728; Köstenberger, *Theology of John's Gospel*, 236.
148. Köstenberger, *Theology of John's Gospel*, 255.
149. Michaels, *Gospel of John*, 968–69.

biology but theology."[150] It was an indelible reminder of "he who believes in me . . . from his innermost being will flow rivers of living water" (7:38).[151] It was a "reminder that life (represented by water) emerges from death, the shedding of blood."[152] The symbolism in the water flowing from the side of Jesus points to the eternal nature of the gift of life that water symbolized by the various texts cited above.

Acts

The story of Philip and the Ethiopian unveils the abiding effect of the application of water in baptism. The Ethiopian appears to be a believer in God who came to Jerusalem to worship (8:27), and continued to demonstrate his interest in spiritual matters by reading from Isa 53 (8:26–34). From that text, Philip preached to him Jesus who Isaiah depicts as the sacrificial lamb slain for the sins of the world (8:35; Isa 53:7–12). Some see in this text a fulfilment of OT prophecies (Ps 68:31; Zech 2:4, 11–12; Zeph 3:10) which are arguably echoed.[153] Luke does not explain in Acts 8 what Philip said, but whatever was said led the Ethiopian to request water baptism, in which Philip assisted (8:36–38).[154]

The justification and redemption from sin spoken of by Isaiah, that came by Jesus, appears to have become realized and appropriated by the Ethiopian's baptism (8:25–28).[155] It is forgiveness of sins that denotes the people of God, and which "was central to the promise of Israel's restoration."[156] Although called an Ethiopian and not an Israelite, by his baptism the Ethiopian responded to the gospel of Jesus just as the Jewish Pentecost crowd responded to Peter's instruction (2:38).[157] His response was the same as Cornelius's, another gentile who came to Christ upon hearing the gospel (10:34–48). The purpose of God in sending the sacrificial lamb to atone for the sins of the world is set in eternity, arising from before the foundations of the world (Eph 1:4; 1 Pet 1:20), and the

---

150. Klink, *John*, 814.
151. Michaels, *Gospel of John*, 968–69.
152. Michaels, *Gospel of John*, 969; see also Klink, *John*, 815.
153. Marshall, "Acts," 573.
154. Marshall, "Acts," 575; Marshall, *Acts*, 174–75.
155. Marshall, *Acts*, 174–75.
156. J. Green, *Conversion in Luke-Acts*, 127.
157. J. Green, *Conversion in Luke-Acts*, 127–28.

effects of his redemptive work continue into the eschaton (Matt 25:34; John 17:24; 1 Tim 6:17–19; 2 Tim 4:8; Heb 9:26). Water baptism connects the believer to the continuous efficacy of Jesus's sacrificial atonement, and it is a confession of one's eternal reconciliation with him.[158]

Romans

As in Acts, the application of water in baptism in Rom 6 points not just to the initiation of life, but to its continuation. Baptism is described as a "burial" (6:4) which means one has died, but it is also a resurrection because one is given new life (6:4–5). Grant R. Osborne compares this new life to moving to a new country, in which one must learn new customs, social orders, patterns of living, and change old habits because one's citizenship has changed.[159] This new life mirrors the life of the resurrected Jesus (6:5), with whom one is unified, and that includes living forever as he does (6:8–11, 23; Heb 7:25).[160] Water then initiates life, and also sustains that life indefinitely.

1 Corinthians

Using agricultural imagery, 1 Cor 3:6–9 explains spiritual life as planting, watering, and growing. The planting was by Paul, the watering by Apollos, but God causes the growth or life. Anthony C. Thiselton says it is important that the works of Paul and Apollos are passing events noted by the two aorists "planted" and "watered," contrasted with "God who causes the growth" which is continuous action and noted by the imperfect tense.[161] He says the work of individual humans passes, but God's sanctifying and life-sustaining work is ongoing to the individual and the church.[162] This metaphor of water is associated with life's start, and with its perpetuation.

---

158. J. Green, *Conversion in Luke–Acts*, 128; Beasley-Murray, *Baptism in New Testament*, 101–2.
   159. Osborne, *Romans*, 147.
   160. Osborne, *Romans*, 148.
   161. Thiselton, *First Epistle to Corinthians*, 302.
   162. Thiselton, *First Epistle to Corinthians*, 302.

Ephesians

The cleansing aspect of "washing of water with the word" (5:26) was discussed in chapter 3, but the continuing work of cleansing and sanctification occurs by the presence of the truth, who is ultimately Jesus (John 14:6; 17:17), by the word (5:26), and by the continuing effect of Jesus's sacrifice of himself (5:25–26).[163] Such sanctification looks forward to an eschatological moment when Jesus presents the church in purity (5:27; 1 Thess 5:23).[164] This work of Jesus is described as "nourishes and cherishes" (5:29), "because we are member of his body" (5:30). This text also describes the Christ/church relationship as that of a marriage (5:23–32).[165] This imagery of intimate union with Christ can hardly conceive of Christ ceasing to sustain the relationship, particularly since Christ and the church have become "one flesh" (5:31; Matt 28:20; John 14:18; Heb 13:5).[166] The "washing of water," however one may define it, results in a purification or sanctification that is initiated, and indefinitely persists.

Titus

The saving act of "washing of regeneration and renewing by the Holy Spirit" (3:5) came by Jesus (3:6). It was a merciful act (3:5) of justification by grace (3:7), so that believers might inherit eternal life (3:7). Because the washing is "by the Holy Spirit" (3:5) it seems that to assume the regenerative work was in any way defective would undermine God's omnipotence. Because eternal life is the ultimate purpose of this "washing . . . by the Holy Spirit" (3:5–7) it is then necessarily implied that the effect of washing has open-ended duration and efficacy to accomplish its intended eternal purpose.[167] The usage of the term "regeneration" in the second and third centuries sometimes referred to the resurrection.[168] Whether the resurrection is intended here is uncertain, but the text points to a washing that sustains life from inception into eternity.

---

163. Best, *Ephesians*, 542–43.
164. Bock, *Ephesians*, 178–80; Liefeld, *Ephesians*, 146–50.
165. Best, *Ephesians*, 531, 545.
166. Best, *Ephesians*, 549–57.
167. Wall, *1 & 2 Timothy*, 366–67.
168. Witherington, *Socio-Rhetorical Commentary*, 160–61.

Hebrews

The "new and living way" (10:20) is contrasted with its shadow, the law of Moses (10:18). This "new and living way" was provided by the personal and bodily sacrifice of Jesus (10:21), who has become the "great priest" (10:21). Because of Jesus's high priesthood, believers are encouraged to "draw near" because we have had our "hearts sprinkled clean from an evil conscience and our bodies washed with pure water" (10:22).[169] It is the high priesthood of Christ that enables one "sprinkled" and "washed" the privilege of approaching Christ, now and forever.[170]

Terry J. Wright connects this text (10:19–22) to the introductory remarks that Jesus "upholds all things by the word of his power" (1:3).[171] Wright notes that "God does not want to discard his creation, to cease his sustaining action ... but through the Son, to continue to sustain it ... to ensure that it may continue to exist in a proper relationship to him."[172] The sprinkling and washing with pure water, a reference to baptism, has been called part of the "foundation of Christian experience." This experience has been "expressed in terms of repentance, faith, and baptism(s) and laying on of hands (6:1–2; 10:22)."[173] It is this experience that serves as the entrée into a new relationship with God, whereby one accesses the heavenly sanctuary, in this life and in the one to come.[174] The interminable effect of this washing in pure water is reflected in the comments about judgment (10:27), "the living God" (10:31), "a great reward" (10:35), "what was promised" (10:36), the coming of Jesus (10:37), and the "preservation of the soul" (10:39).

1 John

The "water and blood" by which Jesus came (5:6), and the "Spirit and the water and the blood" that testify and are "in agreement" (5:7–8), are set in the context of overcoming the world (5:4–5) and "eternal life" (5:11–13). It is Jesus who overcame the world (John 16:33), and who enables others to overcome (4:4; 5:4–5) and inherit eternal life (5:11, 13, 20). The

---

169. Cockerill, *Epistle to the Hebrews*, 462.
170. Cockerill, *Epistle to the Hebrews*, 462–63.
171. T. Wright, "Seal of Approval," 146–47.
172. T. Wright, "Seal of Approval," 147.
173. Marshall, "Soteriology in Hebrews," 264.
174. Marshall, "Soteriology in Hebrews," 263–77.

statement "For there are three that testify" (5:7) emphasizes the ongoing nature of their testimonial work by the use of the present participle (ὅτι τρεῖς εἰσιν οἱ μαρτυροῦντες).[175] It is this constant testimony that remains current in the believer.[176] First John 5:10 says, "The one who believes in the Son of God has the testimony in himself." The testimony that remains active within the believer "is this, that God has given us eternal life" (5:11). In 1 John 5 the water, along with the Spirit and the blood, expresses a testimony that occurred in the past and is still in progress, and aims at overcoming the world and providing eternal life.[177] The victorious life (5:4) of which the water (and the Spirit and the blood) witnesses exists now, but it also extends into eternity.[178]

Revelation

The sound of many waters is heard in the heavenly realm (1:15; 14:2; 19:6). It is to the heavenly "springs of the water of life" (7:17) that those who have "washed their robes" will be invited (22:14) and led (7:14), and it is those who have "washed their robes" who will "have the right to the tree of life" (22:14). The "water of life" is reserved for those who have overcome (21:6–7; 22:1–2; 1 John 5:4–5).

In these texts water symbolizes not just life, but "imperishable life."[179] Reminiscent of creation, water is the symbol of God establishing again his dominion over all.[180] Just as the heavens and earth were created and sustained by water (2 Pet 3:5; Gen 1–2), so those living in eternity are sustained by water (21:6–7; 22:1–5, 12–15, 17).[181] The imagery of the "water of life" (7:17; 21:6; 22:17) seems to imply "the divine resources of eternal life are deep and never-ending."[182] In offering the "water of life" Jesus says, "I am the Alpha and the Omega, the beginning and the end" (21:6), which speaks to the beginning of history and to its end.[183] In this

---

175. Yarbrough, *1–3 John*, 284.
176. Yarbrough, *1–3 John*, 288–89.
177. Yarbrough, *1–3 John*, 290–92.
178. Crowe, *Hope of Israel*, 148–49.
179. Roloff, *Revelation*, 100.
180. Roloff, *Revelation*, 212, 237, 246, 252–53; Smalley, *Revelation of John*, 481.
181. Beale, *Book of Revelation*, 1103.
182. Smalley, *Revelation of John*, 541.
183. Beale, *Book of Revelation*, 1055.

text, it is at or after the end of history that the water of life is offered.[184] This indicates it is eternally availability and never ceases to sustain.[185]

CHAPTER SUMMARY

The intent of this chapter has been to substantiate that God uses water to sustain life physically and spiritually. Sustaining presupposes life already exists. The sustaining of life by water in the physical realm is well known and has needed little or no verification. Sustaining life spiritually has been demonstrated by numerous OT and NT texts that use water as a metaphor or symbol of spiritual life that exists now, and also beyond the end of time or history. God has consistently been credited with sustaining life, even though life originated by the means of water. For example, it was water that sustained and revived Hagar and Ishmael, but it was God who directed Hagar to the well (Gen 21:19). In the New Testament the water of baptism is said to result in "newness of life" (Rom 6:4), but the spiritual and eternal dimension of that life is that it is a "gift of God" (Rom 6:23).

Many biblical texts have been cited, but these were necessary to demonstrate the pervasiveness of the subject of water, and its use as God's metaphor or mechanism to sustain spiritual life. This usage of water begins in Gen 1–2 and continues throughout the Bible to Rev 21–22. The prevalence of the message, repeated in so many circumstances by many different voices, spread over the lifespan of biblical history, forces one to acknowledge that God uses water as a means or symbol to sustain physical and spiritual life, now and forever.

---

184. Beale, *Book of Revelation*, 1055–56.
185. Beale, *Book of Revelation*, 1103–11, 1149.

5

Synthesis of Evidence

THE FIRST FOUR CHAPTERS introduced this research and discussed, in what may appear a somewhat cursory fashion, the underlying biblical texts that support the portion of the thesis that asserts a biblical theology of water exists in which God uses water to initiate physical and spiritual life, provide physical and spiritual cleansing, and sustain physical and spiritual life. Because of the breadth of this portion of the thesis, it is important to synthesize these findings into a unified whole so their implications can be more readily discussed, and additional aspects of the thesis can be more easily examined. One aspect of the thesis to be argued in this chapter is that these findings form an inclusio bookended with Gen 1–2 and Rev 21–22. Another consideration is *Chaoskampf* theory and polemic theology as they relate to these findings.

CHAOSKAMPF AND POLEMIC THEOLOGY

Chapter 2 includes numerous references to *Chaoskampf* theory and polemic theology. Because of the ancient historical setting of the Genesis creation story, questions surrounding cosmology naturally arise and lend themselves to more scrutiny than water-related matters farther removed from creation, such as affairs during the days of Israel's prophets and kings, events during the postexilic period, or happenings in the

NT.¹ Enuma Elish dates back to almost 2000 BCE, and has been widely utilized in creation studies seeking to promote *Chaoskampf*.² Writing over seventy years ago, Alexander Heidel noted that Enuma Elish was "the principle source of Mesopotamian cosmology," but that it "is not primarily a creation story at all." He calls the creation account "brief and meager."³ More recently, others agree with Heidel that *Chaoskampf* theory is not a credible creation source, and many have dismissed the theory in whole or in part.⁴

Heidel states that the most important cosmological discovery from Mesopotamia dates from the sixth century BCE, and its central theme is the justification of Marduk as king.⁵ If the HB is a postexilic product, perhaps non-Israelite cosmology of roughly the same era may be of interest when compared to the biblical account.⁶ But if the HB is taken on its face, where authorship of Genesis is attributed to Moses (Josh 1:7; 8:31; Ezra 3:2; 6:8; Dan 9:11, 13; Mark 1:44; 7:10; John 1:17, 45) who lived more than five hundred years earlier, then these late secular poems, stories, and myths may be almost inconsequential as they relate to biblical cosmology.⁷ If one accepts the NT assertion that "all Scripture is inspired by God" (2 Tim 3:16), then Moses, with the assistance of God, wrote about things prior to his life and beyond the scope of his observation and experience. Even with God's participation in writing the Genesis creation story, Richard Averbeck says, the author "shaped the story of creation around what was observable and understandable to the ancient Israelites."⁸

Michael Coogan notes that around the time of Moses "a shift occurred in the pantheons of much of the ancient world" in which the older

---

1. Rackley, "Kingship, Struggle, and Creation"; Tsumura, "Creation Motif."

2. V. Matthews and Benjamin, *Old Testament Parallels*, 21; Gunkel, "Influence of Babylonian Mythology"; Coogan, *Brief Introduction*, 32–38; Tsumura, "*Chaoskampf* Myth."

3. Heidel, *Babylonian Genesis*, 10.

4. Rackley, "Kingship, Struggle, and Creation"; Tsumura, "*Chaoskampf* Myth"; Ballentine, *Conflict Myth*; Tsumura, *Creation and Destruction*; Scurlock and Beal, *Creation and Chaos*; Walton and Sandy, *Lost World of Scripture*; Lu, "Deification and Demonization."

5. Heidel, *Babylonian Genesis*, 61.

6. Meyers, *Exodus*, 2–3.

7. Meyers, *Exodus*; Childs, *Introduction to Old Testament*, 134–35; Coogan, *Brief Introduction*, 89–92; Hoffmeier, "What Is Biblical Date."

8. Averbeck, "Literary Day," 8.

gods were replaced by younger and more powerful gods.[9] If true, the importance of ancient documents, gods, and processes related to biblical cosmology and *Chaoskampf* may be diminished. While seeming to discount these ancient documents as being only peripherally related to the biblical account of creation, Heidel does note parallels between the early chapters of Genesis and some of the Mesopotamian myths, such as the existence of a watery chaos prior to creation, the presence of light, and the separation of heaven and earth.[10] As previously stated, it is not the purpose of this presentation to enter into debate about other cosmologies, but to determine the biblical use of water, and its cognate terms, with a view to uncovering a biblical theology of water, if one exists. While ancient Near Eastern writings, songs, stories, and myths may be interesting and may share some of the same concepts found in the Bible, they do not detract from the biblical usage of water, even though they may enhance understanding of the subject and its related metaphors found throughout Scripture.

John Currid says, "The primary purpose of polemic theology is to demonstrate emphatically and graphically the distinction between the worldview of the Hebrews and the beliefs and practices of the rest of the ancient Near East."[11] Based upon this definition, the presence of polemic theology seems difficult to deny throughout the Bible. When Jesus said he was "the way, the truth, and the life" (John 14:6), he was in essence claiming all other ways, all alleged truths, and all other promises of life to be erroneous. His message was polemic. It was Jesus and Jesus alone who provided these blessings.[12] As it relates to water, there are many circumstances in which polemics are likely present in biblical accounts. For example, in the biblical creation story water is prevalent, but associated with that is a disciplined systematic order that is absent in the ancient Near Eastern creation myths.[13] The biblical account of creation also differs in that what was created was separate from God, and not part of his being.[14] When Elijah confronted the prophets of Baal on Mount Carmel (1 Kgs 18), the use of water, the foretelling of rain, and the cloud in the distance graphically point to the power of Israel's God over the pagan

9. Coogan, *Brief Introduction*, 93.
10. Heidel, *Babylonian Genesis*, 81.
11. Currid, *Against the Gods*, 25.
12. Klink, *John*, 617–19; Köstenberger, *Theology of John's Gospel*, 180.
13. Westermann, *Genesis*, 1:1–6.
14. Walton, "Genesis," 1:16–17.

storm god, Baal. The polemic against foreign gods and promotion of Israel's God is likely the reason this story appears.[15] Similar polemics are common throughout Scripture, such as with the plagues of Moses (Exod 7–13), in David's speech to Goliath (1 Sam 17:45–47, with the writing on the wall (Dan 5), or in John's plea for repentance (Matt 3:7–12).

Whether *Chaoskampf* or polemic theology is present in some or even all of the water texts of the Bible does not eliminate the presence of water texts, nor diminish their meanings. A broader understanding of the water-related terms may be provided by ancient Near Eastern worldviews or by polemic writing, so they are not to be dismissed, particularly when detailed exegesis is undertaken. Detailed exegesis of each text, however, has not been required to this point. The intent of this presentation has primarily been to sufficiently explore enough of each text to portray the widespread use of water and its cognate terms, and to garner a general impression of each to substantiate the thesis. Such a broad review may seem superficial and lacking in scholastic acumen, but it is believed to be essential to underscore the prevalence of the subject throughout the Bible so that its ramifications can be explored in more detail. In the end, it is the Bible's repetitive use of these terms, and the association of theological concepts surrounding these terms, that is under consideration. Any help obtained from worldviews contemporaneous with the times of the biblical writing is welcomed. It seems such worldviews are not detrimental, but additive to the discussion. Accepting or rejecting *Chaoskampf* or polemic theology, partially or completely, is not required to accept the fact of God's use of water to accomplish some of his objectives.

SYNTHESIS

The thesis of this research begins by stating that the Bible uses water as an element initiating physical and spiritual life, providing physical and spiritual cleansing, and sustaining physical and spiritual life. While the physical aspect is somewhat obvious, the spiritual aspect of these three components has been examined with numerous biblical texts verifying the veracity of this portion of the thesis. Table 1.1 identifies uses of water in the OT that have been examined. Each OT text supports at least one component of this part of the thesis. The component is identified by an

---

15. Na'aman, "Contest on Mount Carmel"; Patterson and Austel, *1 and 2 Kings*, 208; Monson, "1 Kings," 77–80.

uppercase *x* if the text primarily supports it. In some cases, more than one component is primarily supported. A lowercase *x* identifies thesis components that the text secondarily supports. Sometimes the text secondarily supports more than one component. Components noted as secondarily supported receive such designation because the support requires some theological or textual networking, or the support is less obvious.

Text	Initiate	Cleanse	Sustain
Gen 1–2	X	X	X
Gen 6–9	X	X	X
Gen 16	X		
Gen 21			X
Gen 26			X
Exod 2	X		X
Exod 7	x		X
Exod 14	X	x	X
Exod 15, 17			X
Exod 29, 40		X	x
Josh 3	X	x	x
2 Kgs 2	X		
2 Kgs 5	x	X	x
Ps 1, 23, 42, 46, 63			X
Ps 18	x		X
Ps 104	X	x	X
Isa			X
Jer	x		X
Ezek 36	x	X	X
Ezek 47	X		X
Jon 1–2	X	x	X
Zech 13		X	X
Zech 14	X		X

Table 1.1 OT uses of water (reviewed)

Ten of the thirty-nine OT books have been cited as referring to water initiating, cleansing, or sustaining life (table 1.1). These ten books range topically from creation to the postexilic era, and may have been originally written from roughly 1400 BCE to 400 BCE, which demonstrates the breadth and scope of the subject of water throughout the OT, and in Israel's history. Using the same format, table 1.2 identifies uses of water in the NT that have been examined. Twelve of the twenty-seven NT books have been cited, and while they occupy only a small time frame compared to the OT, the volume of water references in the NT make the topic a major one.

Text	Initiate	Cleanse	Sustain
Matt 28	X	x	x
Luke 3, 7	X	X	
John 1	X	X	x
John 2	X		
John 3	X	x	X
John 4	X	x	x
John 7	X	x	x
John 9	x	X	
John 19	X	X	X
Acts 2	X	X	X
Acts 8	X		
Rom 6	X	X	X
1 Cor 3	X		X
1 Cor 6	X	X	x
1 Cor 10	X	X	X
Eph 5		X	X
Titus 3	X	X	X
Heb 10	X	X	X
1 Pet 3	X	X	X
1 John 5	X	X	X
Rev 7, 21–22	X	X	X

Table 1.2 NT uses of water (reviewed)

While the categorizations in tables 1.1 and 1.2 may appear somewhat arbitrary, this is part of what is argued in this presentation, and part of what substantiates that a biblical theology of water exists. It has been said that theology is "reasoned discourse about God."[16] Thomas Aquinas is credited with turning this reasoned discourse into a science, and this science has as its task the explication of truths revealed in Scripture.[17] The pervasiveness of the subject of water in Scripture cannot be ignored. When multiple uses of water are presented or multiple theological concepts arise within a single water text, it strengthens the assertion that a biblical theology of water exists. The task of this presentation to this point has been to identify, briefly explain, and categorize these numerous biblical texts for further inquiry. This synthesis hopes to concretize these findings such that they are better understood, and also to establish their interrelatedness as part of an overall theology. Such fits with "faith seeking understanding," a phrase credited to Anselm which describes theology.[18]

An abridgment of the numerous water texts cited in prior chapters and summarized in tables 1.1 and 1.2 may be represented from the examination of two specific texts, Gen 1–2 and Rev 21–22. Within each of these two texts, each of the three components of the thesis is found. Because these two texts are also the beginning and end of the Bible, they also support the presence of an inclusio, which will be discussed in more detail.

Genesis 1–2

Although much of this material has already been presented as it relates to individual components of the thesis, here that information is supplemented and consolidated to establish the three components of the thesis as a unified whole within this isolated biblical text or context. It is first important to note the multiple uses of water or its cognate terms in Gen 1–2 expressed in table 1.3. In table 1.3, each *x* indicates one use of the term in that verse. In some verses, more than one usage occurs so more than one *x* is supplied. A parenthetical *x* means the term is not stated, but implied. Category headings include both singular and plural forms of the term, and they also include related words built upon the same English root where tense changes the spelling, such as "flows" and "flowed."

---

16. Plantinga et al., *Introduction to Christian Theology*, 6.
17. Plantinga et al., *Introduction to Christian Theology*, 9.
18. Plantinga et al., *Introduction to Christian Theology*, 8.

Synthesis of Evidence

Text	Deep	Water	Sea	Rain	Mist	River	Flow
1:2	X	X					
1:6		XXX					
1:7		XX					
1:9		X					
1:10		X	X				
1:20		X					
1:21		X	X				
1:22		X	X				
1:28			X				
2:5				X			
2:6		X			X		
2:10		X				XX	X
2:11						(X)	X
2:13						X	X
2:14						XX	X

Table 1.3 Water and water-related terms used in Gen 1-2

Thirty times in Gen 1-2, water, or a related term, is used (table 1.3). Considering that the book of Genesis is the beginning of the Bible for both Jews and Christians, the proliferation of water terms in these introductory chapters carries substantial importance. The "deep" (*tĕhôm*) (Gen 1:2) has been considered primeval water, but beyond that it has been difficult to define with more precision.[19] Rosanna Lu has stated, as suggested previously, that "*tĕhôm* has been unduly linked to the Mesopotamian Tiamat and interpreted as the embodiment of chaos and conflict."[20] Bruce Waltke defines the term, along with the darkness in which it is shrouded, as "surd evil."[21] Contradicting Waltke, Eric Ortlund says, "The darkness and water in Gen 1:2 are not bad, but are just unorganized and unfruitful (chaotic)."[22] More aligned with Ortlund, John

---

19. Lu, "Deification and Demonization," ii; תְּהוֹם, *HALOT*, 2:1690-91; Niehaus, *Ancient Near Eastern Themes*, 24.
20. Lu, "Deification and Demonization," ii.
21. Waltke with Fredricks, *Genesis*, 60.
22. Ortlund, *Piercing Leviathan*, 8.

Walton describes the deep more technically as "material in existence" that is part of the "(functional) nonexistence."[23]

However one defines the deep of Gen 1:2, it appears as part of God's "formless and void," covered in "darkness," which is transformed by light, order, and functionality, which includes life. Figure 1.1 portrays the untransformed image.

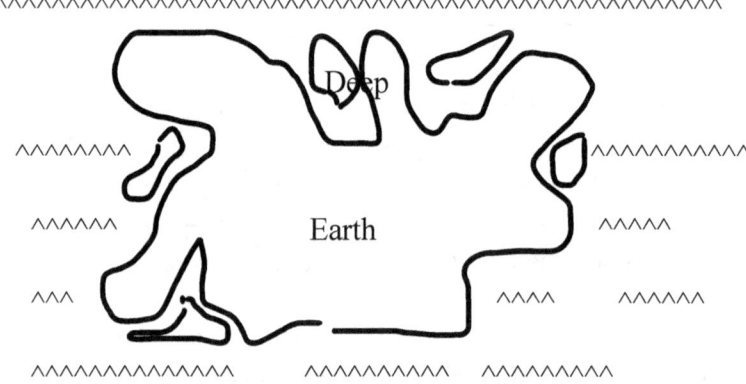

Figure 1.1. Representation of author's visual image of Gen 1:2

The image depicted in Gen 1:6–7 is of the waters of the deep being separated by an expanse or sky.[24] This occurred after light was created on the first day (Gen 1:3). Water above the expanse has typically been identified with clouds and rain.[25] Figure 1.2 pictures this developmental stage. The water below the expanse was pooled to form seas, enabling dry land to emerge from the deep (1:9–10). This continued separation and ordering is imaged in figure 1.3.

---

23. Walton, *Lost World*, 48.
24. Westermann, *Genesis*, 1:15.
25. Westermann, *Genesis*, 1:115–16; Waltke with Fredricks, *Genesis*, 62; Sailhamer, *Genesis Unbound*, 123–26.

Synthesis of Evidence

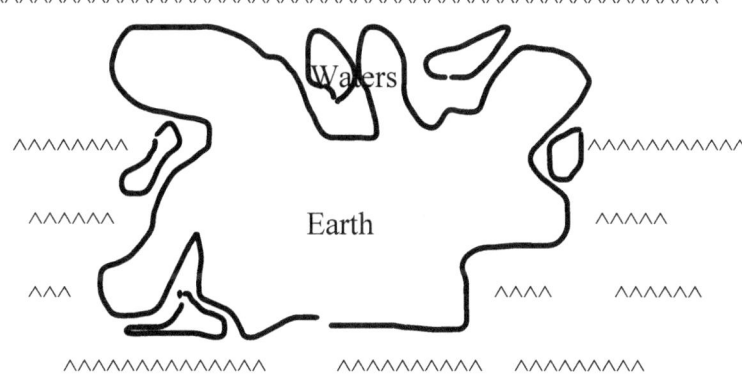

Figure 1.2. Representation of author's visual image of Gen 1:6–7

In these ten references to water in nine verses (Gen 1:2–10), God's creative work "is bound up with its orderliness and organization as a secure and fertile environment for life ... to flourish."[26] Earlier it was detailed how these orderly and creative movements by God are mirrored by human birth as sperm and egg meet and grow in dark watery environs until the appointed time of change from the developmental darkness, water, and unfruitfulness, to the maturity of light, earth, and productivity. John Walton calls this mature state "functional creation."[27] It is this process in which life is born "out of water and by water" (2 Pet 3:5) that undergirds the first proposition of the thesis that God uses water to initiate life.

---

26. Ortlund, *Piercing Leviathan*, 82.
27. Walton, *Lost World*, 48.

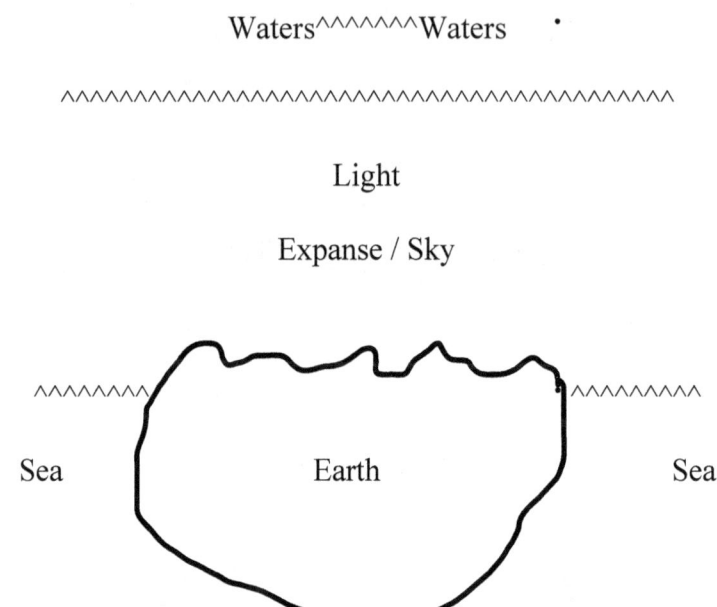

Figure 1.3: Representation of author's visual image of Gen 1:9–10

That this water of creation also cleanses, the second component of the thesis, is ascertained first by the presence of the Spirit of God hovering over the "surface of the deep" (1:2). God would dwell in the garden he was creating (Gen 3:8), and nothing unclean is permitted in God's presence (Exod 3:5; 19:23; 29:4; 40:30–32; Lev 11:44; Josh 5:15; Ezek 42:14; Rev 22:15). The hovering Spirit of God presents a picture of God readying things to prepare this new habitation.[28] Second, cleansing by the water of creation is implied because for God to create something unholy would be to countermand his own character, and God cannot deny himself (2 Tim 2:13). Third, for God to call his creation "good" or "very good" seven times (Gen 1:4, 10, 12, 18, 21, 25, 31) underscores the purity of what was born from water. As previously stated, it was not sin, but the primeval chaos, darkness, and uselessness that were washed away so that order, light, and purpose might replace it.[29] This water birth and its accompanying cleansing announced and enabled the transformation that old things had passed away, and a new purpose and existence had

28. Sailhamer, *Genesis Unbound*, 118; Waltke with Fredricks, *Genesis*, 60.
29. Dunn, "Jesus and Purity."

arrived, which was in keeping with God's holy character.[30] This cleansing of the heavens and the earth supports the second element of the thesis, that God uses water to spiritually cleanse.

The third component of the thesis is that God uses water to sustain life. That fish and sea creatures need the water to maintain life is common knowledge, and it is into these life-sustaining waters that God placed "swarms of living creatures" so they could "be fruitful and multiply, and fill the waters in the seas" (1:20–22). Genesis 2 speaks to water supporting life by explaining that shrubs and plants of the field had not yet sprouted because the Lord had not yet sent rain (water), even though a mist (water) from the ground moistened the earth (2:5–6). The Hebrew term translated "mist" is אֵד, a word with an unclear meaning, which appears to refer to a mist or seepage arising from a subterranean pool of water or spring.[31] What is clear is that this mist was insufficient to enable and sustain the life that more water, in the form of rain and a river, could support (2:5, 10). It is worth noting that the rain was to be sent by God (2:5), but in contrast, the mist seems to arise at will from outside sources (2:6).[32] Some find in this text (2:5–6) that God controls the life-giving rain as he also awaits the presence of humanity for whom the pending vegetation is intended. The mist may be viewed ultimately as a work of God, but the rain as an extraordinary work of God for the purpose of sustaining humanity and the vegetation which supports it.[33] Additional water was provided by a river flowing "out of Eden to water the garden: and from there it divided and became four rivers" (2:10). The river arising from within the garden is contrasted with the mist that (2:5) may have arisen from forces outside the garden.[34] This river arising from within the garden represents the life-giving and life-sustaining presence of God that supports life in the garden, but trickles outside the garden into the entire world advertising its potency.[35] John Walton says of this text, "Genesis uses a familiar picture of fertile waters flowing from the

---

30. G. Cole, *God Who Became Human*, 33.

31. Westermann, *Genesis*, 1:200–201; Wenham, *Genesis*, 1:58; אֵד, *HALOT*, 1:11; Walton, "Genesis," 1:25; Hasel and Hasel, "Hebrew Term 'ed'"; אֵד, *NIDOTTE*, 3:50–51.

32. Westermann, *Genesis*, 1:199–201.

33. Westermann, *Genesis*, 1: 199–201; Wenham, *Genesis*, 1:57–58.

34. Waltke with Fredricks, *Genesis*, 86–87.

35. Waltke with Fredricks, *Genesis*, 86–87; Wenham, *Genesis*, 1:64–66; Westermann, *Genesis*, 1:215–20.

seat of deity."³⁶ Walton appears to agree with others that the four rivers that are spawned from the river flowing out of Eden refer to the four corners of the earth, or the rest of the earth that is outside the garden of God.³⁷ Walton acknowledges God has different roles, but that "both initiating and sustaining are the acts of the Creator God."³⁸

These thirty references to water in Gen 1–2 demonstrate that God uses water to initiate life, to cleanse, and to sustain life.³⁹ This profuse use of water and water-related terms in the introductory chapters of the Bible is not accidental, but is likely for emphasis, to identify a theme, or to stress key points.⁴⁰ It forces the reader to examine why such a focus on water exists, and why it exists immediately in the opening words of Scripture.

Revelation 21–22

Just as the prominent use of water and its cognate terms is found in the opening words of Scripture (Gen 1–2), such also finds prominence in the final two chapters of the Bible (Rev 21–22). As with Gen 1–2, the previous discussion of Rev 21–22 will be supplemented and consolidated to establish the three components of the thesis as a unified whole within this single biblical text or context. This text has a similar emphasis, thematic identification, and stressing of key points as occurs in Genesis.⁴¹ As table 1.3 identifies uses of water and water-related terms in Gen 1–2, table 1.4 identifies those terms in Rev 21–22 using the same legend.

---

36. Walton, "Genesis," 1:29.

37. Walton, "Genesis," 1:29; Westermann, *Genesis*, 1:216–19; Sailhamer, *Genesis Unbound*, 75–84.

38. Walton, *Lost World*, 122.

39. Walton, *Lost World*, 122.

40. Osborne, *Hermeneutical Spiral*, 52; Fuhr and Köstenberger, *Inductive Bible Study*, 123; Michael Gorman, *Elements of Biblical Exegesis*, 40, 64.

41. Osborne, *Hermeneutical Spiral*, 52; Fuhr and Köstenberger, *Inductive Bible Study*, 123; Michael Gorman, *Elements of Biblical Exegesis*, 40, 64.

Text	Sea	Thirst	Spring	Water	Lake	River	Wash
21:1	X						
21:6		X	X	X			
21:8					X		
22:1				X		X	
22:2						X	
22:14							X
22:17		X		X			

Table 1.4 Water and related terms used in Rev 21–22

While thirty uses of water or water-related terms were identified in Gen 1–2, the shorter chapters of Rev 21–22 offer eleven appearances of water terms. The first term is "sea," which is said to no longer exist in the new heaven and new earth (21:1). Because Rev 21 describes God's restored cosmic temple,[42] it may be easy to just exclude the sea as a symbol of the "forces of evil, chaos, and hostility towards God and his people."[43] But the sea represents the holding place of the dead, as does "death and hades," which were thrown into the lake of fire (Rev 20:13–15).[44] The water terms, "sea" and "lake," are used multiple times in this text in a negative manner and this usage continues into 21:1 where that sea ceases to exist, and in 21:8 where the lake is the locus for the second death.

In ancient Near Eastern culture, the sea was "a recurring symbol for comic chaos" as evidenced in Job 7:12; 38:8–11.[45] It represented unfruitfulness, darkness, and the opposite of orderliness, which continuously and unsuccessfully attempted to defy God.[46] When Jesus walked on the water he demonstrated his power over this symbolic force (John 6:16–25).[47] In Rev 21 the sea that had been so negatively associated with death, hades, and defiance of God is finally gone, and in its place "the new heaven and earth represent God's faithfulness to creation, not his abandonment of it."[48] G. K. Beale identifies five potential usages of the

42. Niehaus, *Ancient Near Eastern Themes*, 136.
43. Tabb, *All Things New*, 42.
44. Osborne, *Revelation*, 730.
45. Ortlund, *Piercing Leviathan*, 71–73.
46. Ortlund, *Piercing Leviathan*, 71–73.
47. Klink, *John*, 311–14; Michaels, *Gospel of John*, 354–58.
48. Koester, *Revelation*, 803.

"sea" as being the source of cosmic evil, unbelieving nations, a place of the dead, the location of the world's idolatrous commercialism, and as a synecdoche for the entire former creation. Beale believes all five of these are represented in 21:1.[49] In the new heaven and earth, this sea does not exist, and whatever unholiness symbolized by it is outside the confines of the new heaven and earth.

In contrast to the sea which is outside the new heaven and earth, inside the new heaven and earth there exists a "spring of the water of life" (21:6). While the sea held the dead (Rev 20:13), the "spring" of this water provides life based on two related things, "thirst" (21:6) and overcoming (21:7). "Thirst designates the need for life with God, who lives forever."[50] Satisfaction of that need for God is met when Christ is enthroned as one's Lord, and commitment to Christ continues until its eternal fruition in the new heaven and earth. Overcoming emphasizes the continuation of faithfulness until one's death or the return of Christ (21:7).[51] This imagery is duplicated in Rev 7:14–17 where those who have "washed their robes" (7:14), becoming purified or cleansed, come into the temple of God, and are led by him to "springs of the water of life" (7:17) where they "thirst" no more (7:16) because they are in God's presence (21:7). It was this "water of life" or "living water" that Jesus offered (John 4:10–14; 7:38–39), and which was prophesied by Isaiah (55:1–3), Ezekiel (47:1–12), and Zechariah (14:8). This water initiated life, as its descriptor indicates, which undergirds the first component of the thesis.

The water of God, relied upon for cleansing in the Levitical system (Lev 8:6; 14:8; 16:26, 28), was prophesied as having a cleansing purpose (Ps 51:2; Isa 1:16; Jer 4:14; Ezek 16:4, 9; 36:25), and may serve as a backdrop for those who "washed their robes" (7:14) prior to receiving the "springs of the water of life" (7:17; 21:6). That this water of life has a cleansing quality is evidenced by the list of those who have not "thirsted" (21:6), have not "overcome" (21:7), and have not "washed their robes" (7:14; 22:14), but remain outside the new heaven and earth, steeped in faithlessness and sin (21:8; 22:15).[52] The water flowing from the temple in Ezek 47 had cleansing properties (Ezek 47:12) and it forecasts the scene

---

49. Beale, *Book of Revelation*, 1041–44.
50. Koester, *Revelation*, 807.
51. Koester, *Revelation*, 834; Osborne, *Revelation*, 738; Smalley, *Revelation of John*, 541; Beale, *Book of Revelation*, 1056.
52. Beale, *Book of Revelation*, 1059.

of Revelation (21:6; 22:1–2).[53] This river is "a sign of God's presence and blessing," a part of which includes cleansing.[54] It remains that only that which has been cleansed can appear in the presence of God (Exod 30:20; Heb 10:22). Those contaminated by sin are removed from God's garden and from the tree of life (Gen 3:22–24; Rev 21:8; 22:15).[55] This cleansing effect of water supports the second component of the thesis.

Perhaps for emphasis, or to identify a theme or to stress key points, the author of Revelation repeats that those who "wash their robes" have the right to eternal life (22:14), and the same "water of life" is again offered for the "thirsty" (Rev 22:17).[56] What differs in Rev 22, compared to Rev 21, is that the "water of life" is termed a "river" (22:1–2) rather than a "spring" (21:6), and the emphasis is on water sustaining life by watering the tree of life that continually nourishes (22:2), as opposed to entering into life or life being initiated (21:6).[57] The idea of a river echoes Ezek 47:1–12 and Zech 14:8. Revelation 22:1–2 is also "modeled on the description of the primeval garden" (Gen 2:10).[58] Ezekiel pictures water flowing from the temple of God, but in Rev 21:22 God and the Lamb are the temple from whom these life-giving and life-sustaining waters flow.[59] This image of continuous life and nourishment substantiates the third component of the thesis, that God uses water to sustain life.

What is evident from this review of Rev 21–22 is that the Bible closes its pages with an emphasis on water. Last words are often considered to be of most importance and if that is the case here, overlooking that living water can initiate life, cleanse, and sustain life indefinitely would disregard the gravity of these final words.

THE FORMATION OF AN INCLUSIO

That the Bible begins (Gen 1–2) and ends (Rev 21–22) with a proliferation of references to water and its cognate terms helps establish that an inclusio exists. An inclusio is "sometimes called a *sandwich structure*"

53. Beale, *Book of Revelation*, 1107–8.
54. Koester, *Revelation*, 834.
55. Koester, *Revelation*, 834–35.
56. Osborne, *Hermeneutical Spiral*, 52; Fuhr and Köstenberger, *Inductive Bible Study*, 123; Michael Gorman, *Elements of Biblical Exegesis*, 40, 64.
57. Smalley, *Revelation of John*, 541.
58. Beale, *Book of Revelation*, 1103.
59. Beale, *Book of Revelation*, 1104.

in which "a word, image, or idea from the beginning of the passage is echoed at the end."[60] It is also called "book-ending."[61] "The result of the inclusio thus formed is to enclose the intervening material so as to form a distinctive section of thought."[62]

Structure

The space between Genesis and Revelation is extensive, creating an inclusio at the macrostructural level, which admittedly is unusually broad.[63] An inclusio, however, can extend beyond a single text to include a collection of texts.[64] In his discussion on the meaning of words in a context, Grant Osborne suggests considering the theology of "the individual book and then of the writer before broadening it to the New Testament as a whole."[65] He thus expands "context" beyond a book, or writer, even as far as an entire testament. Osborne also states that "unless we can grasp the whole before attempting to dissect the parts, interpretation is doomed from the start."[66]

This inclusio is identifiable as a "theological-canonical" context that tends "to emphasize the covenant relationship that God has with his people."[67] It involves how "individual books of the Bible function together to form one comprehensive book."[68] This water inclusio is about the "whole" of which Osborne spoke and extends not just to one testament, but to both testaments, or the Protestant canon. It is a "synthetic approach" that seeks the "whole counsel of God in the Scriptures" and is a "correlation of the individually observed, interpreted, and applied texts."[69] It is vital that arbitrary textual divisions, such as chapters and verses, previous exegetical efforts, and in this case, intervening books,

---

60. Michael Gorman, *Elements of Biblical Exegesis*, 40.
61. Köstenberger and Patterson, *Invitation to Biblical Interpretation*, 247.
62. Köstenberger and Patterson, *Invitation to Biblical Interpretation*, 282; Fuhr and Köstenberger, *Inductive Bible Study*, 161–64.
63. Köstenberger and Patterson, *Invitation to Biblical Interpretation*, 602–5.
64. Köstenberger and Patterson, *Invitation to Biblical Interpretation*, 768–69.
65. Osborne, *Hermeneutical Spiral*, 111.
66. Osborne, *Hermeneutical Spiral*, 37.
67. Fuhr and Köstenberger, *Inductive Bible Study*, 26–27.
68. Fuhr and Köstenberger, *Inductive Bible Study*, 27.
69. Fuhr and Köstenberger, *Inductive Bible Study*, 340.

do not inhibit identifying repetitive words, similar images, or a common theme at both the beginning and the end.[70]

Michael Gorman acknowledges that "frequently we cannot reconstruct the exact or even an approximate occasion for a biblical text."[71] The truth of Gorman's statement makes the widespread use of water and water-related terms throughout Scripture even more impressive because the topic is mentioned by multiple writers, using different languages, in varied settings, stretching over centuries. Such accentuates the pervasiveness of the topic, but also its importance to the purposes of God as revealed in the Bible as a whole. The coalescence of the copious biblical texts into an identifiable and coherent beginning (Gen 1–2) matched by a similar ending (Rev 21–22) condenses the sundry parts into an identifiable and manageable whole enhancing better discussion of the topic, while also confirming the presence of an inclusio that bookends the Bible.[72]

Alpha and Omega

Jesus himself may be most influential in identifying this inclusio when he says, "I am the Alpha and the Omega, the beginning and the end" (Rev 21:6). Jesus then repeats this declaration with a slight modification when he says, "I am the Alpha and the Omega, the first and the last, the beginning and the end" (Rev 22:13). In this statement Jesus connects in "the beginning" (Gen 1:1) and "the end" (Rev 21:6; 22:13), which is exactly what the thesis advocates. What is meant by these opposite terms, however, is debated. Craig Koester connects these statements to the immediate context in which the old "heavens and earth" is contrasted with the "new heaven and earth" (21:1), and the water that previously brought judgment under the old creation (Rev 8:10–11; 16:4–5) to the unending water of life in the new (21:6; 22:1–2).[73] Others have focused more on linguistics to see in these declarations the claim of Jesus's exclusivity, or as a polemic against opposition to Jesus's authority, bypassing the obvious contextual references to original creation and its contrast with the new

---

70. Michael Gorman, *Elements of Biblical Exegesis*, 43, 64, 99; Köstenberger and Patterson, *Invitation to Biblical Interpretation*, 394.

71. Michael Gorman, *Elements of Biblical Exegesis*, 77.

72. Osborne, *Hermeneutical Spiral*, 54.

73. Koester, *Revelation*, 806–8.

heaven and earth.[74] John's Apocalypse consistently elevates Jesus as the only one worthy (1:4–8; 4:1; 5:9, 12), and any statement of his exclusivity is a polemic against all opposition. But such claims cannot eviscerate the context where contrast between the first creation and the last is expressed in such terms as the passing away of the old creation (21:1, 4); the arrival of a new city (21:2); a new relationship between humans, God, and Christ (21:2, 22; 22:3); the presence of new things (21:5); presence of the tree of life and the water of life (21:6; 22:1–2, 14, 17, 19); overcoming in the first creation to inherit in the new creation (21:7; 22:3, 12, 14); and a description of those who existed in the prior creation, but not in the new (21:8; 21:15). Koester's focus is contextually accurate without diminishing the presence of a polemic or the claim of Jesus's exclusivity.

The Genesis creation account that opens the Bible (Gen 1–2) and the creation of the new heaven and earth that closes the Bible (Rev 21–22) are end points of the same story, one past and one future. These end points depict both creation accounts using water and its related terms. These water terms are used numerous times in between the end points, together forming a well-defined theology of water. G. K. Beale says of these terms describing Jesus, that they "are figures of speech (merisms) in which the figurative point is to mention the opposite poles of something in order to emphasize the totality of all that lies between."[75]

Considering the various writers, languages, settings, the time span between one end point and the other, and the statements of Jesus, the presence of this inclusio seems certain and is hardly accidental.[76]

CHAPTER SUMMARY

This chapter has synthesized the prior three chapters making their findings more manageable. A brief discussion of *Chaoskampf* and polemic theology acknowledged the possibility of their influences on the terminology and concepts surrounding water and its related terms. The essential meanings of the biblical texts, however, remain unchanged. The presentation of tables and figures were designed to facilitate smoother handling of the materials from the prior three chapters, as well as to highlight the prominence of water across the Bible.

74. Hansen, "Alpha and Omega," 148–78; Linicum, "Origin."
75. Beale, *Book of Revelation*, 1055.
76. Beale, *Book of Revelation*, 1055.

This chapter demonstrated the existence of a biblical theology of water from the plethora of individual biblical texts supporting the thesis, and further emphasized through the literary device of an inclusio, established with end points in Gen 1–2 and Rev 21–22. Each of these bookends encapsulates the three components of the thesis which shows their interrelatedness.

All of this authenticates the thesis that there exists a biblical theology of water within the traditional canon of Protestant Scripture whereby water is an instrument that initiates physical and spiritual life, provides physical and spiritual cleansing, and sustains physical and spiritual life, and that these three aspects are interrelated.

6

Theological Ramifications

INTRODUCTION

Since the thesis has been validated in the previous five chapters, it seems important to make use of it by considering some of its theological ramifications. Those of immediate interest include the Holy Spirit, salvation, and baptism. Each of these three is connected theologically to the topic of water, and there also exists a thematic connection to water for each. These connections will be examined along with their implications.

THE HOLY SPIRIT

The Holy Spirit is one of the persons in the Trinity, along with the Father and the Son. Several biblical texts indicate the unity of character and purpose all three, in spite of functional differences.[1] Examples of this unity include Jesus instructing disciples to be baptized in the name of the Father, Son, and Holy Spirit (Matt 28:19). At his baptism, Jesus was physically present on earth, the Father's voice from heaven was heard calling Jesus his Son, while the Holy Spirit descended upon Jesus (Luke

---

1. The early church heavily debated the nature of the Trinity, but such is not intended here. For further discussion see: Plantinga et al., *Introduction to Christian Theology*, 109–46, 227–83; Reeves, *Delighting in the Trinity*; González, *From the Beginnings*, 261–90; Placher and Nelson, *From Its Beginnings*, 37–61.

3:21–22). The apostle Paul prayed to the Father about the Spirit's power that enabled Christ (Jesus) to indwell the believer by faith (Eph 3:14–19). Jesus promised the Holy Spirit would be sent by the Father (John 14:26). In each of these examples all three persons of the Trinity exist separately, yet function in consort with each other.[2]

It is essential to establish the presence of the Holy Spirit in God's use of water to initiate life, to cleanse, and to sustain life, in order to understand this portion of his work. It is also critical to corroborate that God's use of water is sometimes described as a work of the Holy Spirit (John 7:38–39). "Who is the Holy Spirit? And what does the Spirit do?" are important questions.[3] The first question will be answered by simply saying (again) that the Holy Spirit is God. The latter question has specific theological significance to this presentation, and the answer to that question will unfold over the next pages where it will be shown the Spirit's presence and activity looms large as it relates to the biblical theology of water.

The Inclusio

It is interesting that the Bible begins with God as its subject (Gen 1:1), then immediately brings into view "the Spirit of God" who was "moving over the surface of the waters" (Gen 1:2). In the other endpoint of the inclusio the water of life is present (Rev 21:6; 22:1–2), which Jesus said was the Spirit (John 7:38–39). The Spirit also invites people to "come" and "take the water of life" (22:17), which essentially is an invitation to partake of himself. Each of these scenes involves creation, first of the "heavens and the earth" (Gen 1:1; 2:1), and then of "the new heaven and earth" (Rev 21:1), which replaced the former ones (Rev 21:4) as was prophesied (Isa 65:17).[4] Each of these texts merits further examination.

Genesis 1–2

The Hebrew term for Spirit is רוּחַ, a term with a wide range of meanings, but which has been typically restricted in Gen 1:2 to terms such as "breeze," "breath," "wind," or "air."[5] Because this "spirit" has been identi-

---

2. Kärkkäinen, *Holy Spirit*, 15–16.
3. Allison and Köstenberger, *Holy Spirit*, 1.
4. Beale and McDonough, "Revelation," 1151; T. Alexander, *From Paradise*, 223.
5. רוּחַ, *NIDOTTE* 3:1073–78; *HALOT*, 2:1197–91.

fied in the text as "from God" (רוּחַ אֱלֹהִים), it is considered by many as not merely a force from God, but God himself, functioning as the Holy Spirit.[6] Such working of God through the Holy Spirit appears to be confirmed by Ps 33:6, which says, "By the word of the Lord the heavens were made, and by the breath of his mouth all their host." In this psalm the term "breath" is translated from the same Hebrew term, רוּחַ. Complementing this text, Ps 104:30 uses the same Hebrew term that has been translated "Spirit" and declares, "You send forth your Spirit, they are created." Creation then "is first and foremost a statement about God," and it involves the Holy Spirit.[7]

In this creative role the Spirit is said to be an "agent in *creation*, preparing the as-yet empty and unformed material world for its future construction."[8] That future construction is indicated when God said, "'Let us make man in our image'" (1:26). The use of "us" and "our" in Gen 1:26 certainly denotes a plurality. At this point in Genesis the only two "persons" definitively indicated are God and the Spirit of God (1:1–2), although some believe the "light" (1:3) refers to Jesus, which if true, would suggest the "us" and "our" references the Trinity.[9] Although arguing a different point, John Walton may lend some support to this "Trinitarian" view by agreeing that viewing the light (1:3) as a material object makes no sense.[10] John Sailhamer said, "The divine plurality expressed in verse 26 can be seen as an anticipation of the human plurality of the man and the woman. In that way, the human relationship between a man and a woman becomes a witness to God's own personal relationship within the Godhead."[11] However one may interpret the "light" of Gen 1:3, "creation is the united work of Father, Son, and Spirit," functioning in an interrelated manner to bring about God's purposes.[12]

Additional construction by the Holy Spirit is extended to the moment God "breathed" into the first human, giving him the "breath" of life,

---

6. Waltke with Fredricks, *Genesis*, 60; Allison and Köstenberger, *Holy Spirit*, 10; Kuyper, *Work of Holy Spirit*, 23–31; Richter, "What Do I Know"; Yong, "Creatio Spiritus"; S. Ferguson, *Holy Spirit*, 12–16.

7. Kärkkäinen, *Creation and Humanity*, 51.

8. Allison and Köstenberger, *Holy Spirit*, 15 (emphasis original); see also Sailhamer, *Genesis Unbound*, 120.

9. Esses, *Jesus in Genesis*; Steinmann, *Genesis*, 51–52.

10. Walton, *Lost World*, 54.

11. Sailhamer, *Genesis Unbound*, 155.

12. Kärkkäinen, *Creation and Humanity*, 51–52.

causing him to become "a living being" (2:7).[13] In this text, the Hebrew term for "breathed" (נפח) refers to blowing or breathing.[14] The Hebrew term for "breath" (נְשָׁמָה) means the movement of air, the breathing of God, or a living being.[15] The terms רוּחַ (spirit) and נְשָׁמָה (breath) may be interchangeable and "in most cases they are used in tandem to refer to the same thing," as in Isa 42:5 or Job 33:4.[16] Gordon Wenham calls the terms "a near synonymity."[17] If this interchangeability exists, we then see the Holy Spirit hovering over the waters prior to the separation of waters and the ordering of the heavens and the earth (1:2), assisting in the creation of the first human (1:26), and also breathing life into the first human (2:7).[18] This portrays the presence of the Spirit at the beginning before light was ordered on the first day (1:3), and at the end of creation week when man was made (1:26), just before God rested (2:1–2). One may infer the Spirit's presence and agency during the intervening days of creation, as well as his ongoing work of "fructifying" what was created.[19]

It is important to note that while the Spirit of God was present at creation and blows breath into the first human such that he became a living being, this connection of the one blowing and the breath being received may not be the impartation of the Holy Spirit to Adam.[20] Rather, many believe it is the ability to breathe that is "a key characteristic of animal life as opposed to plant life."[21] What the Holy Spirit breathed into Adam was at least the principle of life and breath so he could become "a living being" (2:7). This is the same "breath of life" attributed to all living creatures (Gen 6:17; 7:15). But because humanity was the only creature made in the likeness of God, it is argued that he was given more than mere life, but additionally, the gift of the Holy Spirit himself. The discussions in Romans and 1 Corinthians about the first and second Adams, the provision of the Holy Spirit upon Jesus's disciples and upon believers in

---

13. Allison and Köstenberger, *Holy Spirit*, 15, 333–34; T. Alexander, *From Paradise*, 41.
14. יָפַח, *HALOT*, 1:708.
15. נִשְׁמַת, *HALOT*, 1:730.
16. Allison and Köstenberger, *Holy Spirit*, 334.
17. Wenham, *Genesis*, 1:60.
18. Allison and Köstenberger, *Holy Spirit*, 334; T. Alexander, *From Paradise*, 41.
19. Allison and Köstenberger, *Holy Spirit*, 335–38.
20. Allison and Köstenberger, *Holy Spirit*, 334–35; Wenham, *Genesis*, 1:60; Westermann, *Genesis*, 1:206–7; Sailhamer, *Genesis Unbound*, 164.
21. Wenham, *Genesis*, 1:60.

Christ, and the promise of the Spirit's abundance in the new heaven and earth help support the view that what was provided in creation, but was lost by sin, is regained in Christ now, but fully realized in the eschaton.[22]

It is not my purpose to debate these details, and irrespective of which of these positions one takes, both agree that the Holy Spirit was present at creation. At a minimum it seems that what was breathed into Adam by the Spirit of God is the "life principle . . . energizing and supporting all life of the cosmos," and in this case, he directly breathes that into humanity demonstrating by his personal touch human uniqueness.[23] Man's origin was from the dust (2:7) and his sin would force him back to this source of his creation (Gen 3:19), which makes the emphasis of his creation in Gen 2 his earthliness, or "creatureliness," as one dependent upon God.[24] The breath of the Spirit into him was an infusion of physical life, and may have also been an infusion of the Holy Spirit himself. Either way, the creative nature of Holy Spirit is displayed in Gen 1–2.

The point of discussing the work of the Holy Spirit in Gen 1–2 is not merely to demonstrate his presence and work, or his position as part of the Godhead, even though his presence is "the biblical way of speaking of God in relation to the world."[25] It is to demonstrate the Holy Spirit's presence and work in conjunction with the waters of creation over which he moved when they were formless and void. It is also to identify the Holy Spirit as active in the creation process by which waters were separated and the heavens and earth were created, which included all life forms, humanity being a subset thereof.

Revelation 21–22

While Gen 1–2 clearly shows the presence and work of the Holy Spirit in creation, the other endpoint of the inclusio shows the Spirit completing creation, but "not a return to the original beginning."[26] Revelation 21–22 expresses the Spirit's creative role as having "continuities with the original creation," while also having discontinuities, including "new realities that have emerged in and though history" as he creates an entirely new heaven

---

22. Smeaton, *Doctrine of Holy Spirit*, 9–99.
23. Kärkkäinen, *Creation and Humanity*, 64; see also M. Green, *I Believe*, 21–22.
24. Sailhamer, *Genesis Unbound*, 164–65.
25. Kärkkäinen, *Creation and Humanity*, 65.
26. Fretheim, *God and World*, 9. See also T. Alexander, *From Paradise*, 66.

Theological Ramifications 149

and earth (21:1–4, 7–8; 22:3–5, 14–15).[27] The continuities include that "the new creation will be a bodily life and an earthly life."[28] The presence of God and his Holy Spirit is also prominent in both settings (Gen 1:2, 26; 2:7; Rev 21:6; 22:1–2, 17). The first living beings were clean following the washing of the heavens and the earth (in which they were included) with water (Gen 1:1—2:7), a part of such work being accomplished by the Spirit (1:2, 26; 2:7). Those in the new heaven and earth are also cleansed because they "washed their robes" (7:14; 22:14). This robe washing results in being led to the Spirit who is portrayed as "springs of the water of life" (7:14–17; 21:6), or the "river of the water of life" (22:1), or just "the water of life" (22:17).

The discontinuities in the presence and work of the Spirit will be seen first in the presence of "the spring of the water of life" (21:6), which elsewhere Jesus has called the Holy Spirit (John 7:38–39). In John 7:38–39 Jesus offered the water of life, the Holy Spirit, to those who believed in him, but in Rev 21 the Spirit is the inheritance for those thirsty who have overcome (21:6–7). There is both a reception of the Holy Spirit possible in the fleshly body based upon faith, and also a reception of the Spirit from inheritance once in the spiritual body. While the first reception requires faith, the second reception requires no faith as it comes after faith has been realized by sight (Rom 8:24–25; 1 Cor 13:12–13; 2 Cor 5:7). The first reception of the Holy Spirit in the physical body was surrounded by flesh, worldliness, and sin, prompting Jesus and the apostles to regularly caution against waning faith, drifting into sin, or allowing the cares of the world to entangle and destroy one's faith (John 15:1–7; 1 Thess 3:2; 2 Tim 2:4; Heb 12:1; 2 Pet 3:17; 2 John 1:8). In contrast, the inherited Spirit is for those who overcame these challenges (21:7), which in the new heaven and earth have been eliminated (21:4, 8, 24–27; 22:3, 14–15).

A second difference in the work of the Spirit in the new creation is his proximate material presence as the "river of the water of life" (22:1) which apparently supports the tree of life that bears different healing fruit monthly (22:2). There is a parallel in Genesis as the tree of life was placed in the garden (Gen 2:9; 3:22, 24), and a river was also present (Gen 2:10), but it was not called the "river of life," nor was its nourishment of the tree of life specifically indicated. After the sin in the garden, the tree of life became protected (Gen 3:22–24), but in the new heaven and earth it

---

27. Fretheim, *God and World*, 9.
28. Fretheim, *God and World*, 9.

appears fully accessible. After completing the creation of the garden, the water of life (the Spirit) was not highlighted within the garden, unless it (he) was the river flowing out of Eden (Gen 2:10). This perhaps was because the creative work of the Spirit was now completed and God had "rested" (Gen 2:2–3), humanity was "very good" (Gen 1:31) and without sin, and there may have been an overshadowing anthropomorphic presence of God "walking in the garden" (Gen 2:8).[29] The Spirit appears later when sin was rampant in the world (Gen 6:3) to judge, destroy, and re-create (Gen 7:22–23; Ps 104:29–30). He also appears in numerous other settings where he works at cleansing and sustaining humanity as part of his work of reconciliation and salvation. Several of these appearances will be discussed in the upcoming pages.

In the new heaven and earth the Spirit and bride invite the thirsty to the "water of life" (22:17), but Genesis offers no such invitation. "In Genesis the focus is on a garden with two human inhabitants; the concluding chapters of Revelation describe a populated city of enormous dimensions."[30] Thus, the story that started about a relationship with God for the beginning couple, concludes with multitudes of their descendants enjoying intimate relations with God as Father, Son, and Spirit.[31]

To summarize, the role of the Spirit in Rev 21–22 appears to be his continued companionship with believers, sustaining them, but in surroundings free from distractions (21:7–8, 22–27; 22:4–5, 14–15).[32] He is portrayed as a river flowing directly from the throne of God (22:1) and accessible to all who have overcome (21:7). Encouragement to drink of the water of the Spirit is a current pleading of the Spirit and the bride, the church (22:17). From the Spirit, the tree of life appears to be nourished and its produce continually heals (22:2). Parallels with Genesis seem obvious, and Terence Fretheim says, "The books of Genesis and Revelation provide a creational bracket for the Bible, and texts in between are a continuing witness to the purposive work of God toward this new creation."[33]

While the Spirit has been shown to be present and at work in both Gen 1–2 and Rev 21–22, the presence and work of the Spirit can also be seen in other water texts. In some of these, the Spirit is plainly present,

---

29. Kärkkäinen, *Creation and Humanity*, 80–81.
30. T. Alexander, *From Paradise*, 223.
31. T. Alexander, *From Paradise*, 23–24; 223–24.
32. T. Alexander, *From Paradise*, 23–24.
33. Fretheim, *God and World*, 9.

such as when Jesus offered living water that referred to the Spirit (John 7:38–39). In other texts the Spirit's presence is more subtle.

Other Pentateuch Appearances

If the Holy Spirit was present in Gen 2:7 breathing into the first human breath to make him a living being, then the Spirit was also present in Gen 7:22–23 when in the flood everything that had the breath (*ruach*) breathed (*neshamah*) into it died. "Thus, he blotted out every living thing that was upon the face of the land" (Gen 7:23). What the Spirit gave, he also took away. "You send forth your Spirit, they are created" (Ps 104:30) is mitigated by "You take away their spirit, they expire" (Ps 104:29). The Spirit does both!

Just prior to initiating the flood, God said, "My Spirit will not strive with man forever" (Gen 6:3), which shows the presence of the Spirit with humanity, and also at the inception of the flood scene.[34] The Spirit was present at creation, and he was present at the re-creation. What he established, he later destroyed. This presence of the Spirit is not stated in overwhelming and direct terms, but can be "inferred through inductive reasoning."[35] What is evident is that just as the Spirit was involved in creation, he was also involved in the re-creation, which included the withdrawal of the breath of life he had previously given. This withdrawal of life is an example of the Holy Spirit functioning in a judgment role.[36]

Numerous texts regarding the purification rites of Israel were previously cited, but of particular interest are those surrounding the tabernacle (Exod 29; 40). In order for these water-cleansing rituals to occur, the tabernacle had to be built and it was built by the power of the Holy Spirit.[37] Exodus 31:3 says of chief builder Bezalel, "I have filled him with the Spirit of God in wisdom, in understanding, in knowledge, and in all kinds of craftsmanship." This Spirit-directed enterprise included making the laver that held purification water (Exod 31:9), and the garments (Exod 31:10) that Aaron and the priests would wear after being cleansed by water (Exod 29:4). It was in these Spirit-made garments that sacrifices and offerings to God would first be washed with water (Exod 29:17). The

---

34. Allison and Köstenberger, *Holy Spirit*, 10.
35. Allison and Köstenberger, *Holy Spirit*, 10.
36. Allison and Köstenberger, *Holy Spirit*, 15.
37. Kaiser, "Indwelling Presence," 309; S. Ferguson, *Holy Spirit*, 18.

Spirit working through Bezalel would also create the altar upon which washed offerings were presented to God (Exod 31:9). There is thus a very close connection in the work of the Spirit and the use of water in, and around, the tabernacle of God, the place of Israel's worship. This work of the Spirit may also foretell the Spirit's work in the new Jerusalem in which the temple of God will be built with unspeakable beauty.[38]

What these water-related appearances of the Spirit of God in the Pentateuch demonstrate is that the Spirit works in creation, re-creation, judgment, and worship, and he works through humans using wisdom, prophetic utterance, powerful signs and wonders, and gifts given to his servants, enabling them to create, supply, judge, and lead.[39]

Joshua

Joshua was a man upon whom the Holy Spirit rested (Num 27:18–23). The book of Deuteronomy ends with the statement that Joshua "was filled with the spirit of wisdom, for Moses had laid his hands on him" (Deut 34:9), which references what occurred in Num 27:18–23. The spirit of Moses that Joshua received is clarified by Deut 34:10–11, which describes that spirit as prophetic (34:10), enabling the conducting of "signs and wonders," with "mighty power" and "great terror" (34:11). Such was obviously not mere human capability, but an indication of the presence of the Holy Spirit on Moses.[40] This Spirit on Moses would have been present at the turning of the Nile to blood, the crossing of the Red Sea, and obtaining water from the rocks, all water events. The Spirit of God was upon Moses, and that Spirit was also partially diminished in Moses in order to share with others, enabling them to assist Moses in his work for God (Num 11:17, 25–29). This same principle is applied to the transfer of the Spirit from Moses to Joshua (Num 27:18–23; Deut 34:9–11). It was by the Spirit dwelling on Joshua that Joshua led Israel across the Jordan River into the land flowing with milk and honey. Here the Spirit of God is involved in a miraculous water event, but that event also reflects God's gift of a promised land, reminiscent of the land promise to Abraham (Gen 15:7; 17:8), and anticipatory of its eschatological fulfillment of which the prophets spoke (Jer 24:5; Ezek 11:17; Rev 21:6; 22:1). While God through

---

38. Allison and Köstenberger, *Holy Spirit*, 301.
39. Allison and Köstenberger, *Holy Spirit*, 11–15.
40. S. Ferguson, *Holy Spirit*, 17.

his Holy Spirit has been active in creation by water, and in re-creation through the flood, he is also active in this water event where Joshua leads Israel to the promised land, just as the Spirit was active in the numerous water events in the life of Moses.

2 Kings 2

Elisha's request for a double portion of Elijah's spirit is not a request for a similar personality, or for enhancement of vigor or stamina. Rather, it is Elisha's request for the Holy Spirit's presence that was on Elijah to come even stronger on himself.[41] Elisha was essentially asking to receive from Elijah what Joshua received from Moses. The Spirit's presence on Elijah was expressed by Obadiah (1 Kgs 18:12), and further verified by the power with which Elijah performed miracles such as, predicting drought (1 Kgs 17:1), providing unending flour and oil (1 Kgs 17:14–16), raising a widow's son from the dead (1 Kgs 17:17–24), calling down fire from heaven (1 Kgs 18:38–39), and causing the Jordan River to part (1 Kgs 2:8). Elisha received this same power which was called "a double portion of your spirit" (2 Kgs 2:9), which was confirmed by another parting of the Jordan River by Elisha, just as had occurred with Elijah (2 Kgs 2:13–14).[42] Observers admitted to this transfer of the "spirit of Elijah" onto Elisha (2 Kgs 2:15–16). Elijah being taken to heaven in a whirlwind (2 Kgs 2:11), a premonition of the ascension of Jesus (Acts 1:9–11), preceded by his parting the Jordan River and followed by the Jordan parting for Elisha, confirms the presence of the Spirit of God with both Elijah and Elisha.[43] The Holy Spirit was on John the Baptist (Luke 1:15) who was said to be in the "spirit and power of Elijah" (Luke 1:17). Such seems another indication that Elijah had God's Holy Spirit dwelling on him, and it was this double portion that Elisha sought and received, and then demonstrated in his ministry.[44] The work of the Spirit dwelling on Elijah and Elisha appears similar to that of Moses and Joshua in that it involves prophesy, signs and wonders, and gifts that enabled them to supply others (1 Kgs 17) and to spiritually lead (1 Kgs 18).

---

41. Allison and Köstenberger, *Holy Spirit*, 23.

42. Allison and Köstenberger, *Holy Spirit*, 23.

43. Allison and Köstenberger, *Holy Spirit*, 23; Croatto, "Jesus, Prophet Like Elijah," 456–58.

44. Nantenaina et al., "Prophet Elijah"; Moore, "Finding the Spirit."

The Prophets

Isaiah connects a future pouring out of water to the pouring out of the Spirit (44:3–4). At this time great blessing will flow from God and faithfulness to God will be heralded (44:4–5). This sounds like Ezek 36:25–27 where in a future scene God will "sprinkle with clean water," and "put a new spirit within," which is called "my Spirit," at which time the fulfillment of the promise of land to Israel will occur. There is to be great blessing of food, productivity of crops, cleansing from sin, revitalization of cities, and abundance (36:28–38). In his end-time vision, Zechariah similarly says the Lord will "pour out" the "Spirit of grace and supplication" (12:10) which seem to be at the same time "living water will flow out of Jerusalem" (14:8). This is a time of salvation, victory over enemies, regret of sin and devotion to God, removal of the curse, and the Lord to be declared King and worshipped (12:10–14; 14:8–21). These prophets speak of water and the Spirit in the same context, and they are the same, even as Jeremiah equated living water with the Lord (17:13).

The work of the Spirit in these prophetic texts is part of a larger context in which the prophets discuss the Holy Spirit. The themes include the fulfillment of past promises, but primarily point forward to a future hope that is messianic in nature.[45] They speak of the outpouring of grace, forgiveness of sins, the removal of the curse, provision of nourishment in abundance, victory over enemies, devotion to God, worship of God, and the presence of the Lord as King. This message is not only messianic, but is equally eschatological even from today's perspective.[46] While the Spirit's work in the Pentateuch and the historical books of the Bible largely speak of the past and present, the prophets' connection of water to the work of the Spirit is yet future. To the prophets, the work of the Spirit then does not include prophecy, as such has been fulfilled, or is being fulfilled. But it does include the Spirit's judging, his ongoing work of sustaining life, restoration, and his re-creation of a new habitation.[47]

---

45. J. Hamilton, *God's Indwelling Presence*, 182–92; Allison and Köstenberger, *Holy Spirit*, 46–52; Kärkkäinen, *Holy Spirit*, 5–6.

46. J. Hamilton, *God's Indwelling Presence*, 186–92.

47. Allison and Köstenberger, *Holy Spirit*, 46–52; Kärkkäinen, *Holy Spirit*, 5–6.

The New Testament

In NT texts that connect water and the Holy Spirit, there appears to be a more direct inclusion of the Trinity, as opposed to the Spirit alone. The Father, Son, and Spirit are each named specifically in certain sentences (Matt 28:19). In numerous other texts, all three are identified directly, but sometimes not in the same sentence (Acts 10:44–48), or they are called by other descriptors such as "Lamb" for Jesus, or "water of life" for the Holy Spirit, as in Rev 22:1–3. Many texts comprise this broader category (Luke 3:21–22; John 1: 32–34; 3:1–5; 4:7–14; Acts 2:36–39; 8:29–39; 1 Cor 6:11; Titus 3:5–6; 1 Pet 3:18–22; 1 John 5:5–9).

By contrast, in the OT the Spirit seems to function without specific mention of the Trinity.[48] In spite of that, God (*Elohim*) is frequently mentioned alongside the Spirit, as in Gen 1:2 where he is called the "Spirit of God," or in Gen 6:3 where the Lord (*Yahweh*) said, "My Spirit shall not strive with man forever." Of note is the Spirit's presence without human knowledge, and his presence upon people without their desire or request. For example, in creation, prior to the existence of humanity, the Spirit of God was moving (Gen 1:2). Just prior to the flood God was prepared to remove his Spirit without human knowledge, request, or dissent (Gen 6:3). Afterward the human instrumentality of Noah helped accomplish God's task (Gen 6:11—9:17). Moses unexpectedly was given the Spirit of God (Exod 3:12; 4:1–9, 12; Num 11:17), which enabled his performance of many miracles, including the water events of turning the Nile to blood, crossing the Red Sea, and delivering water from rocks.[49] Even though Joshua was said to be indwelled by the Spirit (Num 27:18), and there is no biblical explanation of when, or how, this was accomplished, Moses's miraculous gifting from the Spirit was passed to Joshua only by God's direction, even though the instrumentality of Moses in this transfer symbolized the exchange, making it indelible in the minds of onlookers

---

48. Schafer, *Two Gods in Heaven*, argues for a binary God in the OT, claiming the Trinitarian concept was rooted in Second Temple Judaism, and was then usurped by Christianity to explain Jesus's incarnation. See also Huijgen, "Traces of the Trinity"; Plantinga et al., *Introduction to Christian Theology*, 82; Gulley, "Trinity in Old Testament."

49. Moses's reception of the Spirit is inferred from God's promises at his calling (Exod 3:12—4:13). That he received the Spirit is stated somewhat retrospectively (Num 11:17). No biblical text states specifically when or under which circumstances the reception occurred. Moses's resistance to becoming God's spokesman and Israel's leader indicates his lack of desire to be a participant with God's plan, which would include Spirit impartation.

(Num 27:18–23). There is no indication Joshua asked for the Spirit, but his reception of the Spirit enabled his leadership of Israel through the Jordan River and into the promised land (Josh 3). Although unrelated to water texts, many other OT characters received the Spirit with little explanation as to the circumstances surrounding their reception, and no indication of any desire or request for the Spirit (Judg 3:10; 6:34; 11:29; 13:25; 1 Sam 10:10; 2 Sam 23:2; 1 Chr 12:18; 2 Chr 15:1). An exception to the lack of human desire, request, or involvement was Elisha, who specifically asked for the Spirit (2 Kgs 2:9).

The NT texts connecting the Holy Spirit and water offer the Spirit as a gift, accessible from Christ who calls the Spirit "living water" (John 4:10–11; 7:38–39).[50] While other unrecorded factors may be relevant, Jesus seems to indicate this gift is available predicated on "knowing," and the overt act of "asking." He said, "If you knew . . . you would have asked him . . . and he would have given you living water" (John 4:10). He then added the element of "drinking" when he said, "Everyone who drinks . . . but whoever drinks of the water that I will give him shall never thirst" (John 4:13–14). The terms of receiving the Holy Spirit then seem to be linked in this text to knowing of the Spirit's existence, asking Jesus for the Spirit, and drinking of the Spirit.

Later, Jesus expanded the terms of receiving the Spirit, making it contingent upon one's desire for him, coming to him, and believing in him: "If anyone is thirsty, let him come to me and drink. He who believes in me, as the Scripture said, from his innermost being will flow rivers of living water" (John 7:38).[51] "Thirst" indicates desire; "come" implies approaching or seeking; "believes" is the present active participle of the Greek word, πιστεύω, which means to consider something as true and therefore, worthy of one's trust;[52] "drink" is the ingestion, or internalization, of the Spirit.

The terms Jesus sets for receiving the Spirit in these two texts from John 4 and John 7 may be summarized as knowing the Spirit is available, desiring the Spirit, asking for, or coming to, the Spirit, believing the Spirit, and drinking of the Spirit. It appears there is more emphasis on the actions of the individual to receive the Spirit than in the OT texts discussed above, excepting the request of Elisha.

---

50. Klink, *John*, 238; Padilla, *Acts of the Apostles*, 197.
51. Klink, *John*, 375.
52. πιστεύω, BDAG, 816.

The Spirit is also presented as a gift arriving at the time one is baptized in water (Acts 2:38; 10:44–48; 19:5–6).[53] Perhaps these statements in Acts reflect those of John the Baptist who proclaimed the baptism of the coming One would include more than water, as his baptism included the Holy Spirt (John 1:33–34).[54] In some of Jesus's last recorded words he commanded his disciples to make more disciples "baptizing them in the name of the Father, and the Son, and the Holy Spirit" (Matt 28:19–20). Thus, John said Jesus would baptize in the Holy Spirit, Jesus said his disciples were to be baptized into the Holy Spirit (concurrently with the Father and the Son), and Acts repeatedly places the reception of the Holy Spirit at baptism.[55] Based on these texts, it seems that in the NT reception of the Holy Spirit and baptism are inseparable.[56]

The reception of the Spirit is connected to baptism further by the apostle Paul who, after listing a series of sinful behaviors that keep one out of the kingdom of God, says, "But you were washed . . . sanctified . . . justified in the name of the Lord Jesus Christ and in the Spirit of our God" (1 Cor 6:11). Here he joins the washing (baptism) to the Spirit of God.[57]

In another passage, Paul says, "We would receive the promise of the Spirit through faith" (Gal 3:14), and that faith makes us his "sons" (Gal 3:26). This sonship is accompanied by reception of the Spirit as both are connected to baptism, in which one is clothed with Christ (Gal 3:27), united with Christ and fellow believers (Gal 3:28), and belongs to Christ as his heir (Gal 3:29).

In Titus 3:5–7 Paul speaks of the "washing of regeneration," and the "renewing by the Holy Spirit," which comes "through Jesus Christ," and makes believers "heirs." The verbal parallels with Gal 3, cited above, are numerous. Those of special interest for our purposes are "baptized" and "washing" (Gal 3:27; Titus 3:5) both of which reference water, the presence of the Holy Spirit (Gal 3:14; Titus 3:5), and "heirs" (Gal 3:29; Titus 3:7). Aside from the verbal parallels, the thematic unity of these texts speaks of being outside the promise of God then becoming "clothed with Christ" (Gal 3:14–27), and the strikingly similar situation of living enslaved to sin but "regenerated" and "renewed" by Jesus Christ, such

---

53. Marshall, *Acts*, 86–87, 206, 325–26; Padilla, *Acts of the Apostles*, 196.
54. Marshall, *Acts*, 324.
55. Padilla, *Acts of the Apostles*, 196.
56. Padilla, *Acts of the Apostles*, 196.
57. Thiselton, *First Epistle to Corinthians*, 453–55.

that in each case one becomes an "heir" (Gal 3:29; Titus 3:7).[58] The text is also similar to John 3:3–5.[59]

The apostle Peter links together the Spirit (1 Pet 3:18), the flood of Noah, and baptism (1 Pet 3:18–22). This text will be discussed in more detail under the discussion of baptism. John connects the Spirit to the water and the blood, all three of which testify together as witnesses that Jesus is the Son of God (1 John 5:6–8). John also records Jesus directly connecting water and the Spirit when he said, "unless one is born of water and the Spirit he cannot enter into the kingdom of God" (John 3:5).

Section Summary

One of the goals of this section has been to look at water-related texts to answer who the Holy Spirit is, and what the Holy Spirit does. He has been identified as part of the Trinity, which means he is God. In the OT, the Spirit is not clearly identified as part of the Trinity, but is frequently seen operating in consort with *Elohim* or with *Yahweh*, while in the NT he specifically and regularly is included with the Father and the Son, denoting his divinity.

As for what the Spirit does in these water-related texts in the OT, the Spirit is active in initiating life by creating the heavens and earth, which also includes his cleansing and sustaining life. This is evident in the separation of waters (cleansing), and breathing life into the first human as part of his creation (initiation) of the heavens and the earth. This human life is also sustained by the breath blown into it. In the NT, the Spirit also initiates, cleanses, and sustains life in the new heaven and earth. Those entering have washed their robes which references cleansing. The water of life (the Spirit) sustains directly and through the tree of life, and this new life is initiated without the distractions and sin of present life. This functioning of the Spirit is found in each bookend of the inclusio, Gen 1–2 and Rev 21–22. Other functions of the Spirit are noted in the texts in between.

In the OT, the Spirit creates, but also destroys, such as in the flood where both occur. In the OT, the Spirit empowers to facilitate the provision of purification rites and worship such as when Bezalel was empowered to make garments, the laver, and altar, all of which had direct and

---

58. Hutson, *First and Second Timothy*, 246.
59. R. Collins, *I & II Timothy*, 356–66.

regular connections with water. In the NT, the Spirit empowers to speak in tongues, praise God, and prophesy which occurred with Cornelius and the believers at Ephesus. In the OT, the Spirit enhanced wisdom, enabled signs and wonders, and provided gifts that facilitated creation, supply, judging, and leadership, as in the cases of Moses and Joshua enabling them to turn the Nile into blood, obtain water from rocks, and cross the Red Sea and the Jordan River. In the OT, the prophets spoke of the Spirit in messianic terms, and eschatologically, which Jeremiah and Zechariah termed "living water," which Zechariah said would flow from the new Jerusalem. Ezekiel spoke of this water flowing abundantly from the temple of God in that new city. In the NT, the Spirit is called a gift, but the Spirit also invites people to himself through knowing him, desiring him, asking for him or coming to him, believing in him, and drinking of him. He is also closely connected to water baptism. This brief summation does not address every work of the Spirit, but it does encapsulate his work in water-related texts, which are a subset of his broader work.

SALVATION

Finding a single meaning for the term "salvation" may be impossible. Considering its use and concept in the Book of Acts, Osvaldo Padilla says, "It is a multifaceted work of God presented from multiple perspectives." He goes on to include in the concept of salvation the forgiveness of sins, deliverance from coming judgment, being justified before God, being liberated from the power of Satan, and being granted inheritance in God's kingdom.[60] If that is a proper assessment of salvation in the Book of Acts, then expanding the field of observation to the entire Bible likely complicates arriving at a concise definition. Salvation has been considered "the beginning point of both the doctrine of reconciliation (atonement) and the doctrine of soteriology," and is "depicted with a number of metaphors in the biblical testimonies."[61] The ideas of rescue, renewal, and the completion of human destiny, as well as that of the cosmos, are bound up in the concept of salvation.[62] In very practical terms salvation is also defined as the bringing of "health and wholeness" the forgiveness of sins, "justice to the poor," and encouragement to "the downtrodden

---

60. Padilla, *Acts of the Apostles*, 197.
61. Kärkkäinen, *Spirit and Salvation*, 203.
62. Kärkkäinen, *Spirit and Salvation*, 203.

and weary."[63] Veli-Matti Kärkkäinen says that "the biblical tradition, both in the Old Testament and in the New, approaches the question of salvation from the perspective of the likeness of God's people to God. For this to happen, a change has to take place in the human person. Of course, this may entail a change of status."[64] To simplify this complex array of possible definitions, the term "salvation" is used herein with reference to being morally, ethically, and spiritually in alignment with God; living in harmony with God and under his blessing; and adhering and adapting to God's creative purpose for humanity. Salvation as a verb, or an act, entails a change to a "saved" position, as Kärkkäinen just described, but salvation is also descriptive of the position of one who already has already made such a change. Salvation then is not merely an act, but is also a descriptor of one's positioning with God at present that extends future into eternity. This is a gift that is spiritual and positional, and has Jesus as its source (Heb 5:9).[65]

Genesis 1–3

This salvation is first seen in the garden when the creation was "good" (Gen 1:25), and upon the creation of humanity it was termed "very good" (Gen 1:31). With a heavens and earth freshly cleansed by the separation of water, and human life arising from one in whom God breathed the breath of life, the first couple made in the image of God had every perk possible living in this pristine paradise. They were on the right side of God, morally upright, sin free, close to the tree of life, in fellowship with God, even co-regent with him over the garden.

Once sin occurred, separation also occurred as the first couple was evicted from the garden (Gen 3:22–24; Isa 59:2). They died spiritually and were separated from the tree of life (Gen 2:17; 3:3, 22–24; Rom 5:12, 17; 1 Cor 15:21–22). Co-regency with God was forfeited (Gen 3:6–7, 16–19), and humanity was distanced from God (Gen 3:22–24; Isa 59:2). Salvation appears to have been lost. Since Adam, sin by each individual person following has resulted in separation from God and ultimately in death (Isa 59:2; Rom 5:12–14, 17–18; 1 Cor 15:21–22).

---

63. Plantinga et al., *Introduction to Christian Theology*, 313.
64. Kärkkäinen, *Spirit and Salvation*, 356–57.
65. González, *From the Beginnings*, 296–97.

The sins of the first couple, albeit horrible and devastating on many levels, did not deter God's plan for humanity. In an act of grace, God made clothing for Adam and Eve, possibly from the killing of animals, which would be the earliest sign of a blood sacrifice for sin (Gen 3:21). He assigned husband and wife roles, which included Eve bearing children in pain and desiring her husband, while Adam named Eve (Gen 3:20) and was to rule over her (Gen 3:16). They both had to live on cursed ground, be engaged in difficult labor, cultivate and eat vegetables, and physically die (Gen 3:15–19). In addition, there was separation from God, the garden, and the tree of life (Gen 3:22–24). But the very fact of these changed circumstances, each determined by God, indicates God had not abandoned humanity, but still had a plan for humanity.

Genesis 3:15 portends a coming conflict between the serpent's descendants and Eve's seed, which would include all humanity, and a specific seed from Eve that would bruise the head of the serpent. Adam and Eve appear to be a part of the overarching plan of God for humanity, but little is said as to their relationship with God after their sin and expulsion from the garden. Bruce Waltke believes that through the making of clothing for the couple God restores them to harmony with him.[66] Gordon Wenham implies the same restoration as he considers the dressing as either the clothing of kings or the clothing of priests.[67] In either case, the first couple would have been restored to a relationship with God in which they functioned to assist God in his overall plan for humankind.

Eve attributed the birth of Cain to God's help (Gen 4:1), and viewed the birth of Seth as a replacement for Abel, and a result of God's effort (Gen 4:25). The comments Eve made at these two birthing incidents may indicate Eve took God's determination regarding her seed seriously (Gen 3:15), and had found reconciliation with God on at least some level. In other words, the salvation that was lost by sin may have been somehow regained, even though the circumstances surrounding these births greatly differed from circumstances in the garden. Terence Fretheim believes Eve is making a theological statement in Gen 4:1.[68] God has helped her create this man-child. The child is not called a baby, or even a boy, but a "man," which reflects God's creative power continuing from Adam to her, and on to Cain.[69] Because Eve takes credit for the first child, saying,

66. Waltke with Fredricks, *Genesis*, 95.
67. Wenham, *Genesis*, 1:84–85.
68. Fretheim, *God and World*, 60.
69. Fretheim, *God and World*, 60–61; Westermann, *Genesis*, 1:289–92; Waltke with

"I have gotten a man-child," it has been suggested trouble was sure to ensue for insufficiently crediting God's involvement, which Eve is more careful to do upon the birth of Seth (Gen 4:25).[70] If these scenes are fairly described, then it may be reasonable to conclude that God continued to work with Eve and Adam after their expulsion from the garden. Even though some of Eve's behavior may have been problematic, God nevertheless utilized Eve and Adam to accomplish his purposes which may speak to their restoration (salvation).

Genesis 6–9

After their removal from the garden, the salvific positions of Adam and Eve are uncertain and many questions are left unanswered. Nevertheless, the population of the world multiplied (Gen 4:17—5:32). Just as consequences followed the first couple when they sinned, the utter degradation of the world's population brought with it devastating destruction and re-creation through the flood (Gen 6–9). God saw "the wickedness of man was great on the earth, and that every intent of the thoughts of his heart was only evil continually," leading God to say, "I will blot out man" (Gen 6:5–7).

It seems that a line is drawn in Gen 6 between the entire wicked world (6:5–7) and Noah, who found favor with God (6:8). Noah was called a "righteous man, blameless in his time," and "Noah walked with God" (Gen 6:9). Based on our definition of salvation, Noah was a saved man since he was righteous and walked with God, but the rest of the world was unsaved or lost. The NT confirms that Noah's faith saved him from the flood, but also eternally (Heb 11:7). The world populace was destroyed, but Noah was saved, and it was water that functioned as the catalyst for both Noah's salvation and the destruction of the wicked world. First Peter 3:20 attests that Noah was saved or rescued through water (ὀκτὼ ψυχαί, διεσώθησαν δι' ὕδατος). "God did not spare the ancient world, but preserved Noah, a preacher of righteousness, with seven others, when he brought a flood upon the world" (2 Pet 2:5). The context in 2 Pet 2 is a discussion about God's power to eternally save those who are upright, but surrounded by wickedness like Noah and Lot (2 Pet 2:4–8). The writer concludes that God "knows how to rescue the godly" (2 Pet 2:9). Noah was not newly saved by the flood, as if he had previously been

---

Fredricks, *Genesis*, 96.

70. Waltke with Fredricks, *Genesis*, 96, 100–101.

lost and was suddenly rescued. Rather, his existing righteous life was corroborated by his obedience to God in building the ark as preparation for the flood (Gen 6:22; 7:5; Heb 11:7). His righteousness or saved status was continued or retained. While others died, Noah lived because he had been righteous and maintained his righteousness even in the face of cataclysmic disaster.

Genesis 16 and 21

When Hagar fled from Sarah, the Lord found her by a spring of water and ordered her to return to Sarah, and to be in submission to her (Gen 16:6–9). A blessing of multiplication of descendants was promised to Hagar (Gen 16:10), and it was announced to her that she was pregnant and that God had heard her cry of struggle (Gen 16:11). While Hagar sought emancipation from stressful living conditions, her solution was even less satisfactory.[71] God sent Hagar back to Sarah and it was her obedience to God that brought about her union with God's purpose.[72] Hagar acknowledged that God had engaged in a relationship with her by calling him "You are a God who sees" (Gen 16:13–14). While it may be argued that Hagar was not lost and in need of saving, it is my position that Hagar was lost, but not necessarily spiritually or eternally lost, because she was single, pregnant, homeless, and likely without any means of survival other than through slave labor or prostitution. God sent her back to Sarah where Sarah and Abraham were under God's blessing, and Hagar could enjoy food, clothing, shelter, and could give birth to the son of a wealthy man who would care for her along with her son. Moreover, God had directed her and made promises to her, aside from those made to Abraham and Sarah. Gordon Wenham notes that God did not promise to remove the oppression Hagar felt from Sarah.[73] Her return to the awkward situation with Sarah indicates her obedience to God, and her acceptance of his lordship in her life. Her return was a dramatic turnaround from the likely horrible life that lay ahead of her, so this was a salvation experience for Hagar.[74] It was a definite change of her present circumstance, and her outlook on life.

71. Westermann, *Genesis*, 1:241–42.
72. Waltke with Fredricks, *Genesis*, 253–54.
73. Wenham, *Genesis*, 1:10.
74. Wenham, *Genesis*, 1:11.

When Hagar was later sent away by Abraham at the insistence of Sarah (Gen 21:9–14), God appeared again to Hagar, who along with Ishmael was near death from dehydration (Gen 21:15–17). God directed Hagar to water which revived both she and Ishmael (Gen 21:18–19). God also made promises to her and was with Ishmael (Gen 21:20–21). In the absence of water, what appeared like certain death was overturned by God's appearance and direction to life-saving water, and by his presence with Ishmael and promise to Hagar. Hagar now has two life-saving events related to water, initiated by the hand of God. Again, significant change in status, and the presence of God, indicate both as salvation events.[75]

Exodus

Just as the water that saved Noah destroyed the surrounding world, the water that saved Israel destroyed their would-be captors when Moses led the Israelites across the Red Sea (Exod 14:1–31). Prior to the crossing, Israel had undergone purification through the offering of a Passover lamb, by a feast of the Passover lamb and unleavened bread, by smearing over the door post and lintel blood from the lamb, and by remaining indoors (Exod 12:1–22). The purpose of these observances are plainly stated as to cause the sparing of the life of Israel, when other life (Egyptian) was destroyed (Exod 12:23–27). In this Israel was obedient to God's instruction through Aaron and Moses (Exod 12:28). These purification rites and acts of obedience to God are part of Israel's salvation experience at the Red Sea. Those crossing the Red Sea are said to have been "baptized into Moses" (1 Cor 10:2). Moses directed Israel to "stand by and see the salvation of the Lord" (Exod 14:13). The term "salvation" is not used here for the departure from Egypt, but for the miraculous intervention of God saving Israel from the Egyptians in the sea.[76] It is this rescue or salvation about which Israel sang (Exod 15).[77] They sang, "He has become my salvation; this is my God, and I will praise him" (Exod 15:2). In this song the changed condition of Israel based on God's deliverance is emphasized.[78] God saved Israel to give them a reason to trust in him (Gen

---

75. Kärkkäinen, *Spirit and Salvation*, 356–57; Westermann, *Genesis*, 1:343; Waltke with Fredricks, *Genesis*, 296.

76. Meyers, *Exodus*, 115.

77. Meyers, *Exodus*, 119; Fretheim, *Exodus*, 163.

78. Fretheim, *Exodus*, 162–63.

Theological Ramifications

14:30).[79] That trust was tested immediately (Exod 15:22–25). Like Hagar, although God had saved, God did not remove all oppressive conditions of the surrounding environment.

Joshua

Joshua leading Israel across the Jordan River was a salvation event. Prior to the crossing Israel was told to "consecrate yourselves" (Josh 3:5). The water of the Jordan River was to stand still to prove God's presence among his people (Josh 3:7–10). The parallel to the Red Sea crossing is noted by Joshua (Josh 4:23–24). The local tribes trembled and melted at the power of God working on behalf of Israel (Josh 5:1). Defeat seemed certain for those tribes while Israel seemed blessed under the hand of God. To further dedicate themselves to God, once across the Jordan, Joshua circumcised all Israelite males, which enabled God to remove "the reproach of Egypt" (Josh 5:9). By any measure God was dwelling among Israel; there was personal and national alignment with God, which is in contrast to the tribes in Canaan. Such meets the definition of "salvation" as stated above.

2 Kings 5

The story of the healing of Naaman has already been discussed, but it is important to note that it too, is a salvation experience.[80] Naaman was not an Israelite (2 Kgs 5:1). He had leprosy, which in spite of his valiant military capabilities (2 Kgs 5:1) and his close relation to the Aramean king (2 Kgs 5:2–5), would seemingly result in his eventual ostracization and loss of status.[81] Naaman was also part of the Aramean army that opposed Israel, and therefore God, and had taken some of the Israelites captive (2 Kgs 5:2). Naaman was not a follower of God. At the instruction of Elisha, the prophet of God, Naaman was cleansed of leprosy in the water of the Jordan River (2 Kgs 5:10–14). Upon his amazement at his cleansing, he professed faith in God, and sought forgiveness for accompanying his

---

79. Meyers, *Exodus*, 115; Fretheim, *Exodus*, 160–61.

80. Cohn, "Form and Perspective"; W. Smith, "Naaman and Elisha."

81. Effa suggests this leprosy was not debilitating Hansen's disease, but more likely a skin illness such as eczema or psoriasis that left Naaman disfigured and in pain ("Prophet, Kings, Servants, Lepers," 306–7).

master to the pagan temple of Rimmon (2 Kgs 5:15–19). Naaman's experience was salvific from the standpoint of his physical cleansing, which was a major change of circumstances, but he more importantly came to faith in God, and sought forgiveness for the things he knew he would be forced to do that would dishonor God. This was a transformation of spirit and allegiance.[82] It fits the expression that "a change has to take place in the human person."[83] The enemy of God has become the servant of God.

The settings and names may differ but the general concept in the texts from Genesis through 2 Kings just reviewed portrays salvation connected to these water events. Adam was part of the heavens and earth which were created by water and he lived as a saved man until his sin (Gen 1:2–10; 2 Pet 3:5). Noah was a righteous man, but the flood that destroyed the wicked did not harm Noah, but enabled him to continue living in righteousness (Gen 6–9). Water appears as the dramatic focal point of the flood story, but Noah's obedience and righteousness also played a role and is contrasted with the surrounding world that lived in wickedness (Gen 6:5–8). On two occasions Hagar likely averted social and financial ruin and physical death, but by the intervention of God, who provided life-giving water, promise, blessing, and his presence, she was saved (Gen 16:21). Water was involved each time, and like Noah, it was accompanied by Hagar's obedience to God, which was exhibited when Hagar returned to submit to a demeaning atmosphere before Sarah (Gen 16:8–9).

Israel crossing the Red Sea and the Jordan provide two additional times water is associated with salvation, redemption, reception of a promise, and blessing (Exod 14; Josh 3). These episodes are also connected to Israel's purification, consecration, and obedience prior to and immediately following the crossings (Exod 12–13; Josh 3–4). In each of these situations, those on the side of God are saved, blessed, protected, and God is present with them. Naaman was transformed physically and spiritually by water, and like others, his obedience and faith were relevant. In each of these cases salvation is related to personal consecration, accepting God's lordship, and obedience to God, even when it is not easy. In each of these cases water was involved, usually as a defining marker of God's power. The answer to whether the water alone saves would have to be answered, "no." Water seem to be the setting, the attention-getting

---

82. Cohn, "Form and Perspective," 172; Effa, "Prophet, Kings, Servants, Lepers."
83. Kärkkäinen, *Spirit and Salvation*, 356–57.

device, the visible instrumentality, but the life-giving, cleansing, healing, life-sustaining power comes from God and it is always accompanied by obedience or faith.

Did all of these receive eternal salvation? Noah (Heb 11:7; 1 Pet 2:4–9) and Moses (Luke 9:30–33; Heb 11:23–29; Rev 15:3) were definitely saved eternally. Eternal salvation appears to be implied for Joshua (Josh 24:1–31). The Bible says little about Hagar, although she is remembered as a key participant in God's grand salvific scheme (Gal 4:24–25). Most of the Israelites who crossed the Red Sea displeased God and later were destroyed in the desert (1 Cor 10:5–6). By contrast, those who followed Joshua across the Jordan remained loyal to God throughout Joshua's lifetime and for the next generation (Josh 24:31). Naaman was physically cleansed and spiritually transformed (saved) (2 Kgs 5:15–19). Whether eternal salvation was involved for each of these may be uncertain based on the biblical record. But it clearly was salvation in the present moment, and each of these saved characters impacted world history in some significant manner. Adam and Noah served as the world's principal procreators. Through Ishmael, Hagar served to birth mighty nations who still exhibit tremendous world attention. Israel's two major salvific water events demonstrate God's work among his chosen people to sustain them and protect them, and they too exert significant influence in world affairs. Naaman's salvation demonstrates God's concern for non-Israelites' physical and spiritual welfare, which was later expressed through the conversion of Cornelius's household (Acts 10–11). Through all of these events runs a messianic thread leading to Jesus the Christ and his salvation for all, even if at times the path seems a bit circuitous.

The Psalms and Prophets

Like the rest of the OT, the Psalms speak of water and human harmony with God, God's presence, his blessing, inner peace, God's provision, cleansing, and sustaining of life. All of these are earmarks of salvation as previously described. These are contrasted with surrounding woes such as in Ps 1 where the one who walks, stands, and sits with the ungodly is contrasted with the one delighted with God, who is firmly planted by streams of water that support life-giving fruit. The result is that the former does not "stand" in the judgment and "will perish" (1:5–6), while the latter "prospers" (1:3). Similarly, Ps 23 contrasts the one shepherded by

God, resting by calm waters and green pastures where continuous feeding and water sustain, even in the "presence of my enemies" (23:5), and this life of blessing is eternal (23:6).

Psalms 42 and 63 speak of water quenching spiritual thirst (42:1; 63:1) and the drinker being in the presence of God, which is a salvation scene (63:2). It is contrasted with those who live otherwise (unsaved) and oppress (42:9; 63:9), revile (42:10), and deny God (42:11), and end up silenced by God (63:10–11). The one lives in harmony with God, while the other is distant and lost.

Psalm 46 references the city of God as being the place of a river bringing happiness (46:4) in the presence of God (46:5), who is the refuge and strength as contrasted with a world in upheaval and at war (46:1–3, 8–10). The refuge and blessing provided here is a salvific redemption from the chaos surrounding the unsaved.

The creation of the world is recalled in Ps 104, where water was used to create the habitat of God and his creatures, including humans (Gen 1–2). The psalmist emphasizes that God established the earth (104:5), and he controlled the creative process in which water was separated to provide dry ground (104:7–9). God used water to sustain the animals and plants (104:10–17). In this psalm, God is creating his personal temple as a place of worship.[84] It is a place where God has no opposition and disorder is absent.[85] God's presence is emphasized.[86] All creation is closely linked to God and his presence, and are part of his world free of sin.[87] But the psalm ends with the assurance that this world is not the place for sinners as they are to "be consumed from the earth" and "be no more" (104:35). This depicts a water-formed, perfect earth made ready for God and his creation, but its purity was marred by sin, which means it cannot remain. Those created beings with God are saved, while those living outside God's design are lost.

The prophets echo similar ideas as when Isaiah compares two paths. Those "who have rejected the gently flowing waters" (8:6) follow one path, and those for whom God is "a sanctuary" follow the other (8:14). Jeremiah is in agreement when he describes the two paths as forsaking "the fountain of living waters" for "broken cisterns that can hold no water" (2:13), and the path of those who repent and return to God to accept his

---

84. Fretheim, *God and World*, 6.
85. Fretheim, *God and World*, 43–44.
86. Fretheim, *God and World*, 26, 36.
87. Fretheim, *God and World*, 260–61.

leadership and receive his reward (3:11–14). Ezekiel says those with God will be given cleansing, a new heart, and abundance in a promised land (36:24–32), while those who reject him receive judgment (36:16–19). Jonah 1–2 is a graphic water scene in which the two ways are juxtaposed. One way attempts to block God and his message only to meet disaster, while the other listens and obeys to receive deliverance. Zechariah 13–14 describes these two ways as those gathered at the living water in new Jerusalem being blessed, and those in rebellion to God being annihilated.

The prophetic writers, like the psalmists, use water as part of their expression of a lifestyle of antagonism to God and his purposes that cannot survive, compared to a lifestyle of alignment with God and his purposes that results in life free of sin, blessings in abundance, and the presence of God. Those following one path are lost, while those following the other path receive salvation. Both the Psalms and the prophets seem to reference the present, such as in Pss 1 and 23, Isa 8, and Jer 2, where the two paths are presented as present reality. But, they also point to a future salvation that is permanent in such texts as Ps 104:35, Ezek 36, and Zech 13–14, where judgment occurs, the earth is cleansed, and living water flows eternally.

The New Testament

The NT advocates the same two-path concept as the OT, those who have been saved by water verses those who have rejected the water and remain unsaved or lost. It also promotes a present salvation, while also pointing to a future realization. Examples include Jesus offering living water to the Samaritan (John 4) and to those at the feast (John 7), Peter declaring salvation that accompanies baptism at Pentecost (Acts 2:38–40, 47) and in his letter (1 Pet 3:18–22), Paul indicating the Holy Spirit's washing regenerates and renews (Titus 3:5), and John recording birth by water (and Spirit) required for a present entering of the kingdom (John 3:3–5). All of these appear to be a present gift.

Like the OT, the NT also points to a future aspect of this salvation. Luke records the Baptizer saying Jesus would come to baptize in "the Holy Spirit and fire," in which he presents a judgment scene using the metaphors of a winnowing fork and unquenchable fire (Luke 3:16–17). This combines both a present and a future aspect of salvation that are related to baptism. John's reliance on the witness of water and blood (1

John 5:6) complement his record of the water and blood flowing from Jesus's side on the cross (John 19:34) to make his case for life present and eternal (1 John 5:11–13). Those already saved see a glimpse into the eternal nature of that salvation in terms of living water, or the river of the water of life (Rev 7:13–17; 21:6–7; 22: 1–4, 14, 17).

It may thus be said that both the OT and the NT speak a single coherent message that God uses water to express salvific concepts, both in the present and in the future, both temporal and eternal. Throughout the Bible the gift of salvation is not forced, but is contingent on positive human response toward God expressed as faith and/or obedience. Examples of this include Adam and Eve expected to live in accordance to God's instruction but losing their relationship with God by disobedience (Gen 2:17; 3:8–24), Noah building the ark (Gen 6:22; 1 Pet 3:20), Hagar returning to Sarah (Gen 16:9, 15), Israel following Moses and Joshua across bodies of water (Exod 14; Josh 3), Naaman dipping in the Jordan (2 Kgs 5), the Samaritan asking (John 4:10–14), feast attendees coming (John 7:38–39), Pentecost attendees repenting and submitting to baptism (Acts 2:38–40), the Ethiopian asking for baptism (Acts 8:36), washing one's robes (Rev 7:13–17), overcoming (Rev 21:6–7), and coming out of free will (Rev 22:17). In each of these water-related situations, salvation was provided by the gift or grace of God, but only for the one acting in faith or obedience, seeking to align with God.

WATER BAPTISM

The linkage of baptism to the Genesis flood was made by the apostle Peter in 1 Pet 3:18–22. The linkage of baptism to Israel's Red Sea crossing was made by the apostle Paul in 1 Cor 10:1–4. That these two apostles correlated Christian baptism to prior water events provides insight into the existence of a biblical pattern that helps establish a biblical theology of water. This pattern begins in Gen 1 and stretches throughout the Bible to Rev 22. By identifying key features and characteristics of the various water events that make up this configuration, the pattern and its theology are identifiable.[88] Of the water events that inform and comprise this arrangement, baptism is prominent in the NT and has arguably generated more controversy than the other events. Each event mentioned by Peter and Paul was salvific, and in each event God exerted his great power and

---

88. Beasley-Murray, *Baptism in New Testament*, 8.

demonstrated his presence. Such warrants a deeper examination of baptism and how it fits in the overall scheme of the Bible's theology of water.

The Holy Spirit and Salvation

The Holy Spirit and salvation, previously discussed, can hardly be considered with a blind eye to the numerus baptismal texts in the NT. Perhaps it should be restated that the numerous baptismal texts in the NT can hardly be discussed with a blind eye to the Holy Spirit and salvation texts previously discussed. The Holy Spirit finds association to baptism in such texts as Matt 28:19 where Jesus directed that disciples be baptized into the name of the Holy Spirit. This association was alluded to by Paul in Col 2:9–12 where he states the fullness of deity, which includes the Holy Spirit, dwells "in Christ," which benefit is received by those "having been buried with him in baptism." In Luke 3:21–22 the Holy Spirit descended upon Jesus at his baptism and this is alluded to by Peter while at the house of Cornelius (Acts 10:37–38). It was followed by Cornelius and his household receiving the Holy Spirit just before their baptisms (Acts 10:45–48). This connection is further cemented in Acts 2:38 where Peter's preaching at Pentecost promised reception of the gift of the Holy Spirit upon baptism, and at the conversion of Saul who was given the Holy Spirit at his baptism (Acts 9:17–18). It should be stated clearly that the Holy Spirit is God (Gen 1:2; Matt 28:19; Luke 3:21–22; Rom 8:9). He and his work are not confined to baptism in spite of his frequent identification with baptism.

Salvation is also noted in connection with baptism, which is no surprise since the Holy Spirit is present. Salvation is specifically connected to baptism in Acts 2 where Peter's Pentecost sermon directed baptism for forgiveness of sins (2:38), and Luke records Peter exhorting the hearers to "be saved" (2:40) through this process. Those who did receive Peter's message were baptized (2:41) and continued in the apostles' teaching (2:42) as Jesus had commanded (Matt 28:19), which was part of "being saved" (2:47).[89] Salvation is also specifically stated as the purpose of Peter's visit to Cornelius (Acts 11:14) in which Peter preached the gospel, resulting in Cornelius's reception of the Holy Spirit associated with his belief, repentance, and baptism (Acts 10:43–48; 11:18).

---

89. J. Green, *Conversion in Luke–Acts*, 127–32.

It has been said that the "connection of baptism to the resurrection makes baptism necessary for salvation."[90] Such a statement may, at least in part, be based on the fact that Peter's sermons at Pentecost and at the household of Cornelius in which the crucifixion and resurrection were central topics, were followed by directives to be baptized (Acts 2:37–38; 10:47–48). Although not presented in the same chronological order in Acts 10, Acts 2:38 cites the reason for baptism as being for "forgiveness of your sins; and you will receive the gift of the Holy Spirit." Both forgiveness of sins and reception of the Holy Spirit would seem to indicate one is saved.[91]

In Acts 10 Peter speaks about forgiveness of sins (10:43) and the Spirit falls prior to the baptismal directive (10:44–48). As he recounts the events at Cornelius's house, Peter claims his purpose was to speak words "by which you will be saved" (Acts 11:14), and he references repentance (11:18). While the order of events in Acts 2 and Acts 10 do not seem to match exactly, the elements are the same. In Acts 2 there was preaching on the crucifixion and resurrection (2:14–35), faith expressed by the hearers (2:37), directive to repent and be baptized (2:38) with the result forgiveness of sins, reception of the Holy Spirit, and salvation (2:38–41). In Acts 10 the preaching on the crucifixion and resurrection occurred (10:34–42), there was a directive to believe and receive forgiveness of sins (10:43), the outpouring of the Holy Spirit occurred (10:44–46), and a baptismal directive followed (10:47–48). In his recollection, Peter adds that his message was to bring salvation (11:14), the Holy Spirit was a gift (11:17), and repentance was involved (11:18). Joel Green considers Acts 2:38 as the prototypical response to the gospel, even though other texts seem to share only certain of the aspects mentioned. He believes "when one or another aspect of this response is mentioned in the narrative, the others can be assumed as well."[92] If that is true, then Acts 2 and Acts 10, although very similar already, offer a consistent message even though framed with slightly different sequencing.

Another text that claims salvific power in baptism is 1 Pet 3:21. It explicitly states "baptism now saves" with a foundational reference back to Noah (1 Pet 3:18–20). In each of these three texts (Acts 2:40; 11:14; 1 Pet 3:21), the Greek term σῴζω (sozo) underlies the English term "save"

---

90. E. Ferguson, *Catechesis, Baptism, Eschatology, Martyrdom*, 94.
91. Kellum, *Acts*, 133; Allison and Köstenberger, *Holy Spirit*, 448–49.
92. J. Green, *Conversion in Luke-Acts*, 127.

Theological Ramifications

in its various forms. The Greek term means to preserve, rescue, save from death, bring out safely, including saving from eternal death.[93] Such fits with the concept of salvation previously noted that describes it as a personal change, including a change in status.[94] It is, as stated above, being morally, ethically, and spiritually in alignment with God, living in harmony with God and under his blessing, adhering and adapting to God's creative purpose for humanity. Such is essentially the statement of the one who believes in Jesus as Messiah, trusts in his resurrection power, has repented, and has been baptized thereby receiving forgiveness of sins, and the Holy Spirit.[95]

It also should be noted that salvation is the gift of God that is not deserved and cannot be earned (Acts 2:38–40; Rom 3:24; 6:23; Eph 2:8). This concept of "gift" is also identified with baptism (Acts 2:38; 8:20; 10:45; 11:17).[96] While the Holy Spirit and salvation are associated with baptism, they are not baptism, and conversely, baptism is not the Holy Spirit or salvation. These three, however, are interconnected, and that relationship is vital to proper understanding of God's use of water to initiate life, to cleanse, and to sustain life.

Historical Considerations

Adela Yarbro Collins finds Christian baptism to have immediate roots in John's baptism.[97] She then looks behind John's baptism to find prior roots in the Levitical ablutions, in prophetic-apocalyptic traditions that had a forward-looking salvific intent, and even in the Qumran community.[98] While there may be some validity to Collins's perspective, its oversimplification fails to appreciate the broader theological foundation for baptism established by God's use of water in which one salvific event after another unfolds, such as with Adam and Eve, Noah, Israel, Naaman, Jonah, and others, as has been repeatedly described herein.

The Levitical ablutions, which Collins references and we have discussed in chapter 3, were primarily cleansing rituals which purified one

---

93. σώζω, BDAG, 982–83.
94. Kärkkäinen, *Spirit and Salvation*, 356–57.
95. Marshall, *Acts*, 86–87.
96. Allison and Köstenberger, *Holy Spirit*, 205–15.
97. A. Collins, "Origin," 28–32.
98. A. Collins, "Origin," 31–35.

spiritually to stand before the presence of God (Exod 29:4; 40:12). It is this cleansing concept, originating from creation when the waters separated eviscerating darkness, formlessness, and unproductivity (Gen 1:2–10), that is experienced again in the flood when wickedness was eliminated (Gen 6–9), and in the Red Sea crossing when Israel was said to have been baptized and their foes were destroyed (Exod 14; 1 Cor 10:1–4). These and other events foreshadow the Levitical cleansing where Collins finds potential baptismal roots. It is the sequence of these many water-cleansing events scattered over prior centuries that lead up to the Levitical use, and later the prophetic statements that Collins references. G. R. Beasley-Murray describes baptismal practices as going back to "immemorial antiquity."[99] He even suggests the efficacy of water to cleanse religiously was originally . . . connected with the veneration of deities resident in the water."[100] Whether Beasley-Murray is correct is beyond the scope of this investigation, but Gen 1 is the biblical starting point for water cleansing.

As a prophetic-apocalyptic baptismal tradition, Collins cites Isa 1:16–17 as an example: "Wash yourselves, make yourselves clean; remove the evil of your deeds from My sight. Cease to do evil, learn to do good, seek justice, correct oppression, defend the fatherless, plead for the widow."[101] Collins also claims Ezek 36:25–28 as an eschatological ablution image.[102] Collins is not in error in identifying these texts, but she isolates them, and fails to recognize them as part of the longer line of cleansing texts that began in Gen 1.

Collins properly identifies the baptism of John as the predecessor of Christian baptism. Some similarities of the two baptisms include that each involved personal repentance and offered forgiveness of sins (Luke 3:3; Acts 2:38), each specifically related baptism to salvation (Luke 3:3–6; Acts 2:38–41), and each claimed that earthly heritage had nothing to do with baptism, forgiveness, and salvation (Luke 3:8–9: Acts 11:15–18). But again, John's baptism was preceded by prophetic-apocalyptic baptismal or washing references, which was preceded by Levitical washings, which was preceded by various other baptismal acts starting at Gen 1. The proper setting and purpose of John's baptism, and Christian baptism, cannot be adequately ascertained without considering each prior water event or reference, not as isolated events or statements, but together as part of

---

99. Beasley-Murray, *Baptism in New Testament*, 1.
100. Beasley-Murray, *Baptism in New Testament*, 3.
101. A. Collins, "Origin," 28–32.
102. A. Collins, "Origin," 28–32.

the long list of interrelated salvific water events and messages unveiled throughout Scripture that comprise the biblical theology of water.

While Collins appears to somewhat segregate John's baptism from the prophetic-apocalyptic that preceded it, Beasley-Murray considers "its eschatological orientation" a "primary factor."[103] More synchronous with the water texts of the OT, Beasley-Murray sees John's baptism as a turning to God, or conversion, in which God receives, forgives, and receives one into his kingdom.[104] The flood, Israel crossing the Red Sea and the Jordan, Naaman's cleansing, and the Jonah story fit closely with this observation in that alignment with God, coupled with faith and repentance, result in the reception of God's protection and favor.

Howard Marshall describes Christian baptism as "an expression of faith and commitment to Jesus as Lord. Just as John's baptism had mediated the divine gift of forgiveness, symbolized in the act of washing, so too Christian baptism was regarded as a sign of forgiveness. . . . But Christian baptism conveyed an additional blessing . . . the Holy Spirit, and this gift accompanied water-baptism."[105] James R. Edwards says of the first three centuries of the church, that the "rite of baptism . . . remained essentially unaltered in the early Christian tradition."[106] He further asserts that "we find no debate over baptism in the New Testament. . . . Our earliest texts assume its essential role in the faith, thereby attesting to its early and widespread acceptance among Jesus followers."[107] Christian baptism then, while similar in some respects to John's baptism, was also different in other respects, and continued to be the uncontroverted norm for the early church.

Symbolism versus Reality

Water baptism has been a boiling pot of controversy for many.[108] One of the issues that looms large is the perspective that baptism is a mere symbol, versus a reality. John Armstrong says, "Early Christians . . . had little

---

103. Beasley-Murray, *Baptism in New Testament*, 32.
104. Beasley-Murray, *Baptism in New Testament*, 35.
105. Marshall, *Acts*, 86–87.
106. Edwards, *From Christ to Christianity*, 185.
107. Edwards, *From Christ to Christianity*, 186.
108. Armstrong, "Introduction," 11–13. See also Guy, *Introducing Early Christianity*, 217.

problem understanding how symbol and reality were intimately connected. They would never have spoken the way many of us do when we refer to baptism as a 'mere' symbol."[109] Yet, there *is* symbolism in baptism. Jesus foretold his death, burial, and resurrection by comparing them to Jonah's three days in the belly of a fish (Matt 12:38–45). Jonah is thus symbolic. The apostle Paul compares baptism to the death, burial, and resurrection of Jesus (Rom 6:4). Jesus's final three days are then symbolized by baptism. By analogy, baptism correlates to the Jonah story. Baptism is, therefore, symbolic of the death, burial, and resurrection of Jesus, which is also symbolized by the Jonah story. The symbolism is palpable. But baptism is not *only* symbolic.

What died in baptism was the "old self," our "body of sin," so we would "no longer be slaves to sin" (Rom 6:6–7). For Jonah, what died was Jonah's dismissal of God's instructions, and his captivity to the storm and the fish (Jonah 1:9–17). The burial of baptism is the immersion in water, for the believer as it was for Jonah (Jonah 2:2–6; Acts 8:36–39; Rom 6:4). It is the symbol of ending one existence prior to emergence to new life, but it is also the reality of that death and new life (Jonah 3:2–4; Rom 6:4–5). Based on Jonah's faith and repentance while buried under the water, what came alive was his commitment to recognize God's sovereignty and direction as the appropriate alignment for his life (Jonah 2:1, 4, 7, 9; 3:3). For the Christian, what comes alive is the same, the recognition of being "freed from sin" (Rom 6:7) and "alive to God in Christ Jesus" (Rom 6:11), living in righteousness (Rom 6:13) as its slave (Rom 6:15–18), which leads to sanctification (Rom 6:19). Baptism language contains a lot of symbolism, but it is more than symbolic. It is "a complex matter involving repentance, faith . . . and reception of the Holy Spirit and joining with the faith community. Baptism was the locus of this initiation, the place where faith and change were expressed bodily in physical washing and where the Holy Spirit was received."[110] It is this inner transformation that occurs in baptism, a salvation experience, that warranted Paul's description of those baptized into Christ as having "clothed yourselves with Christ" (Gal 3:27).

Just as John's baptism had an eschatological focus, so does Christian baptism. Everett Ferguson says, "The discussion of baptism as a likeness of the death of Christ leads into the consideration of the likeness of his

---

109. Armstrong, "Introduction," 14.
110. Guy, *Introducing Early Christianity*, 218.

resurrection and so to the eschatological dimension of baptism."[111] Symbolism surrounds baptism regarding events past, present, and future, but the reality is not diminished by the symbols. John expresses this duality regarding eternal life when he calls it both a promise yet to be fulfilled (1 John 2:25) and also a present reality (1 John 5:11, 13). He echoes Jesus, who said one could have eternal life now, but he also presented it as an eschatological hope (John 6:40). In his discussion of baptism in Rom 6, Paul speaks of baptism resulting in a present new life (6:4), but then speaks of the new life as future, "we shall live with him" (6:8). There is both a present sense and an eschatological sense surrounding baptism, as well as other biblical topics, and the abundant symbolism surrounding baptism should not obscure the realities, whether present or eschatological.

Gift versus Human Participation

Another area of confusion is that reception of the Holy Spirit and salvation are considered gifts one cannot work for, earn, or merit (Eph 2:8–9), yet the gifts are also said to be dependent upon one's repentance and baptism (Acts 2:37–38; 11:16–17). The apparent tension between these two concepts may needlessly lead to polarization, but the numerous OT water texts already cited herein demonstrate the cooperation of the power of God working in tandem with the actions of humanity to provide salvation. For example, Noah built the ark, Israel trusted Moses and crossed the sea, the priests washed with water, Israel trusted Joshua and crossed the Jordan, Naaman trusted Elisha and washed in the Jordan, Jonah repented, trusted God, and was saved from and by water. In each of these examples, the gift and the power were God's, but the expression of human faith was required to actuate God's saving power and gift his Spirit, forgiveness, and salvation. "Both the conversion and the baptism involve human and divine actions."[112] Joel Green sees the divine act as Jesus Messiah being the "necessary but insufficient condition for conversion," which "involves a journey with companions and choices as the converted experience an ongoing makeover with respect to their patterns of faith

---

111. E. Ferguson, *Catechesis, Baptism, Eschatology, Martyrdom*, 94.
112. Beasley-Murray, *Baptism in New Testament*, 35.

and life."[113] Howard Marshall sees baptism as "the outward accompaniment and sign of being inwardly baptized by the Spirit."[114]

Peter expressed that "baptism now saves you," but plainly attributes the power within the act to Christ's death that would "bring us to God" (1 Pet 3:18). Keith D. Stanglin states that it is not "that there is something magic in the water," but "that God chooses to use visible and tangible signs in creation to make his promises manifest."[115] Peter sees the power as "an appeal to God for a good conscience" based on the "resurrection of Jesus Christ" who has subjected all powers under himself (1 Pet 3:21–22). Baptism then unites one with Jesus's resurrection and exaltation.[116] Jesus spoke of being born again and linked the visible water and the invisible spirit as participants together accomplishing new creation (John 3:3–8). Everett Ferguson agrees with Jesus and Peter by saying, "Rebirth brings life (ζωή), and washing produces purification. These gifts that result from invoking the divine power are received in the water, but not from the water, for they are connected with the divine activity and the faith and repentance of the recipient."[117] Jesus's directive to make disciples by teaching and baptizing them did not hint of any tension between the outward human expression and the inward spiritual activity (Matt 28:19). There should not then, be tension between the gift of the Holy Spirit or the gift of salvation, and corresponding human participation, the two in tandem making effectual the gift. This was the case throughout the OT, and the same is affirmed in the NT.

It is important to recognize baptism not as a work of humanity by which one achieves salvation and the Holy Spirit, but as something to which one acquiesces. It is passive, not active. The term "baptize" is an aorist passive imperative in Acts 2:38, which means it is a directive to become baptized, or to submit to baptism, as opposed to baptizing oneself. In Acts 10:48, the directive to be baptized is an aorist passive infinitive, which similarly means to acquiesce to baptism, not to actively baptize oneself. This same passivity on the part of the one being baptized is expressed in other texts (Acts 8:38; 9:18; 10:47; 11:16; 16:15, 33; 18:8; 19:3, 5; 22:16; Rom 6:3; 1 Cor 6:11; Gal 3:27; Col 2:12; Heb 10:22). Representative of these texts, Acts 16:22 is translated by Joel Green as "have

---

113. J. Green, *Conversion in Luke–Acts*, 142.
114. Marshall, *Acts*, 206.
115. Stanglin, *Letter and Spirit*, 244.
116. Stanglin, *Letter and Spirit*, 245.
117. E. Ferguson, *Catechesis, Baptism, Eschatology, Martyrdom*, 99.

yourself baptized," which carries a causative or permissive force.[118] While L. Scott Kellum may agree to the passive nature of the baptismal act itself, he focuses on the prior causative consent required in Acts 22:16.[119] G. R. Beasley-Murray agrees that baptism is passive when he translates 1 Cor 6:11 as "you had yourselves washed."[120] While Kellum denies baptism is a salvific act,[121] Beasley-Murray more appropriately acknowledges that "forgiveness, cleansing, and justification are the effect of baptism in Acts 2:38; 22:16; 1 Cor 6:11."[122] He further identifies baptism as an expression of God's grace in which faith is a corollary, and in which identification with the death, burial, and resurrection of Christ occurs.[123] Beasley-Murray does not see an elevation of faith over baptism or faith as a mere vehicle to baptism, nor does he envision elevating baptism over faith, but a conjoining of the two, faith and baptism, resulting in the reception of God's intended blessings of grace, forgiveness, justification, and union with Christ, which is the goal of faith.[124]

Salvation without Baptism

The essential nature of baptism has been suggested above based on baptism's connection to the resurrection.[125] While the resurrection is one aspect of baptism, and while it may be sufficient to conclude baptism is essential to salvation, other considerations broaden the basis for such a claim. First, starting at Gen 1 and continuing through the Bible, the numerous examples of God or his Spirit working through water to bring people to salvation cannot be dismissed as independent or unrelated texts. Together they form a biblical theology of water whereby or wherein God initiates life, cleanses, and sustains life. Baptism is merely one interaction in this long line of salvific water scenes. Denying baptism's essentiality breaks with this very strong biblical tradition in which numerous examples herald the saving presence and work of God through

118. J. Green, *Conversion in Luke–Acts*, 72.
119. Kellum, *Acts*, 255.
120. Beasley-Murray, *Baptism in New Testament*, 163–64.
121. Kellum, *Acts*, 255.
122. Beasley-Murray, *Baptism in New Testament*, 272.
123. Beasley-Murray, *Baptism in New Testament*, 272–73.
124. Beasley-Murray, *Baptism in New Testament*, 271–75.
125. Beasley-Murray, *Baptism in New Testament*, 92; Ferguson, *Catechesis, Baptism, Eschatology, Martyrdom*, 94.

water. As it relates to baptism, Keith D. Stanglin warns that "the spiritual significance does not nullify the literal command."[126] Those rejecting God's water wind up lost, such as Adam in the garden, or the world in the flood, while those embracing the water are saved, as with Adam prior to sin, Noah in the flood, Israel in their crossing the Sea and the Jordan, the Levitical priests and their offerings, Naaman, and Jonah. Although lacking empirical proof, I am convinced that those who reject baptism as essential to salvation do so because they have not been apprised of this repetitive and powerful messaging of water as a salvific instrument that God systematically used starting in Gen 1 and continuing to Rev 22.

Second, on a more granular level, we have already discussed the gift and presence of the Holy Spirit at baptism (Acts 2:38; 10:43–48).[127] If the means to receiving salvation and the Holy Spirit is baptism, and such is claimed in the NT (Acts 2:38; 19:5–6; 22:16; 1 Pet 3:21), then expecting salvation and the Holy Spirit without baptism seems little more than a whimsical wish. The first Christians never considered coming to Christ, expecting the Spirit, or seeking salvation without baptism, and such a notion seems to have arisen only centuries later.[128] In discussing the necessity of baptism, G. R. Beasley-Murray asks about the necessity of church membership, the Lord's Supper, preaching, or the Bible, saying, "Such matters are self-evident for they belong to the very structure of the Christian life."[129] His point was that baptism is also just as essential because "it meant committal to obedience to Christ."[130] Along this same line of reasoning, we have already discussed that forgiveness of sins occurs at baptism (Acts 2:28; 10:43–48; 22:16; Rom 6:3–23; 1 Pet 3:18–22), and that those baptized are considered saved whether such is explicitly stated (Acts 2:38–40; 11:14; 22:16; 1 Pet 3:21), or implied (Acts 3:19; 8:39; 16:15, 31–34; 19:4–7; Rom 6:3–11; 1 Cor 6:11; Gal 3:27; Eph 4:4–6; 5:26; Col 2:9–12; Titus 3:3–5; Heb 10:22). Baptismal salvation in the NT is similar to water salvation in the OT, and is built upon that OT tradition, becoming part of it, with Peter citing Noah's salvation by water as a prototype of Christian baptism (1 Pet 3:18–22) and Paul citing Israel's baptism in the Red Sea as the delivering mechanism by which they were saved. In the

---

126. Stanglin, *Letter and Spirit*, 27.

127. Baptism here presupposes faith and repentance.

128. Edwards, *From Christ to Christianity*, 185–87; Beasley-Murray, *Baptism in New Testament*, 298.

129. Beasley-Murray, *Baptism in New Testament*, 297.

130. Beasley-Murray, *Baptism in New Testament*, 298.

Theological Ramifications

first sermon at Pentecost, Peter preached to "be saved" (Acts 2:40) and in response "those who had received his word were baptized" (Acts 2:41).

This topic often creates antagonism. Exegetical or doctrinal hair-splitting can fracture adherents of common faith. Such is not intended. Without attempting to pinpoint any exact moment when one crosses the line from lost to saved, which is surely within God's prerogative, it remains that in the NT water baptism is stated as offering forgiveness of sins and the gift of the Holy Spirit; it is the place that the old person of sin dies and new life in Christ begins; it offers hope based on the resurrection of Christ; and therefore, it is said to save (Acts 2:38–40; 22;16; Rom 6:3–23; Col 2:9–12; 1 Pet 3:18–22). Including these NT statements about baptism into the realization that baptism is one of a long line of texts in which God has saved by water leads me to conclude that baptism is necessary for salvation. Could God provide salvation without baptism? It appears he did just that with Enoch (Gen 5:22–24) and the thief on the cross (Luke 23:39–43). Aside from these exceptional cases, in his wisdom God purposefully chose baptism as the means by which to accomplish his task of initiating life, cleansing, and sustaining life just as he did from the beginning. God could have saved Noah by means other than the floodwater, or saved Israel without a Red Sea baptism, but he didn't. To quote again a concise and accurate statement, "The spiritual significance does not nullify the literal command."[131]

CHAPTER SUMMARY

For reasons known only to God, God has chosen water as an instrument through which he initiates life, cleanses, and sustains life. A pattern of water events that starts in Gen 1 and extends to Rev 22 reveals a biblical theology of water that showcases God's work of initiating, cleansing, and sustaining life. Having recognized this divine scheme, it has seemed important to consider its ramifications for other doctrines or concepts, which have included the Holy Spirit, salvation, and baptism. Certainly, many others could have been included.

In each of the water events, the Holy Spirit was present, whether being specifically named (Gen 1:2) or as part of the Trinity (2 Kgs 5:15, 17). His power was exerted in some events where he gave life (Gen 2:7), and in other events he destroyed the enemy (Gen 6:13, 17; 7:21–23). In

---

131. Stanglin, *Letter and Spirit*, 27.

other cases he provided sustenance to his followers (Gen 21:15–21), and in many events he demonstrated his presence in more than one of these expressions (Gen 1–2; 6–9; Exod 14–15; Josh 3; 2 Kgs 5; Jon 1–2). Typical in these water events salvation resulted, not necessarily eternal salvation, but some form of salvation, such as rescue from an enemy (Gen 14), or from the result of sin (Jon 1–2). Since the Holy Spirit was involved, being aligned with him one might expect salvation to be part of the equation.

In the NT, the well-developed pattern of water events tends to take the form of baptism. The continuity of baptism to the OT pattern of water events is emphasized by Peter who connects baptism to the ancient water event of Noah and the flood (1 Pet 3:18–22), and by Paul who connects baptism to the Israelite Red Sea crossing (1 Cor 10:1–4). It is believed that controversy surrounds baptism largely because it has been isolated as a stand-alone doctrine or event, and has not been recognized as part of a larger pattern through which God has operated since the beginning, in spite of apostolic connection to such.

The NT repeatedly states in various forms that baptism saves and that the Holy Spirit is received and accessed through baptism (Matt 28:19; Luke 3:16; John 3:3–15; Acts 2:38–41; 10:43–48; 22:16; 1 Cor 6:11; Eph 4:4; Col 2:9–12; Titus 3:5–8). Romans 6 cites baptism as the act in which believers identify with the death, burial, and resurrection of Jesus Christ, and in which sin is abolished and new life begins that is both present and eternal. The giving of life and its eternal nature is heralded by Peter, who also connects baptism with the resurrection of Jesus (1 Pet 3:21–22).

Baptism has been considered by some to be a symbol, and it is, but it is more than a symbol. The Jonah story was a symbol of the death, burial, and resurrection of Christ, but it was no less real. Baptism proclaims the same, and it is also real. Symbol and reality merge in baptism.

Whether baptism is essential for salvation may not be the right question to be asking. Such a question may fail to see the close inner workings of grace, faith, repentance, and baptism. Instead, the question may be asked as to why one would not want to obey Jesus (Matt 28:19), receive forgiveness of sins and the gift of the Holy Spirit (Acts 2:38; 22:16), live a new life free of sin (Rom 6:6–7), and be saved just as Noah was saved by water (1 Pet 3:18–22). One may also ask why one would accept salvation occurring by water throughout many OT events, but then decline the same in the NT, where baptism is but one in a long line of salvific water events God has used to initiate, cleanse, and sustain life, starting in Gen 1.

7

Summary

THE INITIAL THESIS STATES that there exists a biblical theology of water within the traditional canon of Protestant Scripture whereby water is an instrument that initiates physical and spiritual life, provides physical and spiritual cleansing, and sustains physical and spiritual life, and that these three aspects are interrelated, forming a biblical theology of water. A shorter thesis was also offered which states that God uses water to initiate, cleanse, and sustain life, and these three constructs interrelate forming a biblical theology of water. It was further claimed that an inclusio exists, bookended with Gen 1–2 and Rev 21–22, and that this supports a biblical theology of water that extends from the beginning of the Bible to its end.

As this research developed, numerous biblical texts provided examples of this work of God using water to accomplish his purposes. Beginning in Gen 1 water comes into focus at creation as "the earth was formless and void, and darkness was over the surface of the deep, and the Spirit of God was moving over the face of the waters" (Gen 1:2). The next image of water is its organization by separation, providing upper and lower waters, and pooling to reveal dry land and to create seas (Gen 1:6–10). In this creation by water, the formerly unproductive "heavens and earth," described as "formless and void, and darkness" (Gen 1:1–2), were transformed by "light," "separation," and "gathering" (Gen 1:3–10), to prepare them for usefulness. That preparation for God's purposes is explained further by the entire creation of the "heavens and earth," which includes humanity (Gen 1:1—2:1). The transforming waters that initiated life in Gen 1 also provided a demonstration of the cleansing of the earth by the separation of waters. Genesis 2 presents water as also sustaining life by watering its vegetation (2:4–6, 10). Genesis 1–2 then offer an example of each component of the thesis that God uses water to initiate life, cleanse, and sustain life.

Because of the antiquity of the creation story, it was deemed necessary to consider the secular creation stories of the surrounding cultures, and to discuss mainly Egyptian and Mesopotamian stories that also involved water in creation. Similarities and differences were noted within the theory of *Chaoskampf*, and were largely dismissed as being directly relevant based upon investigations of recent scholarship. Polemic theology was also considered and it was noted to have likely been present in at least some of the examples, not just in the creation account, but also in other water-related texts. It was suggested that the presence or absence of polemic theology did not change the positive affirmation of Scripture, so while it is interesting to locate it, and be aware of its use, in the end it fails to change the biblical story.

Other examples proving the thesis continue throughout the Bible in such water-laden examples as Noah and the flood (Gen 6–9); the two scenes with Hagar where water was present (Gen 16; 21); Isaac finding a wife at the water well (Gen 24); God's blessing to Isaac being declared at a well (Gen 26); Isaac negotiating a peace treaty with the Philistines at a well (Gen 26); Jacob seeking and finding a wife at a well (Gen 28); preserving Moses, deliverer of Israel, in the Nile (Exod 2); Moses turning water to blood (Exod 7); Israel being saved by crossing the Red Sea (Exod 14); Israel being saved from death by dehydration through God's miraculous supply of water on at least two occasions (Exod 15; 17); Israel using water for purification under the Levitical priesthood (Exod 20–40); Israel crossing the Jordan to enter the promised land (Josh 3); Elijah being taken to heaven after miraculously crossing the Jordan and Elisha being blessed by God at that crossing with Elijah, and once without him (2 Kgs 2); Naaman being cleansed of leprosy by dipping in the Jordan (2 Kgs 5); and Jonah being saved from the water (Jonah 1–2). These examples do not include the numerous water texts in the Psalms or the Prophets, the totality of which makes the OT rife with examples and references to God using water to initiate, cleanse, and sustain life.

The NT is also full of the same, including John's claim to baptism for forgiveness of sins (Luke 3:3); Jesus being baptized to announce his

Summary

transformation into his new messianic role (Luke 3:21–22); Jesus turning water to wine announcing the inadequacy of the Jewish system and the arrival of a new way (John 2); Jesus announcing rebirth in water and spirit as the entrée into the kingdom (John 3); Jesus offering living water to the Samaritan woman (John 4); Jesus healing at the pool of Bethesda (John 5); Jesus walking on water, demonstrating his power over it (John 6); Jesus offering living water to feast attendees (John 7); Jesus healing at the pool of Siloam (John 9); water flowing from Jesus's side, reflecting the purification of the world (John 19); Jesus associating water baptism with discipleship (Matt 28:19); Peter offering baptism for forgiveness of sins and the gift of the Holy Spirit (Acts 2); Peter claiming baptism saves (1 Pet 3; Acts 10–11); Ananias telling Paul baptism washes away sin (Acts 22); Paul explaining baptism as the place of identification with the death, burial, and resurrection of Jesus, as well as the place where sin dies and new life begins (Rom 6); John describing the spring of the water of life in the new Jerusalem (Rev 21) and as the river of the water of life (Rev 22).

Other OT and NT texts could have been explored, but these were deemed sufficient to demonstrate the Bible, both the OT and the NT, abounds with incidents and references to water in which God initiates, cleanses, and sustains life. The presence of the water texts in Gen 1–2 and Rev 21–22, the endpoints of the inclusio, along with all the many texts in between, help establish the existence of the inclusio and help establish that a biblical theology of water exists. This theology overlaps and informs other biblical or spiritual concepts, with ramifications to the presence and work of the Holy Spirit, to the locus of, or access to, salvation, and to Christian baptism in terms of its background, meaning, and purpose.

It is essential that this work is not seen as a sneaky way to expound a particular baptismal dogma. Instead, what is presented identifies a multi-millennial old mechanism used by God to accomplish some of his purposes. It started at creation, and continues until today, with a yet future use of water forecast in the eschaton. In this biblical theology of water God has regularly used water to initiate, cleanse, and sustain life. In some cases he performs only one of these tasks, but in others he often performs two of these tasks, or even all three. While many of these events and references are historical and we view them in a past tense, baptism is God's present tense water instrument designed to accomplish his present purposes, but its effect is forward looking to a new Jerusalem where even more water is forecast, and such is pointed to by other prophetic or eschatological texts (Ezek 47; Zech 14; Rev 21–22). It is important to envision God's present use of water, baptism, as one event in the long line of other water events, just as Peter linked it to the flood (1 Pet 3:18–22) and Paul linked it to Israel crossing the Red Sea (1 Cor 10:1–4). It should not, then, be isolated from those many other water events of the Bible, either to exalt it or to diminish it.

This work began with a quote from Graham Cole that is worth repeating. Cole said:

> Biblical theology as a discipline traces the great themes of Scripture from their first appearance in the canon to the last, whether the key term (or terms) appears or the idea does. Key ideas such as covenant, election, sacrifice, kingdom, the land, inheritance, and presence, among many others, become the lens through which the unfolding biblical story is viewed.[1]

It is not advocated that the biblical theology of water is the lens through which the Bible should be exclusively viewed. But at the same time, it cannot be ignored. Awareness that such a lens exists demands that it is included among other lenses through which Scripture is viewed. Cole believes it is important one knows what one sees in Scripture, and states that "biblical theology . . . helps me to know what I see."[2] It is my hope that this book will help the reader to see through the lens of the biblical theology of water, and to know what one sees.

---

1. G. Cole, *God Who Became Human*, 115.
2. G. Cole, *God Who Became Human*, 173.

Bibliography

Abernathy, Andrew T. *The Book of Isaiah and God's Kingdom: A Thematic Approach.* New Studies in Biblical Theology 40. Downers Grove, IL: IVP Academic, 2016.
Achtemeier, Paul J. *1 Peter.* Hermeneia. Minneapolis: Fortress, 1996.
Albrektson, Bertil. *History and the Gods.* Winona Lake, IN: Eisenbrauns, 2011.
Alexander, Ralph H. *Ezekiel.* Rev. ed. Expositors Bible Commentary. Grand Rapids: Zondervan, 2010.
Alexander, T. Desmond. *From Paradise to the Promised Land: An Introduction to the Pentateuch.* 4th ed. Grand Rapids: Baker Academic, 2022.
Allison, Gregg R., and Andreas J. Köstenberger. *The Holy Spirit.* Theology for the People of God. Nashville: B&H Academic, 2020.
Amit, Yairah. "Hidden Polemic in the Conquest of Dan: Judges XVII–XVIII." *VT* 40 (1990) 4–20.
Anderson, Joel Edmund. "Jonah's Peculiar Re-Creation." *BTB* 41 (2011) 179–88.
Ansberry, Christopher B. "Wisdom and Biblical Theology." In *Interpreting Old Testament Wisdom Literature,* edited by David G. Firth and Lindsay Wilson, 174–93. Downers Grove, IL: IVP Academic, 2017.
Anthony-Llorens, Rafael. "'Water from the Rock': A Comparative Analysis of Exodus 17:1–7 and Numbers 20:1–13." Master's thesis, Florida Baptist Theological College, 2008.
Armstrong, John H. "Introduction." In *Understanding Four Views on Baptism,* edited by Paul E. Engle and John H. Armstrong, 11–22. Counterpoints: Church Life. Grand Rapids: Zondervan, 2007.
Arnold, Bill T., and Brent A. Strawn, eds. *The World around the Old Testament: The People and Places of the Ancient Near East.* Grand Rapids: Baker Academic, 2016.
Averbeck, Richard E. "A Literary Day, Inter-Textual, and Contextual: Reading of Genesis 1–2." In *Reading Genesis 1–2: An Evangelical Conversation,* edited by J. Daryl Charles, 7–34. Peabody, MA: Hendrickson, 2013.
Baker, David W. "Isaiah." In *Zondervan Illustrated Bible Backgrounds Commentary,* edited by John H. Walton, 4:2–227. Grand Rapids: Zondervan, 2009.
Ballentine, Debra Scoggins. *The Conflict Myth and the Biblical Tradition.* Oxford: Oxford University Press, 2015.
Balogh, Csaba. "Historicising Interpolations in the Isaiah-Memoir." *VT* 64 (2014) 519–38.

Baltzer, Klaus. *Deutero-Isaiah: A Commentary on Isaiah 40–55*. Translated by Margaret Kohl. Hermeneia. Minneapolis: Fortress, 2001.

Baron, David. *Zechariah: Visions and Prophecy*. Kansas City: Forerunner, 2012.

Barrick, William D. "Living A New Life: Old Testament Teaching about Conversion" *Masters Seminary Journal* 11 (2000) 19–38.

Batto, Bernard F. *In the Beginning: Essays on Creation Motifs in the Ancient Near East and the Bible*. Winona Lake, IN: Eisenbrauns, 2013.

Bauer, David R. *The Gospel of the Son of God: An Introduction to Matthew*. Downers Grove, IL: IVP Academic, 2019.

Beal, Lissa M. Wray. *Joshua*. The Story of God Bible Commentary 6. Grand Rapids: Zondervan Academic, 2019.

Beale, G. K. *The Book of Revelation*. NIGTC. Grand Rapids: Eerdmans, 1999.

———. "Eden, the Temple, and the Church's Mission in the New Creation." *JETS* 48 (2005) 5–31.

Beale, G. K., and Mitchell Kim. *God Dwells among Us: A Biblical Theology of the Temple* Downers Grove, IL: IVP Academic, 2014.

Beale, G. K., and Sean McDonough. "Revelation." In *Commentary on the New Testament Use of the Old Testament*, edited by G. K. Beale and D. A. Carson, 1081–161. Grand Rapids: Baker Academic, 2007.

Beasley-Murray, G. R. *Baptism in the New Testament*. Grand Rapids: Eerdmans, 1962.

Best, Ernest. *A Critical and Exegetical Commentary on Ephesians*. ICC. London: Bloomsbury T. & T. Clark, 1998.

Blaising, Craig A., and Carmen S. Hardin, eds. *Psalms 1–50*. ACCS: Old Testament 7. Downers Grove, IL: IVP, 2008.

Block, Daniel L. *Covenant: The Framework of God's Grand Plan of Redemption*. Grand Rapids: Baker Academic, 2021.

Blumenthal, Fred. "Jonah, the Reluctant Prophet: Prophecy and Allegory." *JBQ* 35 (2007) 103–8.

Bock, Darrell L. *Ephesians: Introduction and Commentary*. TNTC. Downers Grove, IL: IVP Academic, 2019.

Bockmuehl, Markus. "The Baptism of Jesus as 'Super-Sacrament' of Redemption." *Theology* 115 (2012) 83–91.

Boda, Mark J. *Zechariah*. NICOT. Grand Rapids: Eerdmans, 2016.

Bodi, Daniel. "Ezekiel." In *Zondervan Illustrated Bible Backgrounds Commentary*, edited by John H. Walton, 4:400–517. Grand Rapids: Zondervan, 2009.

Brown, Francis, et al. *The Brown-Driver-Briggs Hebrew and English Lexicon*. Reprint, Peabody, MA: Hendrickson, 2018. First published 1906.

Bruce, F. F. *The Epistle to the Hebrews*. Rev. ed. NICNT. Grand Rapids: Eerdmans, 1990.

Brueggemann, Walter. *The Message of the Psalms: A Theological Commentary*. Augsburg Old Testament Studies. Minneapolis: Augsburg, 1984.

———. *Praying the Psalms*. 2nd ed. Eugene, OR: Cascade Books, 2007.

Campbell, Antony F., SJ. "Preparatory Issues in Approaching Biblical Texts." In *The Blackwell Companion to the Hebrew Bible*, edited by Leo G. Perdue, 3–18. London: Blackwell, 2005.

Carnazzo, Sebastian A. "Seeing Blood and Water: A Narrative-Critical Study of John 19:34." PhD diss., Catholic University of America, 2011.

Carson, D. A. *The Gospel according to John*. Pillar New Testament Commentary. Grand Rapids: Eerdmans, 1991.

Carter, Charles E. "Social Scientific Approaches." In *The Blackwell Companion to the Hebrew Bible*, edited by Leo G. Perdue, 36–57. Blackwell Companions to Religion 3. London: Blackwell, 2005.

Castelein, John D. "Believers' Baptism as the Biblical Occasion of Salvation." In *Understanding Four Views on Baptism*, edited by Paul E. Engle and John H. Armstrong, 129–44. Counterpoints: Church Life. Grand Rapids: Zondervan, 2007.

Chaplin, Martin F. "Water: Its Importance to Life." *Biochemistry and Molecular Biology Education* 29 (2001) 54–59.

Chen, Diane G. *Luke*. New Covenant Commentary. Eugene, OR: Cascade Books, 2017.

Childs, Brevard S. *Introduction to the Old Testament as Scripture*. Philadelphia: Fortress, 1979.

Chisholm, Robert B., Jr. "Suppressing Myths." In *The Psalms: Language for All Seasons of the Soul*, edited by Andrew J. Schmutzer and David M. Howard Jr., 85–96. Chicago: Moody, 2013.

Ciampa, Roy E., and Brian S. Rosner. *The First Letter to the Corinthians*. Pillar New Testament Commentary. Grand Rapids: Eerdmans, 2010.

Cockerill, Gareth Lee. *The Epistle to the Hebrews*. NICNT. Grand Rapids: Eerdmans, 2012.

Coetzee, Johan. "And Jonah Swam, and Swam, and Swam: Jonah's Body in Deep Waters." *OTE* 17 (2004) 521–30.

Cohn, Robert L. "Form and Perspective in 2 Kings 5." *VT* 33 (1983) 171–85.

Cole, Graham A. *The God Who Became Human: A Biblical Theology of Incarnation*. NSBT 30. Downers Grove, IL: IVP Academic, 2013.

Cole, R. Dennis. "Numbers." In *Zondervan Illustrated Bible Backgrounds Commentary*, edited by John H. Walton, 1:338–417. Grand Rapids: Zondervan, 2009.

Collins, Adele Yarbro. "The Origin of Christian Baptism." *Studia Liturgica* 19 (1989) 28–46.

Collins, Raymond. *I & II Timothy and Titus: A Commentary*. NTL. Louisville: Westminster John Knox, 2013.

Conzelmann, Hans. *1 Corinthians*. Translated by James W. Leitch. Hermeneia. Philadelphia: Fortress, 1975.

Coogan, Michael D. *A Brief Introduction to the Old Testament: The Hebrew Bible in Its Context*. New York: Oxford University Press, 2006.

Crawford, Matthew R. "Confessing God from a Good Conscience: 1 Peter 3:21 and Early Christian Baptismal Theology." *JTS* 67 (2016) 23–37.

Croatto, J. Severino. "Jesus, Prophet Like Elijah, and Prophet-Teacher Like Moses in Luke-Acts." *JBL* 124 (2005) 451–65.

Crowe, Brandon D. *The Hope of Israel: The Resurrection of Christ in the Acts of the Apostles*. Grand Rapids: Baker Academic, 2020.

———. *The Message of the General Epistles in the History of Redemption: Wisdom from James, Peter, John, and Jude*. Phillipsburg, NJ: P&R, 2015.

Currid, John D. *Against the Gods: The Polemical Theology of the Old Testament*. Wheaton, IL: Crossway, 2013.

Dozeman, Thomas B. *Joshua 1–12: A New Translation with Introduction and Commentary*. AYBRL. New Haven: Yale University Press, 2015.

Drey, Philip R. "The Role of Hagar in Genesis 16." *Andrews University Seminary Studies* 40 (2002) 179–95.

Dunn, James D. G. "Jesus and Purity: An Ongoing Debate." *New Testament Studies* 48 (2002) 449–56.

Ebert, William. "John 2:1–11: Sign, Symbol, and Structure in Johannine Theology." PhD diss., Trinity Theological Seminary, 2005.

Edwards, James R. *From Christ to Christianity: How the Jesus Movement Became the Church in Less Than a Century*. Grand Rapids: Baker Academic, 2021.

Effa, Allan L. "Prophet, Kings, Servants, and Lepers: A Missiological Reading of an Ancient Drama." *Missiology* 35 (2007) 305–13.

Erickson, Amy. *Jonah: Introduction and Commentary*. Illuminations. Grand Rapids: Eerdmans, 2021.

Esses, Michael. *Jesus in Genesis*. Plainfield, NJ: Logos International, 1974.

Estes, Daniel J. "The Transformation of Pain into Praise." In *The Psalms: Language for All Seasons of the Soul*, edited by Andrew J. Schmutzer and David M. Howard Jr., 170–82. Chicago: Moody, 2013.

Ferguson, Everett. "Baptism According to Origen." *Restoration Quarterly* 78 (2006) 117–35.

———. *Catechesis, Baptism, Eschatology, and Martyrdom*. Vol. 2 of *The Early Church at Work and Worship*. Eugene, OR: Cascade Books, 2014.

Ferguson, Sinclair B. *The Holy Spirit*. Contours of Christian Theology. Downers Grove, IL: IVP Academic, 1996.

Firmage, Edwin. "Genesis 1 and the Priestly Agenda." *JSOT* 24 (1999) 97–114.

Floyd, Michael H. "Habakkuk in the Book of the Twelve." In *The Book of the Twelve: Composition, Reception, and Interpretation*, edited by Lena-Sofia Tiemeyer and Jacob Wöhrle, 201–13. VTSup. 184. Leiden: Brill, 2020.

Fowler, William G., and Michael Strickland. *The Influence of Ezekiel in the Fourth Gospel: Intertextuality and Interpretation*. Biblical Interpretation 167. Leiden: Brill, 2018.

Fretheim, Terence E. *Exodus*. Interpretation. Louisville: Westminster John Knox, 2010.

———. *God and World in the Old Testament: A Relational Theology of Creation*. Nashville: Abingdon, 2005.

Fritz, Volkmar. *1 and 2 Kings*. Translated by Anselm Hagedorn. CC. Minneapolis: Fortress, 2003.

Frymer-Kensky, Tikva. "Creation Myths Breed Violence." *Bible Review* 14 (1998) 17–47.

Fuhr, Richard Alan, Jr., and Andreas J. Köstenberger. *Inductive Bible Study: Observation, Interpretation, and Application through the Lenses of History, Literature, and Theology*. Nashville: B&H, 2006.

Futado, Mark D. "Psalms 16, 23." In *The Psalms: Language for All Seasons of the Soul*, edited by Andrew J. Schmutzer and David M. Howard Jr., 255–62. Chicago: Moody, 2013.

Gallagher, Sarita. "In the Times of Elijah and Elisha: The Universal Mission of God in the Narratives of the Sidonian Widow and Naaman the Aramean." George Fox University, 2014. Paper 133. https://digitalcommons.georgefox.edu/ccs/133/.

Gane, Roy E. "Leviticus." In *Zondervan Illustrated Bible Backgrounds Commentary*, edited by John H. Walton, 1:284–337. Grand Rapids: Zondervan, 2009.

Garcia, Juan Carlos Moreno, ed. *Dynamics of Production in the Ancient Near East: 1300–500 BC*. Oxford: Oxbow, 2016.

George, Andrew, trans. *The Epic of Gilgamesh*. London: Penguin Random House, 2020.

Gesenius, Wilhelm. *Gesenius' Hebrew Grammar*. Edited and enlarged by E. Kautzsch. Translated by A. E. Cowley. Mineola, NY: Dover, 2006.

Godbey, William B. *Buried by Baptism*. Whitmore, KY: First Fruits, 2018.

Goldingay, John. *Ezekiel*. Eerdmans Commentary on the Bible. Grand Rapids: Eerdmans, 2003.

———. *Isaiah 56–66: A Critical and Exegetical Commentary*. ICC. London: Bloomsbury, 2014.

———. *Psalms*. 3 vols. BCOTWP. Grand Rapids: Baker Academic, 2006.

Goldingay, John, and Pamela J. Scalise. *Minor Prophets II*. Understanding the Bible Commentary. Grand Rapids: Baker, 2009.

González, Justo L. *From the Beginnings to the Council of Chalcedon*. Vol. 1 of *A History of Christian Thought*. Rev. ed. Nashville: Abingdon, 1987.

Gorman, Mark C. "Reading with the Spirit: Scripture, Confession, and Liturgical Imagination." *Liturgy* 28 (April 2013) 14–22.

Gorman, Michael J. *Elements of Biblical Exegesis: A Basic Guide for Students and Ministers*. 3rd ed. Grand Rapids: Baker Academic, 2020.

Grabbe, Lester L. *1 & 2 Kings: History and Story in Ancient Israel*. T. & T. Clark Study Guides to the Old Testament. London: Bloomsbury T. & T. Clark, 2017.

Green, Michael. *I Believe in the Holy Spirit*. Rev. ed. Grand Rapids: Eerdmans, 2004.

Green, Joel B. *1 Peter*. THNTC. Grand Rapids: Eerdmans, 2007.

———. *Conversion in Luke-Acts: Divine Action, Human Cognition, and the People of God*. Grand Rapids: Baker Academic, 2015.

———. *The Gospel of Luke*. NICOT. Grand Rapids: Eerdmans, 1997.

———. *The Theology of the Gospel of Luke*. New Testament Theology. Cambridge: Cambridge University Press, 1995.

Greer, Jonathan S., et al, eds. *Behind the Scenes of the Old Testament: Cultural, Social, and Historical Contexts*. Grand Rapids: Baker Academic, 2018.

Gruenwald, Ithamar. "The Baptism of Jesus in Light of Jewish Ritual Practice." *Neot* 50 (July 2016) 301–25.

Gulley, Norman R. "Trinity in the Old Testament." *Journal of the Adventist Theological Society* 17 (2006) 80–97.

Gunkel, Hermann. "The Influence of Babylonian Mythology upon the Creation Story." In *Creation in the Old Testament*, edited by Bernhard W. Anderson, 25–52. Issues in Religion and Theology. London: SPCK, 1984.

Guy, Laurie. *Introducing Early Christianity: A Topical Survey of its Life, Beliefs & Practices*. Downers Grove, IL: IVP Academic, 2004.

Haenchen, Ernst. *John 1: A Commentary on the Gospel of John, Chapters 1–6*. Translated by Robert W. Funk. Hermeneia. Philadelphia: Fortress, 1984.

———. *John 2: A Commentary on the Gospel of John, Chapters 7–21*. Translated by Robert W. Funk. Hermeneia. Philadelphia: Fortress, 1984.

Hamilton, James M., Jr. *God's Indwelling Presence: The Holy Spirit in the Old and New Testaments*. NAC Studies in Bible and Theology. Nashville: B&H, 2006.

Hamilton, Victor P. *Exodus: An Exegetical Commentary*. Grand Rapids: Baker Academic, 2011.

———. "Introduction." In *Reading Genesis 1–2: An Evangelical Conversation*, edited by J. Daryl Charles, 1–4. Peabody, MA: Hendrickson, 2013.

Hansen, Fred. "The Alpha and Omega and Lampstands Metaphors: A Linguistic Theory of Metaphor as Applied to the Book of Revelation." PhD diss., Radboud University, 2017.

Hasel, Gerhard F. "The Polemical Nature of the Genesis Cosmology." *EvQ* 46 (1974) 81–102.

Hasel, Gerhard F., and Michael G. Hasel. "The Hebrew Term 'ed' in Gen 2:6 and Its Connection in Ancient Near Eastern Literature." *ZAW* 112 (2000) 321–40.

Hays, Christopher B., and Peter Machinist. "Assyria and the Assyrians." In *The World around the Old Testament: The People and Places of the Ancient Near East*, edited by Bill T. Arnold and Brent A. Strawn, 31–105. Grand Rapids: Baker Academic, 2016.

Heidel, Alexander. *The Babylonian Genesis: The Story of Creation*. 2nd ed. Chicago: University of Chicago Press, 1951. https://isac.uchicago.edu/sites/default/files/uploads/shared/docs/misc_genesis.pdf.

Henriquez-Hernandez, Luis Alberto, et al. "Assessment of 22 Inorganic Elements in Human Amniotic Fluid: A Cross-Sectional Study Conducted in Canary Islands (Spain)." *International Journal of Environmental Health Research* 29 (2019) 130–39.

Hicks, John Mark. *Enter the Water, Come to the Table: Baptism and Lord's Supper in the Bible's Story of New Creation*. Abilene, TX: Abilene Christian University Press, 2014.

Hoffmeier, James K. "What Is the Biblical Date for the Exodus? A Response to Bryant Wood." *JETS* 50 (2007) 225–47.

Huijgen, Arnold. "Traces of the Trinity in the Old Testament: From Individual Texts to the Nature of Revelation." *International Journal of Systematic Theology* 19 (2017) 251–70.

Hutson, Christopher R. *First and Second Timothy and Titus*. Paideia: Commentaries on the New Testament. Grand Rapids: Baker Academic, 2019.

Jang, Yung Gyu. "The Water Rite and Conversion: The Significance of the Naaman Story in 2 Kings 5:1–27 for Christian Baptism." ThD diss., Boston University, 2002.

Jensen, Aaron Michael. "Does τετέλεσται Mean 'Paid in Full' in John 19:30? An Exercise in Lexical Semantics." *Wisconsin Lutheran Quarterly* 116 (2019) 6–15.

Johnstone, William D. *Exodus*. Eerdmans Commentary on the Bible. Grand Rapids: Eerdmans, 2003.

Kaiser, Walter C., Jr. "Exodus." In *The Expositors Bible Commentary*, edited by Tremper Longman III and David E. Garland, 395–672. Rev. ed. Grand Rapids: Zondervan, 2008.

———. "The Indwelling Presence of the Holy Spirit in the Old Testament." *EvQ* 84 (2010) 308–15.

Kaiser, Walter C., Jr., with Tiberius Rata. *Walking the Ancient Paths: A Commentary on Jeremiah*. Bellingham, WA: Lexham, 2019.

Kalengyo, Edison M. "The Sacrifice of Christ and Ganda Sacrifice: A Contextual Interpretation in Relation to the Eucharist." In *The Epistle to the Hebrews and Christian Theology*, edited by Richard Bauckham et al., 302–18. Grand Rapids: Eerdmans, 2009.

Kaltner, John, et al. "Jonah in the Book of the Twelve." In *The Book of the Twelve: Composition, Reception, and Interpretation*, edited by Lena-Sofia Tiemeyer and Jacob Wohrle, 164–75. VTSup. 184. Leiden: Brill, 2020.

Kärkkäinen, Veli-Matti. *Creation and Humanity*. Vol. 3 of *A Constructive Christian Theology for the Pluralistic World*. Grand Rapids: Eerdmans, 2015.

———. *The Holy Spirit: A Guide to Christian Theology*. Basic Guides to Christian Theology. Louisville: Westminster John Knox, 2012.

———. *Spirit and Salvation*. Horizons. Grand Rapids: Eerdmans, 2016.

Katz, Hayah. "He Shall Bathe in Water, Then He Shall Be Pure: Ancient Immersion Practice in the Light of Archaeological Evidence." *VT* 62 (2012) 369–80.

Keating, Daniel. "The Baptism of Jesus in Cyril of Alexandria: The Re-Creation of the Human Race." *Pro Ecclesia* 8 (1999) 201–22.

Kee, Min Suc. "A Study on the Dual Form of *Mayim*, Water." *JBQ* 40 (2012) 183–87.
Keel, Othmar. *The Symbolism of the Biblical World: Ancient Near Eastern Iconography and the Book of Psalms*. Translated by Timothy J. Hallett. Winona Lake, IN: Eisenbrauns, 1999.
Keener, Craig S. *1 Peter: A Commentary*. Grand Rapids: Baker Academic, 2021.
———. *The Gospel of John: A Commentary*. 2 vols. Grand Rapids: Baker Academic, 2003.
Kelle, Brad E. *Ezekiel: A Commentary in the Wesleyan Tradition*. NBCB. Kansas City: Beacon Hill, 2013.
Kellum, L. Scott. *Acts*. Edited by Andreas J. Köstenberger and Robert W. Yarbrough. Exegetical Guide to the Greek New Testament. Nashville: B&H Academic, 2020.
Kelsey, Marian. "The Book of Jonah and the Theme of Exile." *JSOT* 45 (2020) 128–40.
Kimmitt, Francis X. "Psalm 46." In *The Psalms: Language for All Seasons of the Soul*, edited by Andrew J. Schmutzer and David M. Howard Jr., 72–83. Chicago: Moody, 2013.
Klein, George. *Zechariah: An Exegetical and Theological Exposition of Holy Scripture*. NAC 21. Nashville: B&H, 2008.
Kline, J. Bergman. "The Day of the Lord in the Death and Resurrection of Christ." *JETS* 48 (2005) 757–70.
Klink, Edward W., III. *John*. ECNT. Grand Rapids: Zondervan Academic, 2016.
Ko, Ming Him. "The Significance of the Omission of Leaven and Honey from Grain Offerings." *VT* 1–14 (2022) 1–14. https://doi.org/10.1163/15685330-bja10087.
Koester, Craig R. *Revelation*. AYBRL. New Haven: Yale University Press, 2014.
———. *Symbolism in the Fourth Gospel: Meaning, Mystery and Community*. 2nd ed. Minneapolis: Fortress, 2003.
Kok, Johnson Lim Teng. *The Sin of Moses and the Staff of God*. SSN 35. Leiden: Brill, 1997.
Kolb, Robert. "God's Baptismal Act as Regenerative." In *Understanding Four Views on Baptism*, edited by John H. Armstrong and Paul E. Engle, 91–109. Counterpoints: Church Life. Grand Rapids: Zondervan, 2007.
Koning, Jacobus D. W. "The Hermeneutic Process Underlying Paul's Exegesis of Exodus 17:6 and Numbers 20:7–11 in 1 Corinthians 10:1–4." *HvTSt* 77 (2022) 1–9.
Köstenberger, Andreas J. *Encountering John: The Gospel in Historical, Literary, and Theological Perspective*. Edited by Walter A. Elwell and Eugene H. Merrill. 2nd ed. Encountering Biblical Studies. Grand Rapids: Baker Academic, 2013.
———. "John." In *Commentary on the New Testament Use of the Old Testament*, edited by G. K. Beale and D. A. Carson, 415–512. Grand Rapids: Baker Academic, 2007.
———. *A Theology of John's Gospel and Letters: The Word, the Christ, the Son of God*. Biblical Theology of the New Testament. Grand Rapids: Zondervan, 2009.
Köstenberger, Andreas J., and Richard D. Patterson. *Invitation to Biblical Interpretation: Exploring the Hermeneutical Triad of History, Literature, and Theology*. Invitation to Theological Studies. Grand Rapids: Kregel Academics, 2011.
Kruger, P. A. "Symbolic Acts Relating to Old Testament Treaties and Relationships." *Journal for Semitics* 2 (1990) 156–70.
Kulbacki, Piotr. "The Memory of Baptism in the Introductory Rites of the Holy Mass." *Roczniki Teologiczne* 62 (2015) 57–70.
Kunder, Amanda Marie. "The Many Waters of the Gospel of John." PhD diss., Loyola University, Chicago, 2019.

Kuyper, Abraham. *The Work of the Holy Spirit*. Grand Rapids: Eerdmans, 1946.

Langston, Scott M. *Exodus through the Centuries*. Blackwell Bible Commentaries. Malden, MA: Blackwell, 2006.

Lemaire, André. "Schools and Literacy in Ancient Israel and Early Judaism." In *The Blackwell Companion to the Hebrew Bible*, edited by Leo G. Perdue, 207–17. London: Blackwell, 2005.

LeMon, Joel M. "Egypt and the Egyptians." In *The World around the Old Testament: The People and Places of the Ancient Near East*, edited by Bill T. Arnold and Brent A. Strawn, 161–96. Grand Rapids: Baker Academic, 2016.

Liefeld, Walter L. *Ephesians*. IVP New Testament Commentary 10. Downers Grove, IL: IVP Academic, 1997.

Linicum, David. "The Origin of 'Alpha and Omega' (Revelation 1.8; 21.6; 22.13): A Suggestion." *Journal of Greco-Roman and Judaism* 6 (2009) 128–33.

Liverani, Mario. *Israel's History and the History of Israel*. New York: Routledge, 2014.

Longman, Tremper, III. *Psalms: An Introduction and Commentary*. TOTC. Downers Grove, IL: IVP, 2014.

———. "What Genesis 1–2 Teaches (and What It Doesn't)." In *Reading Genesis 1–2: An Evangelical Conversation*, edited by J. Daryl Charles, 103–28. Peabody, MA: Hendrickson, 2013.

Lu, Rosanna Anna. "The Deification and Demonization of Tĕhôm: From Deity to Deep." PhD diss., University of California, Los Angeles, 2018.

Lynch, Matthew J. "Monotheism in Ancient Israel." In *Behind the Scenes of the Old Testament: Cultural, Social, and Historical Contexts*, edited by Jonathan S. Greer at al., 340–48. Grand Rapids: Baker Academic, 2018.

Mabie, Frederick J. *1 and 2 Chronicles*. Rev. ed. Expositor's Bible Commentary. Grand Rapids: Zondervan, 2017.

MacDonald, Nathan. "Anticipations of Horeb: Exodus 17 as an Inner-Biblical Commentary." In *Studies on the Text and Versions of the Hebrew Bible in Honour of Robert Gordon*, edited by Geoffrey Khan and Diana Lipton, 7–19. VTSup 149. Leiden: Brill, 2012.

Mahdy, Heba, et al. "Amniotomy." National Center for Biotechnology Information, last updated Apr. 10, 2023. https://www.ncbi.nlm.nih.gov/books/NBK470167/.

Marshall, I. Howard. *Acts*. TNTC. Downers Grove, IL: IVP Academic, 1980.

———. "Acts." In *Commentary on the New Testament Use of the Old Testament*, edited by G. K. Beale and D. A. Carson, 513–606. Grand Rapids: Baker Academic, 2007.

———. *The Epistles of John*. NICNT. Grand Rapids: Eerdmans, 1978.

———. "Soteriology in Hebrews." In *The Epistle to the Hebrews and Christian Theology*, edited by Richard Bauckham et al., 253–77. Grand Rapids: Eerdmans, 2009.

Martin, Francis, and William M. Wright IV. *The Gospel of John*. Edited by Peter S. Williamson and Mary Healy. Catholic Commentary on Sacred Scripture. Grand Rapids: Baker Academic, 2015.

Matthews, Kenneth A. *Genesis 1—11:26: An Exegetical and Theological Exposition of Holy Scripture*. NAC 1A. Nashville: B&H, 1996.

Matthews, Victor H., and Don C. Benjamin. *Old Testament Parallels: Laws and Stories from the Ancient Near East*. Rev. and expanded 4th ed. New York: Paulist, 2016.

McConville, J. Gordon. *Joshua: Crossing Divides; An Introduction and Study Guide Crossing Divides*. T. & T. Clark Study Guides to the Old Testament. London: Bloomsbury T. & T. Clark, 2017.

McConville, J. Gordon, and Stephen N. Williams. *Joshua*. THOTC. Grand Rapids: Eerdmans, 2010.

McHugh, John F. *John 1–4: A Critical and Exegetical Commentary*. ICC. London: T. & T. Clark, 2009.
McKane, William. *A Critical and Exegetical Commentary on Jeremiah*. 2 vols. ICC. London: Bloomsbury T. & T. Clark, 1986.
McKenzie, Steven L. *Introduction to the Historical Books: Strategies for Reading*. Grand Rapids: Eerdmans, 2010.
Meyers, Carol. *Exodus*. New Cambridge Bible Commentary. New York: Cambridge University Press, 2005.
Michaels, J. Ramsey. *The Gospel of John*. NICNT. Grand Rapids: Eerdmans, 2010.
Miles, John A., Jr. "Laughing at the Bible: Jonah as Parody." *JSOT* 65 (1975) 168–81.
Monson, John. "1 Kings." In *Zondervan Illustrated Bible Backgrounds Commentary*, edited by John H. Walton, 2–109. Grand Rapids: Zondervan, 2009.
Moore, Rickie. "Finding the Spirit of Elijah in the Story of Elisha and the Lost Axe Head: 2 Kings 6:1–7 in the Light of 2 Kings 2." *OTE* 31 (2018) 780–89.
Morris, A. W. "The Lost Truth of Genesis." *Journal of Ministry and Theology* 23 (2019) 39–67.
Morris, Leon. *1 Corinthians: An Introduction and Commentary*. TNTC. Downers Grove, IL: IVP Academic, 1985.
Na'aman, Nadav. "The Contest on Mount Carmel (1 Kings 18:19–40) as a Reflection of a Religious-Cultural Threat." *BZ* 64 (2020) 85–100.
Najman, Hindy, and Konrad Schmid. "Reading the Blood Plague (Exodus 7:14–25): The Hermeneutics of a Composite Text." *JBL* 141 (2022) 23–42.
Nantenaina, Lollo Zo, et al. "The Prophet Elijah as an Agent of Change for Community Development." *Journal of Applied Christian Leadership* 9 (2015) 1–12.
Nettles, Thomas J. "Baptism as a Symbol of Christ's Saving Work." In *Understanding Four Views on Baptism*, edited by Paul E. Engle and John H. Armstrong, 25–41. Counterpoints: Church Life. Grand Rapids: Zondervan, 2007.
———. "A Baptist Response." In *Understanding Four Views on Baptism*, edited by Paul E. Engle and John H. Armstrong, 73–77. Counterpoints: Church Life. Grand Rapids: Zondervan, 2007.
Nevader, Madhavi. "Creating a *Deus Non Creator*: Divine Sovereignty and Creation in Israel." In *The God Ezekiel Creates*, edited by Paul M. Joyce and Dalit Rom-Shiloni, 56–70. LHBOTS. London: Bloomsbury T. & T. Clark, 2016.
Ng, Wai-Yee. "Johannine Water Symbolism and Its Eschatological Significance with Special Reference to John 4." PhD diss., Westminster Theological Seminary, 1997.
Niehaus, Jeffrey. *Ancient Near Eastern Themes in Biblical Theology*. Grand Rapids: Kregel Academic, 2008.
Nissen, Hans Jörg, et al. *The Early History of the Ancient Near East, 9000–2000 B.C.* Translated by Elizabeth Lutzeier and Kenneth J. Northcott. Chicago: University of Chicago Press, 1988.
Noegel, Scott B. "Moses and Magic: Notes on the Book of Exodus." *JANESCU* 24 (1996) 45–59.
O'Day, Gail R. *Revelation in the Fourth Gospel: And Eight Johannine Essays*. Edited by Paul N. Anderson. Johannine Monograph 9. Eugene, OR: Wipf & Stock, 2021.
Oropeza, B. J. *1 Corinthians*. NCCS. Eugene, OR: Cascade Books, 2017.
Ortlund, Eric. *Piercing Leviathan: God's Defeat of Evil in the Book of Job*. NSBT 56. Downers Grove, IL: IVP Academic, 2021.
Osborne, Grant R. *The Hermeneutical Spiral: A Comprehensive Introduction to Biblical Interpretation*. Rev. and expanded ed. Downers Grove, IL: IVP Academic, 2006.

———. *Matthew*. Edited by Clinton E. Arnold. ECNT. Grand Rapids: Zondervan Academic, 2010.

———. *Revelation*. BECNT. Grand Rapids: Baker Academic, 2002.

———. *Romans*. IVP New Testament Commentary 6. Downers Grove, IL: IVP Academic, 2004.

Oughton, Julie, and Michael Peters, eds. *British Medical Association A–Z Family Medical Encyclopedia*. 5th ed. London: Dorling Kindersley, 2008.

Padilla, Osvaldo. *Acts of the Apostles: Interpretation, History and Theology*. Downers Grove, IL: IVP Academic, 2016.

Painter, John. *1, 2, and 3 John*. Edited by Daniel J. Harrington, SJ. SP. Collegeville, MN: Liturgical, 2008.

Pao, David W., and Eckhard J. Schnabel. "Luke." In *Commentary on the New Testament Use of the Old Testament*, edited by G. K. Beale and D. A. Carson, 251–414. Grand Rapids: Baker Academic, 2007.

Parker, Edmund Alfred. "Studies in the Use of Blood in the Old Testament." Master's thesis, Andrews University, 1981.

Patrasescu, Vlad-Emanuel. "Naaman and the Jordan: The Symbolic and Expiatory Role of Water in the Old Testament Texts." *CICSA Journal Online*, n.s., vol. 5 (2019) 55–68. https://www.ceeol.com/search/article-detail?id=881138.

Patterson, Richard D., and Hermann J. Austel. *1 and 2 Kings*. Expositor's Bible Commentary. Grand Rapids: Zondervan, 2009.

Petersen, David G. *Hebrews: An Introduction and Commentary*. TNTC. Downers Grove, IL: IVP Academic, 2020.

Petersen, David L. *Zechariah 9–14 and Malachi*. OTL. Louisville: Westminster John Knox, 1995.

Pitkänen, Pekka. *A Commentary on Numbers: Narrative, Ritual, and Colonialism*. Routledge Studies in the Biblical World. London: Routledge, 2017.

Placher, William C., and Derek R. Nelson, eds. *From Its Beginnings to the Eve of the Reformation*. Vol. 1 of *Readings in the History of Christian Theology*. Rev. ed. Louisville: Westminster John Knox, 2015.

Plantinga, Richard J., et al. *An Introduction to Christian Theology*. Introduction to Religion. New York: Cambridge University Press, 2010.

Poythress, Vern S. "Genesis 1:1 Is the First Event, Not a Summary." *WTJ* 79 (2017) 97–121.

Pratt, Richard L., Jr. "A Reformed Response." In *Understanding Four Views on Baptism*, edited by Paul E. Engle and John H. Armstrong, 42–46. Counterpoints: Church Life. Grand Rapids: Zondervan, 2007.

Pregill, Michael. *The Golden Calf between Bible and Qu'ran: Scripture, Polemic, and Exegesis from Late Antiquity to Islam*. Oxford Studies in the Abrahamic Religions. Oxford: Oxford University Press, 2020.

Provan, Iain. "2 Kings." In *Zondervan Illustrated Bible Backgrounds Commentary*, edited by John H. Walton, 110–219. Grand Rapids: Zondervan, 2009.

Quarles, Charles L. *Matthew*. Edited by Andreas J. Köstenberger and Robert W. Yarbrough. Exegetical Guide to the Greek New Testament. Nashville: B&H Academic, 2017.

Quine, Cat. "Ritual and Polemic in the Hebrew Bible." In *Casting Down the Host of Heaven: The Rhetoric of Ritual Failure in the Polemic against the Host of Heaven*, 61–84. OtSt 78. Leiden: Brill, 2020.

Rackley, Rosanna. "Kingship, Struggle, and Creation: The Story of *Chaoskampf*." Master's thesis, University of Birmingham, 2015.
Rad, Gerhard von. *Genesis: A Commentary*. Rev. ed. OTL. Philadelphia: Westminster, 1972.
Redditt, Paul L. *Zechariah 9–14*. IECOT. Stuttgart: Kohlhammer, 2012.
Reeves, Michael. *Delighting in the Trinity: An Introduction to the Christian Faith*. Downers Grove, IL: IVP Academic, 2012.
Rendtorff, Rolf. "Creation and Redemption in the Torah." In *The Blackwell Companion to the Hebrew Bible*, edited by Leo G. Perdue, 311–20. London: Blackwell, 2005.
Richard, Earl. "Polemics, Old Testament, and Theology: A Study of 2 Cor 3:1—4:6." *RB* 88 (1988) 340–67.
Richter, Sandra L. *The Epic of Eden: A Christian Entry into the Old Testament*. Downers Grove, IL: IVP Academic, 2008.
———. "What Do I Know of Holy? On the Person and Work of the Holy Spirit in Scripture." In *Spirit of God: Christian Renewal in the Community of Faith*, edited by Jeffrey W. Barbeau and Beth Felker Jones, 23–38. Wheaton Theology Conference. Downers Grove, IL: IVP Academic, 2015.
Roberts, J. J. M. *First Isaiah: A Commentary*. Hermeneia. Minneapolis: Fortress, 2016.
Rollock, Robert. *Commentary on Ephesians*. Translated by Casey B. Carmichael. Grand Rapids: Reformation Heritage, 2021.
Roloff, Jurgen. *Revelation*. CC. Minneapolis: Fortress: 1993.
Sailhamer, John H. *Genesis Unbound: A Provocative New Look at the Creation Account*. Colorado Springs: Book Villages, 2011.
———. *The Meaning of the Pentateuch: Revelation, Composition and Interpretation*. Downers Grove, IL: IVP Academic, 2009.
Sandy, D. Brent. *Plowshares & Pruning Hooks: Rethinking the Language of Biblical Prophecy and Apocalyptic*. Downers Grove, IL: IVP Academic, 2002.
Schafer, Peter. *Two Gods in Heaven: Jewish Concepts of God in Antiquity*. Princeton: Princeton University Press, 2020.
Schnabel, Eckhard J. "The Viability of Premillennialism and the Text of Revelation." *JETS* 64 (2021) 785–95.
Schreiner, Thomas R. *1–2 Peter, Jude*. NAC 37. Nashville: B&H, 2003.
———. *Commentary on Hebrews*. Biblical Theology for Christian Proclamation 36. Edited by T. Desmond Alexander et al. Nashville: B&H, 2015.
———. *1 Corinthians: An Introduction and Commentary*. TNTC. Downers Grove, IL: IVP Academic, 2018.
———. *Covenant and God's Purpose for the World*. Short Studies in Biblical Theology. Wheaton, IL: Crossway, 2017.
Scurlock, JoAnn. "Introduction." In *Creation and Chaos: A Reconsideration of Hermann Gunkel's* Chaoskampf *Hypothesis*, edited by JoAnn Scurlock and Richard H. Beal, ix–xx. Winona Lake, IN: Eisenbrauns, 2013.
Scurlock, JoAnn, and Richard H. Beal, eds. *Creation and Chaos: A Reconsideration of Hermann Gunkel's* Chaoskampf *Hypothesis*. Winona Lake, IN: Eisenbrauns, 2013.
Shulman, Dennis G. "Jonah: His Story, Our Story; His Struggle, Our Struggle; Commentary on Paper by Avivah Gottleib Zornberg." *International Journal of Relational Perspectives* 18 (2008) 329–64.
Smalley, Stephen S. *The Revelation of John: A Commentary on the Greek Text of the Apocalypse*. Downers Grove, IL: IVP Academic, 2005.
Smeaton, George. *The Doctrine of the Holy Spirit*. Eugene, OR: Wipf & Stock, 2016.

Smith, Gary V. *Interpreting the Prophetic Books: An Exegetical Handbook*. Handbooks for Old Testament Exegesis. Grand Rapids: Kregel Academic, 2014.

Smith, Ralph L. *Micah–Malachi*. WBC 32. Grand Rapids: Zondervan, 1984.

Smith, Robert Houston. "Exodus Typology in the Fourth Gospel." *JBL* 81 (1962) 329–42.

Smith, W. Alan. "Naaman and Elisha: Healing, Wholeness, and the Task of Religious Education." *Religious Education* 89 (1994) 205–19.

Sonik, Karen. "From Hesiod's Abyss to Ovid's *rudis indigestaque moles*: Chaos and Cosmos in the Babylonian 'Epic of Creation.'" In *Creation and Chaos: A Reconsideration of Hermann Gunkel's* Chaoskampf *Hypothesis*, edited by JoAnn Scurlock and Richard H. Beal, 1–25. Winona Lake, IN: Eisenbrauns, 2013.

Stallard, Mike. "Reflections on 'Baptism Now Saves Us' in 1 Peter 3:21." *Journal of Ministry and Theology* 22 (2018) 5–17.

Stanglin, Keith D. *The Letter and Spirit of Biblical Interpretation: From the Early Church to Modern Practice*. Grand Rapids: Baker Academic, 2018.

Steinmann, Andrew E. *Genesis: An Introduction and Commentary*. TOTC. Downers Grove, IL: IVP Academic, 2019.

Stibbs, Alan M. *The Finished Work of Christ*. Carol Stream, IL: Tyndale, 1954.

Sweeney, Marvin A. *I and II Kings: A Commentary*. OTL. Louisville: Westminster John Knox, 2007.

Tabb, Brian J. *All Things New: Revelation as a Canonical Capstone*. NSBT. Downers Grove, IL: IVP Academic, 2019.

Terblance, M. D. "An Abundance of Living Waters: The Intertextual Relationship between Zechariah 14:8 and Ezekiel 47:1–12." *OTE* 17 (2004) 120–29.

Thiselton, Anthony C. *The First Epistle to the Corinthians*. NIGTC. Grand Rapids: Eerdmans, 2000.

Thompson, Marianne Meye. *John: A Commentary*. NTL. Louisville: Westminster John Knox, 2015.

Tsumura, David Toshio. "The *Chaoskampf* Myth in the Biblical Tradition." *Journal of the American Oriental Society* 140 (2020) 963–70.

———. *Creation and Destruction: A Reappraisal of the* Chaoskampf *Theory in the Old Testament*. Winona Lake: Eisenbrauns, 2005.

———. "The Creation Motif in Psalm 74:12–14? A Reappraisal of the Theory of the Dragon Myth." *JBL* 134 (2015) 547–55.

———. *The Earth and the Waters in Genesis 1–2: A Linguistic Investigation*. Edited by David J. A. Clines and Philip R. Davies. JSOTSup 83. Sheffield: University of Sheffield Press, 2009.

Udoibok, Offiong Etuk. "The Significance of the Son of Man Terminology in Ezekiel." *West African Theological Seminary* 1 (January 2013) 85–86.

Van de Mieroop, Marc. *A History of the Ancient Near East ca. 3000–323 BC*. 3rd ed. Blackwell History of the Ancient World. Chichester, UK: Wiley, 2016.

Vanderhooft, David S. "Babylonia and the Babylonians." In *The World around the Old Testament: The People and Places of the Ancient Near East*, edited by Bill T. Arnold and Brent A. Strawn, 107–37. Grand Rapids: Baker Academic, 2016.

Van der Loos, H. *The Miracles of Jesus*. NovTSup 9. Leiden: Brill, 1968.

Van Dorn, Douglas. *Waters of Creation: A Biblical-Theological Study of Baptism*. Erie, CO: Waters of Creation, 2009.

Vawter, Bruce. "Ezekiel and John." *Catholic Bible Quarterly* 26 (1964) 450–58.

Von Wahlde, Urban C. *The Gospel and Letters of John*. 2 vols. ECC. Grand Rapids: Eerdmans, 2010.
Voth, Steven. "Jeremiah." In *Zondervan Illustrated Bible Backgrounds Commentary*, edited by John H. Walton, 228–371. Grand Rapids: Zondervan, 2009.
Wall, Robert W. *1 & 2 Timothy and Titus*. THNTC. Grand Rapids: Eerdmans, 2012.
Wallace, Daniel B. *Greek Grammar beyond the Basics: An Exegetical Syntax of the New Testament with Scripture, Subject, and Greek Word Indexes*. Grand Rapids: Zondervan, 1996.
Waltke, Bruce K., with Cathi J. Fredricks. *Genesis: A Commentary*. Grand Rapids: Zondervan, 2001.
Walton, John H. "Creation in Genesis 1:1—2:3 and the Ancient Near East: Order out of Disorder after *Chaoskampf*." *CTJ* 43 (2008) 48–63.
———. "Genesis." In *Zondervan Illustrated Bible Backgrounds Commentary*, edited by John H. Walton, 1:2–159. Grand Rapids: Zondervan, 2009.
———. "Interactions in the Ancient Cognitive Environment." In *Behind the Scenes of the Old Testament: Cultural, Social, and Historical Contexts*, edited by Jonathan S. Greer et al., 333–39. Grand Rapids: Baker Academic, 2018.
———. "Jonah." In *Zondervan Illustrated Bible Backgrounds Commentary*, edited by John H. Walton, 5:100–119. Grand Rapids: Zondervan, 2009.
———. *The Lost World of Genesis One: Ancient Cosmology and the Origins Debate*. Lost World. Downers Grove, IL: IVP Academic, 2009.
Walton, John H., and Brent Sandy. *The Lost World of Scripture: Ancient Literary Culture and Biblical Authority*. Lost World. Downers Grove, IL: IVP Academic, 2013.
Wells, Bruce. "Exodus." In *Zondervan Illustrated Bible Backgrounds Commentary*, edited by John H. Walton, 160–283. Grand Rapids: Zondervan, 2009.
Wenham, Gordon J. *Genesis 1–15*. 2 vols. WBC 1–2. Grand Rapids: Zondervan, 1987.
Westall, Frances, and Andre Brack. "The Importance of Water for Life." *Space Science Reviews* 214 (2018) 1–23.
Westermann, Claus. *Genesis*. Translated by John J. Scullion. 3 vols. CC. Minneapolis: Fortress, 1995.
Williamson, H. G. M. *A Critical and Exegetical Commentary on Isaiah*. 2 vols. ICC. London: T. & T. Clark, 2006.
Witherington, Ben, III. *A Socio-Rhetorical Commentary on Titus, 1–2 Timothy, and 1–3 John*. Vol. 1 of *Letters and Homilies for Hellenized Christians*. Downers Grove, IL: IVP Academic 2006.
———. *Troubled Waters: Rethinking the Theology of Baptism*. Waco, TX: Baylor University Press, 2007.
Woudstra, Marten H. *The Book of Joshua*. NICOT. Grand Rapids: Eerdmans, 1981.
Wright, Christopher J. H. *Knowing the Holy Spirit through the Old Testament*. Knowing God through the Old Testament. Downers Grove, IL: IVP, 2006.
Wright, Daniel F. "The Origins of Infant Baptism—Child Believer's Baptism." *SJT* 40 (1987) 1–23.
Wright, Terry J. "The Seal of Approval: An Interpretation of the Son's Sustaining Action in Hebrews 1:3." In *The Epistle to the Hebrews and Christian Theology*, edited by Richard Bauckham et al., 140–48. Grand Rapids: Eerdmans 2009.
Yarbrough, Robert W. *1–3 John*. BECNT. Grand Rapids: Baker Academic, 2008.
———. *Romans-Galatians*. Edited by Iain M. Duguid et al. ESV Expository Commentary. Wheaton, IL: Crossway, 2020.

Yong, Amos. "*Creatio Spiritus* and the Spirit of Christ: Toward a Trinitarian Theology of Creation." In *Spirit of God: Christian Renewal in the Community of Faith*, edited by Jeffrey W. Barbeau and Beth Felker Jones, 168–82. Wheaton Theology Conference. Downers Grove, IL: IVP Academic, 2015.

Zimmerli, Walther. *Ezekiel 2: A Commentary on the Book of the Prophet Ezekiel Chapters 25–48*. Hermeneia. Philadelphia: Fortress, 1983.

www.ingramcontent.com/pod-product-compliance
Lightning Source LLC
Chambersburg PA
CBHW070257230426
43664CB00014B/2558